MOSCOW
An Architectural History

MOSCOW
An Architectural History

Kathleen Berton

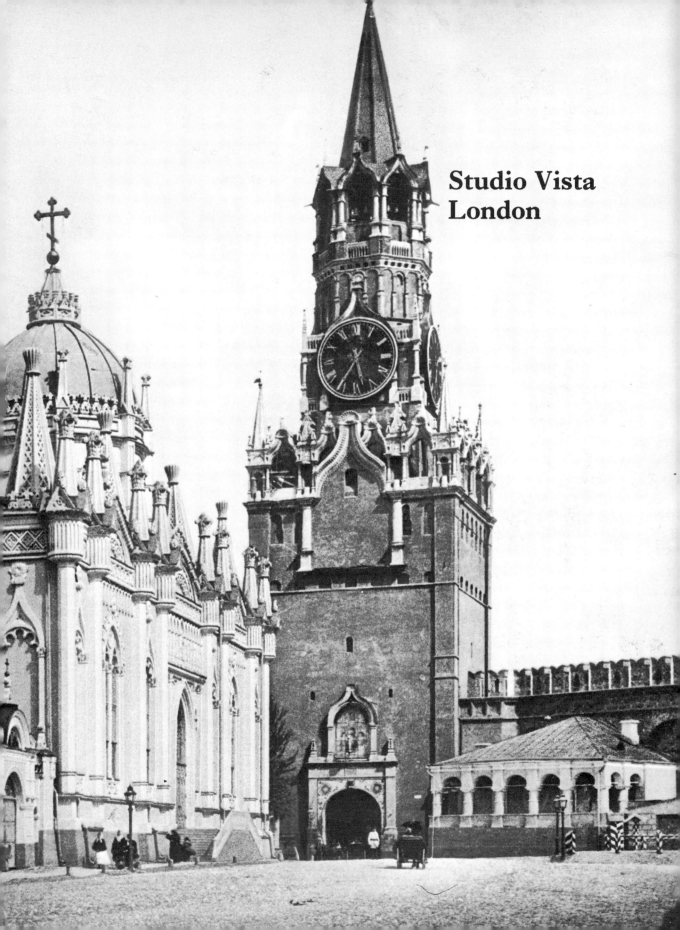

Studio Vista
London

Acknowledgments

Apart from acknowledging the kind assistance of the staffs of the Lenin Library and the British Library, I particularly wish to thank Anthony Day, who not only drew all the maps but in his capacity as an architect carefully reviewed the text. I wish to express gratitude also to all those who generously provided the illustrations (listed in detail at the back of this book), and especially to Valery Plotnikov, whose photography has a special quality. Most important of all has been the constant support given by my husband.

A Studio Vista book published by
Cassell & Collier Macmillan Publishers Ltd,
35 Red Lion Square, London WC1R 4SG
and at Sydney, Auckland, Toronto, Johannesburg,
an affiliate of
Macmillan Publishing Co. Inc.
New York

ISBN 0 289 70647 5

Designed by Sandra Schneider

Filmset in Monophoto Ehrhardt and printed by
BAS Printers Limited, Over Wallop, Hampshire
Bound by Webb Son & Co. Ltd.

Table of Contents

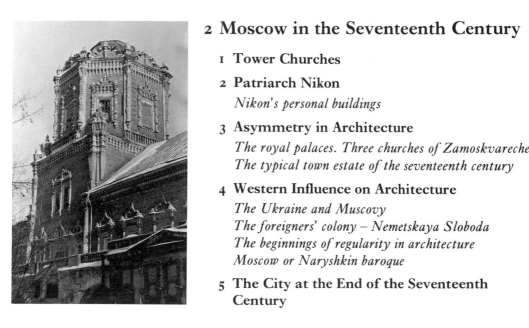

Introduction

The approaches to Moscow are crisscrossed by broad, relentlessly straight avenues of dull, featureless eight-storey buildings monotonously stretching away to the horizon on either side. Apart from the vivid flash of the Kremlin and St Basil's, Moscow at first glance seems to have nothing to offer in its dense mass of tedious building. It would hardly seem possible that the history of its architecture could be worthy of attention. Yet how wrong that impression would be.

Here is an ancient city on the very outer fringes of Europe which, except for the brief period of St Petersburg's hegemony, has been the arbiter of architectural style in Russia for five hundred years, the faithful successor to Kiev, to Novgorod, and to Vladimir and Suzdal. Although the wooden architecture which prevailed in the city until recent times has with few exceptions not survived the frequent fires, stone buildings still exist in numbers great enough to illustrate the turbulent history of the city since the fifteenth century. There are gaily painted medieval dwellings like the Palace of Averky Kirillov, the secretary to Tsar Aleksei Mikhailovich; and the building that housed the first English emissary at the time of Ivan the Terrible. There are rectangular formal façades of the eighteenth century like the elegant Gubin House on the Petrovka or the large Catherine Palace, now the Soviet Tank Academy, in Lefortovo. The nineteenth century is represented by imitations of earlier styles, some of them garish like the Igumnov House – now the French Embassy – some more subtle like the Kremlin Great Palace. Art Nouveau had its adherents in Moscow and the results can be seen in buildings like the Metropole Hotel, designed by an Englishman, and in the gay whirls and trills of the Ryabushinsky house by F. O. Shekitel. The 1920s were a time for experimentation and brilliant design and have left such surprising monuments as the *Izvestiya* building and the Centrosoyuz building designed in 1929 by Le Corbusier.

Many of the magnificent monasteries that encircled Moscow and acted as defence bastions against Tartar attacks still survive, like the Vysoko-Petrovsky with its decorative Moscow baroque, the Andronikov and Rozhdestvensky with their fine fifteenth-century cathedrals, the quaintness of the Donskoi, the unrivalled splendour of Novodevichy and the immense fortress walls of the outermost, the Simonov. Although no longer in possession of the skyline, the churches are everywhere. Their forms and their designs are exceptionally varied. From the beautiful simplicity of the early Moscow style like the Deposition of the Robe in the Kremlin (1484–5) to the riotous colours and superficially eccentric design of St Basil's (1560), from the pyramid-towered churches to those with the classic five cupolas, from the explosion of exterior sculpture and decoration in the height of Moscow baroque to the finely moulded forms of neo–classicism, the churches are the faithful recorders of the past. Like its other buildings, they are the tangible evidence of Moscow's dramatic and exceptional history. More than other European cities nearly all major buildings in Moscow until quite recently were erected by the personal fiat of its autocratic rulers. Yet these witnesses to history are not to be found easily. The curious must enter the courtyards, pierce the hostile street façades to penetrate to the incongruous jumble of buildings that make up the seemingly monolithic blocks. They must explore the lanes and alleyways of the old parts of central Moscow within the Ring Road and only then will they find these unusual buildings.

Some buildings which have disappeared or were never built and which were planned by Moscow's rulers to enhance the glory of the state are also of great interest. They include the grandiose Kremlin palace and the evocative ruins of Tsaritsyno, both whims of Catherine the Great, the immense Cathedral of Christ the Redeemer actually built as a memorial to the victory over Napoleon but blown up in 1932, the tall palaces of labour and industry planned in the twenties which would have completely overwhelmed the centre of the city, and the most notorious of all, the Palace of Soviets, begun in 1936 but never completed, which would have been higher than the Empire State Building.

It is only recently that the architecture of Moscow has departed from its strongly individual character to take on the patina of the international modern style. Certainly in the late-medieval period before the eighteenth century, architecture evolved in a most particular way. With the eighteenth century and after, it belongs more closely within the framework of European architecture. Yet always, because of the specific conditions prevailing in Russia – a strong autocracy, remoteness, an extreme climate, the slow acquisition of technical knowledge – it has continued to display characteristic attributes. Yet it is important to stress that Europe, too, has exerted its influence on the development of architecture in Russia even from earliest times. The first and major influence was the Greek-type church, a form relayed through Byzantium after the eleventh century. But other styles also found their way to Moscow, sometimes barely recognizable, like the High Gothic which filtered in through Poland, and the ideas of the Renaissance, which came more directly via the Italian masters working on the buildings of the Kremlin in the fifteenth century. The fascinating, perhaps most attractive thing about the architecture of Moscow is its sense both of the familiar – because of the frequent times it has been touched by the European tradition – and of the unfamiliar in the extraordinary, idiosyncratic way in which it has developed and in its close alliance with the vicissitudes of the history of Moscow and its powerful rulers from Ivan the Terrible to Stalin. It all combines to bring about an amalgam of known and unknown elements that might at first seem to be outlandish and barbarian but, on closer examination, reveal a complex but lucid and vivid pattern.

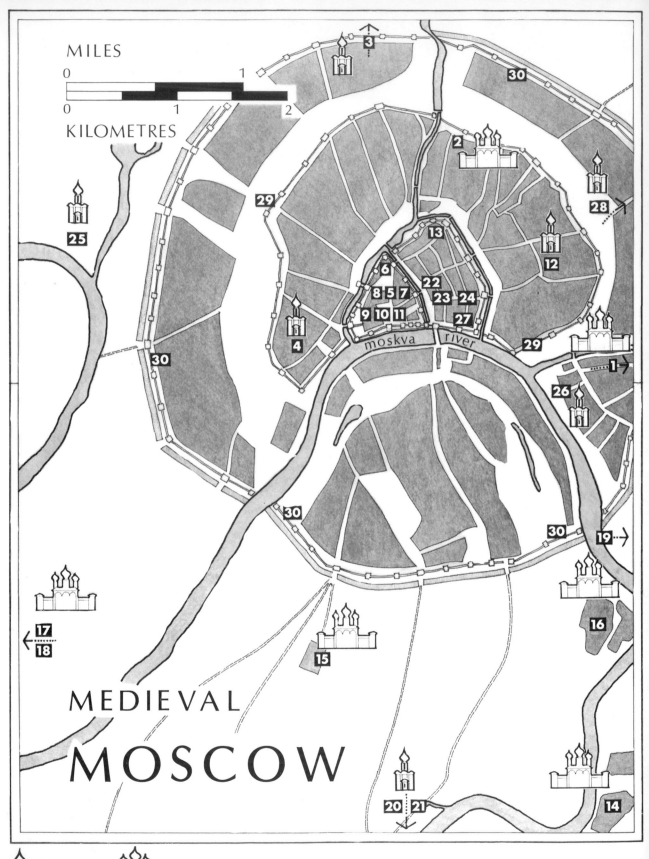

MILES

0   1

0   1   2

KILOMETRES

moskva river

MEDIEVAL

MOSCOW

 Cathedral/ Church/ Chapel

 Convent/ Monastery

 Palace/ Estate/ Mansion/ House

 Apartment/ Hotel

 Railway station

1 Medieval Moscow

I THE EMERGENCE OF MUSCOVY

The beginnings of Moscow

The beginnings of the recorded history of Moscow coincide with the demise of the splendid princedom of Kievan Rus. The vast Russian plain is bounded by the Baltic Sea to the north, the Carpathian Mountains to the west, the Black Sea and the Caspian Sea to the south, the low lying Ural Mountains to the east, and the even lower Valdai Hills to the north-west. Its principal geographic feature is that it is watered by long, grand rivers: the Volga, the Dnieper, the Dvina and the Don. This huge area was settled in the sixth and seventh centuries by the eastern branch of the Slav tribes during the great Migration of the Peoples. The Dnieper River, which formed the main highway between the energetic people of Scandinavia to the north and the highly civilized citizens of Byzantium to the south, became one of the busiest trade routes in Europe and the Slav tribes who settled on the southern reaches of the Dnieper were inexorably drawn into complex trading relationships that involved Byzantium, Asia Minor, Bokhara and Samarkand, Europe and even North Africa. In the ninth century, the Norse (Varangian) chieftain, Ryurik, began to move into the Slav lands and seized the Russian town of Novgorod the Great. The Chronicle tactfully states that Ryurik was formally invited thus: 'Our land is great and rich but there is no order in it. Come, then, to rule as princes over us.' In succeeding years his successor, Oleg, captured and brought unity to the numerous Slav towns and made Kiev on the Dnieper his capital. The Norse rulers were gradually absorbed into Slavic society, but the only proof of conquest was the adoption of the Norse gods.

Although Kiev's economy as everywhere else at the time was firmly based on agriculture, commerce with Byzantium was of great importance and dictated the course of its foreign policy. In 907 Prince Oleg extracted a favourable trade treaty with Constantinople ensuring access to its markets. In the latter half of the tenth century Prince Vladimir, soon to be first native saint of the Russian Church, decided to adopt a new religion. According to the chronicles, he received envoys representing the principal religions of the western and mediterranean world, Muslims, German Catholics, Jews and Byzantine Orthodox Christians. The Council of Boyars and

---

1 Spassky Cathedral, Andronikov Monastery, 1420–27   2 Rozhdestvensky Convent Cathedral, 1501–05   3 St Trifon v Naprudnom, late 15th century   4 Antipy Church shto na Kolymazhnom Dvore, first half of the 16th century   5 The Kremlin Uspensky Cathedral, 1475–79   6 Kremlin wall, 18 towers and 5 gates, 1475–1525   7 The Kremlin: Spassky Gate, 1491   8 The Kremlin: Rizpolozheny Church, 1484–5   9 The Kremlin: Granovitaya Palace, 1487–91   10 The Kremlin: Blagoveshchensky Cathedral, 1484–9   11 The Kremlin: Cathedral of the Archangel Michael, 1505–9
12 Cathedral of St Vladimir bez glavy, first half of the 16th century   13 Kitaigorod walls, 1534–38   14 Dulo Tower of the Simonov Monastery, late 16th century   15 'Old' Cathedral of the Donskoi Monastery, 1593   16 Danilov Monastery
17 Smolensk Cathedral of the Novodevichy Convent, 1525   18 Novodevichy Convent: St Ambrose Church, early 16th century   19 Novospassky Monastery   20 Voznesenskaya Church, Kolomenskoe, 1532   21 The Church of St John the Baptist at Dyakovo, 1547   22 St Basil's Cathedral, 1555–60   23 Angliskoe Podvore, early 16th century   24 The Romanov Palace, early 16th century   25 The Church at Khoroshevo, 1598   26 Nikita shto za Yauzy Church, 1595   27 Zachatiya Anny shto v uglu, late 15th century and late 16th century   28 Church Pokrova v Rubtsova, 1619–26   29 Belgorod walls, 1586–93   30 Earthen ramparts at Zemlyany Gorod, late 16th century

Wardens of the towns, a more democratic institution of government than any that ever existed in Muscovy, was convened to discuss the matter. The choice finally fell on Orthodox Christianity probably because of the importance of the trading relationship with Byzantium. However, the beauty and mystery of the Byzantine churches also seem to have played their part. The Chronicle tells of the great impression the churches of Constantinople made on Vladimir's envoys: 'We knew not whether we were in heaven or on earth. For on earth there is no such splendour or beauty and we are at a loss to describe it. We only know that God dwells there among men, and their service is fairer than the ceremonies of other nations. For we cannot forget that beauty.'

Thus, Greek culture, which had always meant visible forms rather than abstract ideas to the Slavs, was imported into their world. Icons, frescoes, and mosaics followed in its wake, together with the rapid building of great churches like St Sophia in Kiev and St Sophia in Novgorod on the Byzantine model of the spherical dome on a square base. Vladimir embraced the new religion so wholeheartedly that he set aside one tenth of his income for church building. Soon after, the Bible was translated into Old Slavonic, the Slav language of the time, by the Greek scholars, St Cyril and St Methodius, who in the process invented the Russian alphabet. Although there was not quite the same link with the Greek culture and language as there was between the western Church and Rome where Latin remained the language of the Church until this century, the head of the Church in Kievan Rus, the Metropolitan, was invariably a Greek. Essential differences between the eastern and western Churches were obvious in the Russian Church from the beginning with its greater emphasis on piety than on knowledge and its influence, which sometimes became direct interference, in the secular power of the Prince.

In the tenth century Kiev was a powerful and wealthy state by the standards of the times, boasting no fewer than 400 churches and eight market places inside heavily fortified walls. Its international importance is illustrated by the marriages of the children of Prince Yaroslav the Wise in the eleventh century. He himself married a princess of Sweden, his sons took German and Polish wives, and three of his daughters married the kings of Norway, Hungary and France. In Kievan Rus there were probably more than 300 towns under the control of the prince advised by a council of boyars and wardens. Town government was controlled by the Vyeche, a sort of popular assembly of free adult males. Although slavery also existed there was a large class of free farmers, the *smerdy*, a sort of yeoman class. The lovely gold and silver filigree work in the Kremlin armoury is eloquent testimonial to the high level of culture and craftsmanship of Kievan Rus.

The death of Yaroslav in 1054 marks the commencement of the decline of Kiev. He inaugurated a method of inheritance that depended on a rota system of princes and led to a dispersal of power in the kingdom. His five sons were to rule collectively, the eldest to govern Kiev, but this led to internecine strife and by 1100 twelve separate principalities in Kievan Rus were feuding with each other. At the same time another raid of nomads, the Cumans, swept in from the east and contributed to the depopulation of the Dnieper basin. The western crusades, too, added to the decline of Kiev by increasing the use of the Mediterranean as an alternative trading route to the Baltic and by the capture of Constantinople in the fourth crusade. Meanwhile, other enemies, the Teutonic Knights, Lithuanians, Swedes and Hungarians, threatened from the north and west.

As a result there was a second Slav migration, this time to the wooded north-west, the *zalessky* (beyond the woods) area of the Upper Volga and the basin of the Oka. In 1169 Prince Andrei Bogolyubsky at the head of a coalition of twelve princes sacked the city of Kiev and established a new capital, Vladimir, in the north-western principality of Rostov-Suzdal. A famous and most revered ancient icon of Greek origin, the Virgin lovingly embracing the Child, the Vladimirsky Bogomatery, accompanied his victorious march north to the site of his new capital. Future movements of this icon were also to indicate changes of political power.

A new style of architecture emerged after the rupture with Kiev. The Byzantine cube was contracted and extended upwards and the cupola, although still not a true onion dome, had acquired an elongated point in the centre. The most perfect example of this type of church is the utterly beautiful simplicity of the little Pokrova na Nerl (the Intercession of the Virgin on the Nerli River) built in 1165. Happily it is still situated alone in the midst of fields on the banks of what is now a minor stream, and its view is not obscured by later buildings. In the twelfth century the little river was a major highway and it was probably crowded by other buildings. Over the centuries the church was altered many times and lost its original simplicity. First attempts to restore it to its twelfth-century aspect were undertaken in the late nineteenth century when it was given the large onion dome it now bears although it was later agreed that it probably first carried a flatter, helmet-shaped dome. Later, in the first ten years after the revolution, extensive restoration was carried out and now, except for the dome and the fact that it is not a functioning church, it is as it was originally.

Barely fifty years after the foundation of the new capital of Vladimir the Mongol hordes, under Genghis Khan, swept across the Russian plain in the years between 1237 and 1240 and conquered Rus by taking nearly all of its major towns and laying them waste. Although Novgorod and Pskov, the northern and western outposts of Rus, remained inviolate, those great cities were obliged together with all the Russian towns to pay tribute to the Khans. All contact with Europe was decisively ended for over two hundred years, an event that, more than anything else, influenced the future development of Moscow.

The rise of Muscovy
Even the writers of the ancient chronicles were amazed at the growth and rise of the little village of Muscovy on the edge of the Rostov-Suzdal lands. Unlike Vladimir,

no great ruler deliberately chose it to be his new capital. It is first mentioned in the chronicle for 1147 when the Grand Prince of Suzdal, Yuri Dolgoruky, invited Sviatoslav, the Prince of Novgorod, to come to Moscow to enjoy a 'mighty banquet'. Prince Dolgoruky kept a small palace at Moscow for resting on his journeys south. In 1156 the chronicle records that the prince built wooden walls around his hall at the confluence of the Moskva and Neglinnaya Rivers probably close to the present Borovitsky Gate in the Kremlin (*bor* means pine wood).

But why should this little village on the border of a great principality become the undisputed centre of a reunited and greatly expanded Rus? It was strategically situated at the junction of the north-south Rostov-Ryazan route and the east-west Smolensk-Vladimir route, i.e. midway between the Rus of the Upper Volga and the Rus of the Dnieper. Klyuchevsky, the great Russian historian, concluded that Moscow's geographical position was in large part responsible for this expansion. He explains that the most vigorous colonization took place along the river systems of the Upper Volga and the Oka; strings of towns grew up alongside the rivers and then these chains extended up their tributaries. Moscow was in the centre of this *mezhdureche* (between the rivers) area, a settlement at the end of the portage between the Yauza, the east-west highway of the time, and the Kama which, through the Sosh, emptied into the Volga. As the north-south route also ran through Moscow, rapid settlement took place there, which included the establishment of a large number of boyars, always in the forefront of colonization.

In the thirteenth and fourteenth centuries Moscow was at the centre of the Russian towns under the hegemony of the Mongol horde, from their capital Sarai, near present-day Volgograd. It was bounded on the north by Novgorod, on the west and south-west by the Lithuanian-Polish empire, on the north-east, east and south by the Mongols and other peoples. Expansion in any direction was impossible but curiously, for those troubled times, the central position of Moscow kept it relatively safe from concerted foreign attack. By the fourteenth century the frequency of the Tartar raids had diminished and popular industry had begun to recover. The subsequent emergence of highly autocratic Muscovy, the absence of all free political institutions, the lack of any real contact with the west during the period of the Renaissance and the Reformation, the forms of Asian servitude including the kowtow, diplomatic protocol and even the wearing of the richly decorated caftan, were indirect results of the lengthy period of Tartar overlordship. The 'backwardness' of Moscow noted by nearly every western traveller from the sixteenth century onwards is in large measure due to this accident of history. With the end of Tartar rule and the rise of Muscovy every tsar from Ivan III onwards, but particularly Peter the Great, strained towards emulating the technologically more advanced west while at the same time dismissing its rational philosophies.

Another factor which helps to explain the rise of Moscow was the role played by its quietly ambitious and politically unscrupulous princes who accepted the invidious role of tribute-gatherer for the Mongols. In the process of collecting the taxes not only did they assert their authority over other princes but they also began gradually to assimilate the lands bordering on Moscow. The Moscow princes also had a source of valuable revenue in their ability to extract dues from the traffic flowing south-west and north-east. The line of Moscow princes was founded by Daniel (1263–1303), the youngest son of the hero Alexander Nevsky of Novgorod, who defeated the German knights in the famous battle on the spring ice covering Lake Peipus. Daniel raised Moscow to the level of a principality and slowly began the process of acquiring neighbouring land, doubling the area of Moscow in his lifetime.

His grandson Ivan (1325–41), nicknamed Kalita (moneybags), adroitly continued to extend the influence of Moscow over lesser principalities some many miles away, such as Uglich, Beloozero, and Gallich on the Upper Volga. By 1353 Ivan Kalita, who already had the right to collect taxes for the Horde, had also assumed judicial authority over the other princes of Rus with the backing of the Mongols. Ivan Kalita is the first of the Moscow Grand Princes to be buried in the Archangelsky Cathedral in the Kremlin (his body was transferred from the old cathedral to the present one in the sixteenth century).

The first Russian offensive against the Tartars, the Battle of Kulikovo, took place near the Don River in 1380. The Russian forces, a coalition of the northern towns led by the Moscow Grand Prince Dmitry Donskoi, resoundingly defeated the Mongol troops. It did not mean the end of the Mongol threat, for two years later they returned to devastate Moscow, Vladimir and Mozhaisk and they were to remain a threat for the next two hundred years, but it signalled the beginning of the end, the first time Russian troops had emerged victorious after an encounter with the Tartars. The splendid Donskoi Monastery in southern Moscow was built over the place from where Dmitry Donskoi and his troops set forth to the battlefield. He received the appellation 'Donskoi' after the location of the battle near the Don River.

By the mid-fifteenth century Moscow had assumed a commanding role over most of northern Rus. Under the far-seeing rule of Ivan III, known as the 'Great' and the grandfather of Ivan the Terrible, the first ruler to claim the title of Tsar, this position was consolidated. By the end of his reign in 1505 the proud independence of Novgorod to the north was broken allowing Muscovy to secure the enormous northern area up to the White Sea. Tribute was withheld from the Tartars to the south who retired ignominiously from a proposed attack on Moscow in 1480. By 1502 the Golden Horde ceased to exist as a united force. Ivan failed to expel his western enemy, the Lithuanians, but did manage to push them back to the upper stretches of the Western Dvina and Dnieper. With the acquisition early in his reign of the remaining Russian lands not yet under Moscow tutelage – Yaroslav, Rostov, Tver, Perm, Pskov and Ryazan – he vastly extended his empire, and the land of Muscovy increased fourfold between 1462 and 1505.

For all its extremely close relationship with the Tsar, the Russian Church was still largely influenced by Byzantine practice and trappings although, significantly, it had not taken over Byzantine intellectual curiosity. During the centuries of Tartar rule it had been cut off from the Orthodox Church in other countries and in the fifteenth century when it began to reassert its independence, Constantinople fell to the Turks. The practices of the Russian Church were based on unquestioning acceptance of dogma combined with exotic ritual and rich decoration that must have seemed to the Russian peasant from his rude hut, as it did to Vladimir's emissaries in the tenth century, like the representation of heaven on earth. At the Easter service, the most important festival of the year, the 'Royal Doors' open into the mysteries of the altar dramatically revealing golden light, silver and sparkle that is intended to represent heaven.

Ivan began to establish contact with countries outside the new borders of Muscovy and in 1472, as a widower, he married Sophia Paleologue, the niece of the last Byzantine Emperor, who had taken refuge in Rome when the Turks took Constantinople. Sophia's entourage, therefore, included the Papal Legate and although his attempt to spread Catholicism went entirely unheeded, Philip, the Metropolitan of Moscow, took great umbrage at the arrival of this heretic in the Kremlin and refused to marry Ivan and Sophia. The Tsar and his bride, according to fond legend, were finally wed after bribing the priest of the small church in the Bolshoi Posad or Kitaigorod as it became known later.

After the fall of Constantinople and Rome a monk from Pskov wrote meaningfully to Ivan's son, Vasily III, 'two Romes have already fallen but the third remains standing and a fourth there will not be'. Already in the fourteenth century the post of Metropolitan of Moscow had been created. In addition in 1395 the revered icon, the Virgin of Vladimir, brought by Andrei Bogolyubsky from Kiev 200 years earlier, had been ceremoniously transferred from the Cathedral of the Assumption in Vladimir to Moscow to give heart to its citizens expecting a siege from Tamerlane. It was never returned. A century later, the icon was placed in the new Cathedral of the Assumption in the Kremlin, finally signifying the pre-eminent position of Moscow.

The earliest buildings of Moscow
Apart from the splendid buildings of the Kremlin, the architecture of the fifteenth and early sixteenth centuries is not well represented in the Moscow of today. At that time as for most of its history Moscow was predominantly a city of wood, the building material which for centuries had been both cheap and easily accessible. As late as 1812 the city was predominantly wooden and even today the old suburbs of Moscow still boast many streets of little wooden houses nestling close to each other, slightly rickety and out of true, reminding one of a painting by Chagall. The devastation wrought by frequent fires that wiped out whole districts without warning meant that houses had to be frequently rebuilt. A large market was located near the present Vysoko-Petrovsky Monastery near the wall of Belgorod (where the

Boulevard Ring Road now is) which specialized in the selling of precut logs for the required number of rooms, an early example of prefabricated houses. The purchaser would trundle away the logs, gables, roofing etc., in a sleigh or cart and reassemble his house within a matter of days. The houses were therefore mostly of the same size and height and placed regularly along the streets which had to be wide enough to allow the digging of firebreaks. A few stone churches were erected as Moscow became richer and more secure from Tartar attack and some of these, remarkably, have survived to our time. The appearance of these churches was such an unusual event that they were recorded in the chronicles; it is not until the seventeenth century that stone buildings became commonplace.

A distinctive early Moscow style with borrowings mostly from the architecture of Vladimir-Suzdal and Pskov became evident by the fifteenth century and its characteristics may be studied in the handful of churches that remain from that time in and near Moscow, many of them having recently received the careful attention of such Soviet restorers as L. A. David and M. Maksimov. Although the most immediate and trenchant influence on the architecture of the new capital came from Vladimir and Suzdal, the highly dignified and harmonious buildings of Novgorod and the more charmingly provincial features of Pskov were also of great importance for its development. Novgorod as a city with its nascent stirrings of democracy and its rich merchants and small but powerful middle class was utterly unlike Moscow. Its citizens built many churches between the twelfth and the fifteenth centuries but then its independence was finally extinguished by Moscow. The Novgorod architects in common with their Vladimir counterparts gradually modified the Kievan-Byzantine legacy of six piers and five domes to four piers and a single central dome. The Kievan triple apse had become by the fourteenth century a single apse incorporated more and more within the body of the church and as a consequence less protuberant. The dome, too, underwent marked modifications from the Saracen helmet shape typical of Kiev and Vladimir. Wood, the material of which most of the early churches were built, was flexible enough to allow the dome to be altered easily by drawing up the apex which made the sides bulge out. This now familiar onion shape was to become even more pointed in the hands of the Moscow architects. By the end of the thirteenth century the slanted gable roof more appropriate to the ice and snow of Novgorod had replaced the flat Byzantine roof. In this way Novgorod churches became simpler, with less external decoration, and considerably smaller than the vast Byzantine-type cathedrals like St Sophia.

In Pskov, on the edge of the Russian lands, the shape of the churches is more squat and bulbous although they convey a great sense of the medieval period with their heavy walls and small apertures. The essential conservatism of the Pskov builders did not prevent them from evolving a system of corbelled arches in place of the pendentives used in Byzantium for supporting the central dome. This allowed for a low church-roof without diminishing the height of the dome and this important innovation was brought to Moscow by the Pskov builders invited by Ivan to help in the reconstruction of the Kremlin.

The strongest influence on Moscow was the architecture of Vladimir and Suzdal. At first the splendid palaces and churches raised by the Suzdalian princes in an attempt to rival Kiev borrowed heavily from the latter although they were built in white limestone and wood. At the beginning also the interior and exterior of the churches were closely integrated but by the fourteenth century this changed with the penchant for exterior sculpture. The lavish reliefs of churches like the Pokrova na Nerli were not imitated in Moscow where the use of sculpture was virtually unknown until the end of the seventeenth century but the more modest use of exterior decoration in early Moscow churches was certainly inherited from Vladimir.

The basic features that distinguish the early Moscow style were a simple plan, four internal columns, the main body of the church a heavy cube mass, material of white stone, the triple apse externally exposed, separate entrances on the remaining three sides, façades divided into three bays with segment-headed gables to each elevation, a modest use of decoration, and the exterior roofing a type of gable or *zakomary* that reflected the complex groined cruciform vaulting of the interior, supporting cupola and drum, a device that had developed in Pskov. Later, as groin vaulting became more common, the interior columns were to disappear allowing for a more spacious nave, and the exterior *zakomary* gables evolved from being primarily structural into multiple gables and purely decorative forms. These purely decorative gables as distinguished from the *zakomary* were known as *kokoshniki* after the high, elaborate, pointed women's headdress of the time. A most characteristic feature of the early Moscow church is its shape: the form of a rough pyramid rising from a heavy square base to the progressively narrower tiers of gables to the drum and thence to the point of the cupola, the latter shaped in the form of a Saracen warrior's helmet. Although early Moscow architecture borrows much from the Vladimir-Suzdal style, there are important differences. The builders in Moscow lacked the skills of their predecessors in Vladimir – the Tartar invasion had caused a decline in the quality of all the arts – and nowhere does one find the spaciousness or the high level of sculpture that was attained in churches like the Dmitriev Cathedral. Basically, the Moscow churches were smaller, simpler, more functional, yet when one sees them today they seem to be lone spokesmen of the pure beauty of simplicity and symmetry of a bygone age.

Three remarkable churches in the early Moscow style, older than anything in Moscow itself, were built in the early fifteenth century in the nearby countryside. The first is the exceedingly beautiful Uspensky (Assumption) Cathedral na gorodke built high on the banks of the Moskva River at Zvenigorod about 1399 by Yuri, the younger son of Dmitry Donskoi. Like many younger sons he had ambitions to rule in Moscow but was foiled in his desire until very late in his life. He tried to make up for it by building churches in his own principality that would excel anything in Moscow itself. In this he was more than successful. The Assumption Cathedral originally occupied the centre of the Zvenigorod Kremlin, the fortified religious-administrative centre, of which all that is left now is the earthen mound encircling the area to the north of the church. Although basically a church on the Vladimir pattern, a cube mass with four columns, triple apse, façade of three bays and a single dome, it differs from the somewhat later churches still extant in Moscow because as a court church standing near the Prince's palace it is unusually fine with its lovely narrow frieze placed midway up the façade, the pattern repeated again at the top of the drum just below the cupola and under the roof of the apse. The magnificent west end is also reminiscent of Vladimir churches with its five recessed arches, the bulbous 'melons' enriching the third and fifth arches. Another unusual feature for a church of this date is the choir-stall inside. The outstanding icon painter Rublyev, or one of his followers, is believed to have painted the frescoes, of which only fragments remain. The church's recent history is unusual. One of the oldest in the Moscow *oblast* (region), it had been closed after the Revolution, but reopened during the war when there was a slight modification of the officially hostile attitude to religion. It is still used. A small village has grown up at its foot and winding one's way up the steep path from the river, one finds oneself in a typical village street of low wooden houses – a street framed at its end with the elegant lines of Prince Yuri's church.

Still in Zvenigorod, about a half a mile from the Assumption Cathedral, is the Savvino-Storozhevsky Monastery with many interesting buildings (the monastery is now used as a military rest home and museum) including the Rozhdestvo Bogomatery (Cathedral of the Nativity of Our Lady),* also built by Prince Yuri in 1395 in a style very similar to that of the Assumption Cathedral although not with such fine proportions. The flat roofs of both the Rozhdestvo Bogomatery and the Assumption Cathedral were originally populated with striking *zakomary* gables that gave these churches a more characteristic silhouette.

A third church of this period is the Troitsa (Trinity) Cathedral of the Troitse-Sergeyev Monastery located some fifty miles north of Moscow in Zagorsk, the most important of the three monasteries still functioning in the Soviet Union. The Trinity Cathedral, built in 1422–23, is very similar to the Zvenigorod churches with its narrow frieze, its opulent portal, single cupola and overall impression of simplicity combined with modest but extremely elegant decoration. The oldest building in the monastery and the object of devotion by pilgrims, this church, perhaps more than any other, seems exclusively Russian. It was one of the first churches to bear an iconostasis (see p. 30), the complete wall of religious paintings partitioning off the altar reducing the already narrow space of the dark interior. The iconostasis was also painted by Rublyev and his pupils and the magnificence of these paintings, lit by candles, the heavy incense, the chanting of the priests in their brocaded robes, the continual coming and going of the black-robed women and bearded men give a sense of the mystery and spirituality that are the hallmarks of the Russian church.

*Rublyev was also active in this church and painted the Deisis row of the large iconostasis. After the revolution panels of this iconostasis were discovered abandoned in the church, some used as steps to a storeroom and some in the storeroom itself. They have now been cleaned and restored and are on view in the Tretyakov Gallery, a magnificent example of the highest art of icon painting.

About three miles east of the Kremlin the Andronikov Monastery perches high up on the banks of the Yauza River, in early times the main highway from Moscow to Vladimir. The monastery was founded in 1359 about the same time as several other strong monastery-fortresses that formed a semi-circle around Moscow's southern and eastern flank to protect it from Tartar raids. These were in addition to the Andronikov, the Novospassky, Simonov, Danilov, Donskoi and Novodevichy monasteries and convents. All have survived in one form or another: the Danilov is now used as a factory and only a few of its buildings have survived; the Simonov is also partly used for the Likhachev Automobile Works, and only the Novodevichy and Donskoi monasteries have functioning churches. The Andronikov Monastery, where Andrei Rublyev, the greatest of the icon painters, lived for the last twenty years of his life, contains the oldest stone building in Moscow, the Spassky Cathedral.

Even today the view of the Andronikov high up on the banks of the Yauza is an unexpected pleasure in an otherwise drably industrial part of Moscow. Its white walls, broken by a wooden grille gate, and the peace of its interior, particularly in the white stillness of winter, contrast sharply with the dusty noisy trams rattling past its east wall. In the centre of the monastery is the Spassky (Saviour) Cathedral, built between 1420 and 1427, a unique example of early Moscow architecture. Again, the similarities with Vladimir architecture are there – helmet-shaped cupolas with

1 Andronikov Monastery, mostly sixteenth and seventeenth centuries. The most ancient of Moscow's defence monasteries.

restrained decoration, an elevation subdivided by giant pilasters and narrow slit windows on the drum lighting the interior, a division of the walls into three arched bays, a recessed entranceway with 'melons'. Yet the complicated tiers of *zakomary* gables and the unequal height of the wall partitions reflecting the vaulted ceiling of the interior, the lack of a horizontal frieze half-way up the walls and the strong silhouette of the heavy base and the climbing gables leading to the point of the tall drum and cupola make it specifically Muscovite.

The restoration of the church is one of the miracles of Russian skill and dedication. It had been much altered over the centuries and was changed beyond recognition after being badly burnt in the fire of 1812, traces of which can be discerned in parts of the gables. In the 1930s it was dismantled almost completely and rebuilt after intensive research and a study of the old stones. At one time the materials of the building lay literally on the ground surrounding the base of the church and one must question the claim of the restorers to know how the church originally looked. Of course the result is partially inspired guesswork and the restorers themselves estimate it is only 90 per cent accurate, but much of the placing of the gables and use of decoration was agreed upon only after twenty years of study. The rebuilt church was not completed until 1960 to coincide with the six hundredth anniversary of Rublyev's birth.

About two miles away on the Boulevard Ring Road where it meets Ulitsa

2 Novospassky (New Saviour) Monastery, transferred from the Kremlin at the end of the fifteenth century. Walls and buildings are of the sixteenth and seventeenth centuries.

3 Blagoveshchensky Sobor (Cathedral of the Annunciation) in the Kremlin. Built by craftsmen from Pskov, 1484–89. (See pages 30–1.)

Zhdanova is the Rozhdestvensky (Nativity) Convent. Like the Andronikov it is also part of a series of fortress monasteries but one that protected the northern and western flank of inner Moscow. The Cathedral of the Nativity, built 1501–05, bears some resemblance to the Spassky Cathedral, its style of architecture belonging more to the fifteenth century than the sixteenth. It is best viewed from the back or apse side in order to avoid the odd, nineteenth-century accretion on the front. Four internal pilasters are no longer free-standing but pushed back into the corner, and support the roof of the cathedral with its groin vaulting and its gables. The gables are staggered, with each of the upper ones rising from midway between two on the lower tier – a feature which marks the beginning of the transition of the gable to a more decorative object.

There is yet another of these very early churches still extant in Moscow. It served a completely different function from the two monastery cathedrals. St Trifon v Naprudnom, in the village of Naprudnoe, is a *posad* church, one belonging to a particular settlement, in other words an ordinary parish church and the only one to survive from the late fifteenth and early sixteenth centuries. Bricks, which had only recently come into use in Moscow, were here used sparingly for the cornices, the drum of the cupola, along the edge of the gable, the odd roof bell-tower and the upper part of the interior roof. As in the Nativity Cathedral, the system of groin vaulting has removed the need for free-standing pillars in the interior of the church. Like the cathedral of the Andronikov Monastery, each elevation is divided into three arched bays, the central section higher than those on either side of it. The most unusual feature is the little bell-tower standing on the roof found in the course of restoration by L. David in the 1950s. This is very rare in Moscow churches where bell-towers soon became buildings separate from the main church. The church, also situated high up on a hill, is becoming completely submerged and isolated by the tall blocks of flats and factories springing up all round it.

4 St Trifon v Naprudnom, end of the fifteenth century. One of the first of the parish churches in Moscow to be built of masonry. Note the unusual roof bell-tower. 4a View of the apse.

Of the same architectural period although built a little later is the Antipy Church shto na Kolymazhnom Dvore. It was built on what is now Ulitsa Marksa i Engelsa in the first half of the sixteenth century near where the old royal carriage house was situated. It is similar to the other early Moscow churches but differs markedly in detail – the apse is divided decisively into two asymmetrical parts and is finished not with the usual cornices but by a row of decorative rounded *kokoshniki*. The pointed gables clustering around the base of the cupola are also decorative for here there are no internal pillars, the roof being supported by the system of groin vaulting. The front of the church on the corner of the street has been altered by the addition of an eighteenth-century chapel.

2 NEW BUILDING IN THE KREMLIN

Ivan the Great began the transition of the former village into a great capital by demolishing the crumbling, small edifices of the Kremlin, the fortified triangular area in the centre of Moscow, and building it anew. No one is quite sure of the sense or from what language the word *Kreml* derives but some think it originates from the Greek words *kremn* and *krimnos* meaning a steep hill over a ravine, while others believe it means thick, coniferous woods in a swampy place. Be that as it may, by the time of Ivan Kalita in the fourteenth century it was being described in the chronicles as the *Kreml. Kreml* also came to mean the fortified citadels of other ancient Russian towns like many near Moscow: Tver (now Kalinin), Tula, Kolomna, Rostov Veliky, Ryazan. As part of improved defence arrangements against frequent Tartar raids during the infancy of Dmitry Donskoi in the fourteenth century, the Moscow Kremlin's old wooden walls, which must have given it the appearance of a stockade, were replaced by those of white limestone. Henceforth the Kremlin symbolized the secular and ecclesiastical power of the state while commercial and financial activities were carried on outside its walls. There are no buildings in the Kremlin earlier than the reign of Ivan III.

The Mediterranean world in the fifteenth century was glorying in the Renaissance, the eruption in philosophy and the arts of a new sense of freedom. Ivan III sent an emissary, Semyon Tolbuzin, to Venice, who found there one Alberti Fioraventi, an architect from Bologna who had acquired some fame in the city. Ivan entrusted this man with his most important project, the rebuilding of the Cathedral of the Assumption in the Kremlin. In 1472 Russian craftsmen had already tried to build a large church on the model of the twelfth-century Assumption Cathedral in Vladimir. However, the Russian builders were not skilled in the techniques for large buildings and the walls cracked before the church was properly finished. Fioraventi, nicknamed 'Aristotle' by admiring Russians, was also obliged to use the Vladimir Cathedral as his inspiration and guide and there is evidence that he visited Novgorod as well. He arrived in 1475 and for a salary of ten roubles a month managed to

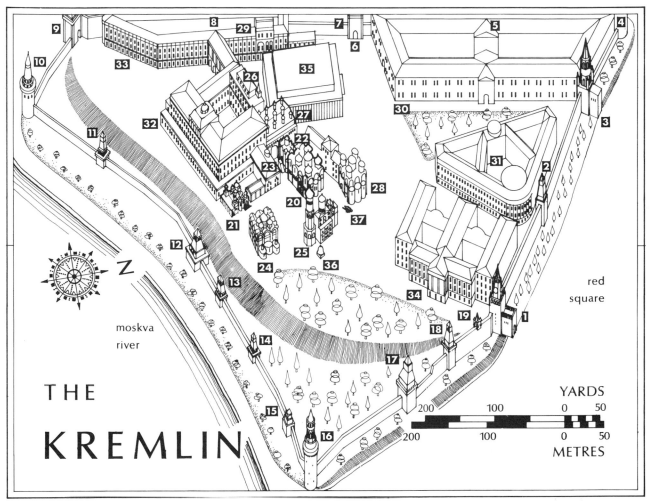

THE

KREMLIN

1 Spassky gate 2 Senate Tower 3 St Nicholas Gate 4 Corner Arsenal Tower 5 Middle
Arsenal Tower 6 Trinity Gate 7 Kutafya Tower 8 Armoury Tower 9 Borovitsky Gate
10 Water Tower 11 Annunciation Tower 12 Tainitsky Tower 13 First Nameless Tower
14 Second Nameless Tower 15 Petrovsky Tower 16 Beklemishev Tower 17 St Constantine
and Helena Gate 18 Alarm Tower 19 Tsar's Tower 20 Uspensky Cathedral, 1475–79
21 Blagoveshchensky Cathedral, 1484–89 22 Rizpolozheny Church, 1484–85 23 Granovitaya
Palace, 1487–91 24 Cathedral of the Archangel Michael, 1505–9 25 Bell Tower of Ivan Veliky,
1505–08 26 Terem Palace, 1635–36 27 Upper Saviour Cathedral, 1635–6 28 Cathedral of the
Twelve Apostles and Patriarch's Palace, 1656 29 Poteshny Palace, 1652, much altered in 19th
century 30 The Arsenal, 1702–36 31 The Senate (Building of the Council of Ministers),
1776–87 32 Kremlin Great Palace, 1838–49 33 The Armoury, 1851 34 Kremlin Theatre,
1930–34 35 Palace of Congresses, 1960–61 36 Tsar Bell, 1733–35 37 Tsar Cannon, 16th
century

5 Uspensky Sobor (Assumption Cathedral) in the Kremlin, by Fioraventi, 1475–79. The most important building in the Kremlin.

complete the cathedral in four years. His achievement still dominates the Kremlin and served as a model for Russian architects until the end of the seventeenth century.

The Uspensky (Assumption) Cathedral on the north side of Cathedral Square is the most important and the most ancient building in the Kremlin ensemble. Fioraventi and his Italian craftsmen were able to build a more spacious church with their advanced technology than could the Russians and they are said to have saved Russia one hundred years of building evolution. Externally, the Assumption Cathedral is similar to the church in Vladimir with its characteristic belt of blind arcading forming a band around the otherwise plain walls, punctuated by windows cunningly hidden among the pilasters to provide the interior with light, and with the division of each wall except the apse into four arched sectors. The lovely stone arched portal with columns receding into the interior, the painting surmounted by a roof over the portal and the paintings over the bulbous apse provide a welcome contrast to the stark simplicity of the massive walls. Finally, five great gilded cupolas in the shape of warrior helmets on their massive drums complete and provide a constant harmony to this lovely church. The Italians left no obvious mark of the Renaissance style on the façade of the church although in small ways their influence can be seen. The way the apse does not protrude but is nearly unnoticeable in the square of the building and the finish on the capitals and pillars indicate their hand.

Inside, the cathedral is unusually light and airy and gives an impression of space and height and grandeur, a very different sort of church from the low, narrow, dark Russian churches of the time. Indeed, until the eighteenth century such spacious places of worship were not generally built. The original iconostasis and wall frescoes were executed by Dionisy, a famous icon painter of his time, but only a few fragments remain of his work in the altar and small Chapel of Praise. New frescoes were painted in 1642–3 but these were touched up several times and painted over with oil paints in the nineteenth century. Cleaning and restoration of the old frescoes began before the Revolution and was finally concluded in 1950, and some of the frescoes on the south wall and in other places are now as they probably were in the seventeenth century. The huge iconostasis which was covered in gilded silver at the end of the nineteenth century until the Revolution contained the most famous of all Russian icons, the Virgin of Vladimir, now replaced in the place of honour, the lower right of the iconostasis, by a copy (the original is in the Tretyakov Gallery). Although it ceased to function as a place of worship in 1918, the cathedral continues as a museum of art treasures, a role it adopted as the most important church in the land from its beginning. Many wonderful icons hang there such as the famous twelfth-century icon of St George.

The cathedral was used only for the grandest ceremonial occasions like royal weddings, coronations, declarations of war, and services of thanksgiving at their conclusion, and after deliverance from calamities. Ivan III broke off relations with the Tartars here by ripping up the Tartar document demanding tribute. The cathedral was the principal church of the metropolitans after they moved to Moscow from Vladimir and of the patriarchs after the establishment of the title in 1589. All the metropolitans and patriarchs from the time of Metropolitan Peter in 1326 are buried here with the exceptions of Tikhon and Aleksei, the two patriarchs of Soviet times. Near the south entrance is the carved Tsar's throne made in 1551 for Ivan the Terrible and, nearby, the Patriarch's stone throne.

During the five decades between 1475 and 1525 the Kremlin was completely transformed, not only with the magnificence of the Assumption Cathedral but also with the appearance of other churches, two more cathedrals (the term cathedral in Russian meant an important church rather than the seat of a bishop), and royal palaces built for the first time in stone instead of wood (the first stone domestic dwelling was built in 1471 for the wealthy merchant, Tarakan). Many of these buildings have survived to our day, a remarkable achievement considering how many times the Kremlin was sacked, occupied, burnt, and fought over. Ivan was wise in choosing Italian builders and many more followed Fioraventi, including Pietro Antonio Solario, Marco Ruffo, Alevisio Novo, and Marco Bono da Caracano. They not only rebuilt the interior of the Kremlin but extended its territory north and east and increased its size by a third. They rebuilt the heavy brick walls with their eighteen towers, five main gates and extruding barbican making it into a true citadel. The shape of the Kremlin was the traditional Russian triangle at the confluence of two rivers, the Moskva and the Neglinnaya, with a wide moat on the third side providing a constant barrier of water. The walls made an indomitable fortress inside which palaces, cathedrals and monasteries were grandly situated. The three corner towers, the Arsenal, Water Tower and the Beklemishev, were round, the others all square. Soon after they were built small pointed tent-shaped towers built in the Russian style to allow snow to slide off were placed over the main gates and towers and pointed wooden roofing along the upper walkways appeared. At first the tent-shaped towers were of wood but in the seventeenth century they were rebuilt of brick looking today much the same as they did then. The walls on the Red Square side were built higher than elsewhere to compensate for the lack of a natural water barrier and three of the main gates of the Kremlin were situated on the market square.

The Spassky (Saviour) was the grandest gate and was used for the entrances and exits of the tsars and ambassadors. This gate bears an inscription on the interior side of the tower over the archway: 'Ivan Vasilievich, by the grace of God, Grand Prince of Vladimir, Moscow, Novgorod, Tver, Pskov, Vyatka, Ugorsky, Perm, Bolgaria and other towns, Lord of All Russia, in the thirtieth year of his reign ordered this tower to be built and so it was done by Pietro Antonio Solario, citizen of the Medici, in the year 1491 from the Incarnation of our Lord . . .' Spassky Gate was graced with the first clock in Moscow in the sixteenth century. Christopher Galloway, an English architect, designed and built the Gothic spire over the tower in 1624–5 and replaced the old clock with a new one with thirteen bells which rang out the hour. According to today's Russian guides describing Red Square, the original Galloway clock was discovered in 1850 in the basement of the Faceted Palace with its chimes intact and it was then replaced on the Spassky Tower, the roman numerals and copper pointers were gilded, the base painted black and the chimes adjusted to play the 'Preobrazhensky March'. In 1917 the clock was damaged during Red Guard attacks on the Kremlin but Lenin personally ordered it to be repaired and its chimes altered so as to play the first bars of the 'Internationale' which it does to this day, forming the signature tune of Moscow Radio.

6 Borovitsky Gate from inside the Kremlin. The base, designed by Italian architects, was built at the end of the fifteenth century, the tower was added in the seventeenth century and the red star was fixed in position in the 1930s.

Beside the Assumption Cathedral is a lowly church, small, perfect, and white, contrasting greatly with the grand features of the cathedral. The Rizpolozheny (Deposition of the Robe) was built by craftsmen from Pskov in 1484–5 and is more typical of the times than the great church beside it. The wide steps and terrace before the entrance may have been originally a covered arcaded gallery. Although tiny and intimate, it is unusually light inside from the tall windows on the drum of the cupola. The frescoes were completed in 1644 and the iconostasis in 1627 but it was damaged many times in fires and partially rebuilt after every disaster. It has been restored in Soviet times, most recently in 1968.

Ranged beside the Rizpolozheny Church is the oldest secular building still extant in Moscow, the Granovitaya or Faceted Palace, built between 1487 and 1491 by the two Italians, Marco Ruffo and Pietro Antonio Solario. It is named after the diamond-shaped pattern on the palace's exterior often encountered in medieval Russian architecture, possibly a derivation of the geometrical shapes dominant in Persian architecture. The palace consists of two floors, the lower one for storage and service rooms, and the upper one, a single, large chamber supported by a magnificent central pillar both functional and decorative supporting a vaulted ceiling. The hall, the largest in Muscovy when it was built, was used mainly for feasts and as an audience chamber where the tsars received foreign ambassadors and accepted gifts and letters of credence watched by black-robed, tall-hatted boyars and nobles forming a dramatic and sinister background to the event. The palace has survived almost unchanged except for enlargement of the windows in the seventeenth century. The heavily painted walls date from the 1880s although the nineteenth-century painters faithfully followed the original plan for the paintings designed by Simon Ushakov in 1668. The chandeliers are nineteenth-century copies of ancient prototypes.

One odd fact about the palace that strikes the visitor is that there appears to be no way of entering it from the square. In fact the palace was meant to be entered from the Terem Palace behind it and a lovely doorway connects the two. However, an elaborate staircase, the famous Red Staircase, was built beside the Faceted Palace to the Terem Palace joining both to the square. In the seventeenth century it had a roofed porch and its iron fretwork was painted gold and red. Although the roof did not survive long, the staircase, flanked by proud eagles and lions, was extant until the 1930s when the Kremlin Great Palace was altered. Its removal seems singularly unnecessary and leaves Cathedral Square incomplete. It was from this staircase in 1682 that Peter the Great as a small boy of ten, newly proclaimed Tsar with his half brother Ivan, witnessed the invasion into the Kremlin of the enraged *streltsy* (or armed mercenaries) and the wild massacre of many of his family.

All this frenzy of building in the late fifteenth and early sixteenth centuries awoke the arts from the long slumber in which they had lain during Mongol hegemony. The iconostasis, the wooden screen of formal rows of icons which separated the body of the church from the altar, developed to its highest level at this time. Although a strict order was not always adhered to, the following pattern was customary: the bottom tier represented local saints or the patron of that particular church, the second tier Christ in Majesty flanked on either side by Mary and John the Baptist with the disciples receding left and right of them, surmounted by a smaller row of icons illustrating the twelve most important church festivals, and finally, at the top, a row of icons representing the patriarchs of the church. The whole effect of such a screen, its brilliant colours on gold backgrounds, the different sizes of the tiers – the second and fourth tiers were much larger than the others – and its gilded wooden frames was one of incredible richness and splendour before the mystery of the hidden altar. The greatest icon painters were those of the fourteenth and early fifteenth centuries: Theophanes, the Greek, Daniel Cherny, and the most outstanding of them all, the master painter Andrei Rublyev. He was the artist responsible for part of the great iconostasis of the Blagoveshchensky (Annunciation) Cathedral.

This golden-headed cathedral on the south side of Cathedral Square was also part of Ivan's building programme. Ten years after the Assumption Cathedral, it was built in 1484–9 by craftsmen from Pskov over the undercroft of an early-fifteenth-century church. It is much smaller than the grand Assumption Cathedral for it was used as the private church of the grand princes and tsars, the nearest place of worship to their palace. Originally it looked quite different from its appearance today. At first it had only three domes and an ambulatory extending around the church on three sides, probably with a roofed arcade. As it was built on the strong stone ground floor of the earlier building used by the grand princes and tsars to store their treasures, it was raised high off the ground. This was an architectural feature of many of the early wooden churches which used the ground floor as a storehouse, and where the main entrance would be up a flight of stairs to the first floor.

In the year of Ivan the Terrible's coronation, 1547, a disastrous fire struck Moscow and damaged the cathedral. By a miracle the iconostasis which came from the earlier church survived unscathed. In 1564 Ivan had the cathedral restored and partially rebuilt adding in the central area on the west side two new domes to harmonize the roof, enclosing the open gallery, and, at the four corners of the gallery, placing four chapels each topped by a small dome, making nine domes in all. In 1572 in the south-east corner a new porch and flight of steps were built, the famous Ivan the Terrible steps. It is said that his many marriages (seven in all not to mention the numerous concubines) caused the Metropolitan to protest that the Tsar could only attend services from his own entrance on the south-east side of the church and could not enter the church proper but must remain behind a grille. The Russian Church does not sanction more than three marriages.

The interior of the cathedral is high but narrow. With every inch of wall and column painted in warm colours, the sixteenth-century floor of red and brown jasper, and the luxury of the gilt-framed iconostasis across the whole of the eastern wall, it gives an impression of enclosed overpowering richness, which is somehow more indigenously 'Russian' than the spaciousness of the Assumption Cathedral. the frescoes, according to a notation on the wall, were completed in 1508. Although they survived the 1547 fire, they were painted over many times, as was the Russian custom when holy pictures began to darken with age. In the late nineteenth century first attempts were made to discover the old paintings underneath and many were thus revealed. However, restoration techniques were crude, some of the paintings were lost, and the rest were painted over once more. After the Revolution, some work was done on the frescoes but it was not until after the Second World War in the general work on the Kremlin that the frescoes were properly cleaned and restored.

The most glorious part of the cathedral is undoubtedly the iconostasis, possibly the best in the USSR. The chronicles say that painting was begun in 1405 by the three most outstanding icon painters ever to paint in Russia. The whole scheme of the iconostasis was the vision of Theophanes the Greek, who is responsible for much of the most brilliant painting in Novgorod. He himself painted the three central icons of the Deisis or second tier: Christ in Majesty is the central figure with Mary on his right and John the Baptist on his left. It is possible that he also painted the Archangel Gabriel and the Apostle Paul in the same tier. Rublyev was responsible for some of the icons of the small delicately detailed third row, the tier of the twelve most important festivals of the church. His work includes the Annunciation, the Birth of Christ, the Transfiguration, and the Purification of the Virgin. Prokhor the Elder from Gorodets was the third artist. The fourth tier, which depicts the patriarchs of the church, dates from the sixteenth century and the first row, containing icons of local saints and of the event after which the church was named, the Annunication, dates from the fourteenth to the seventeenth centuries. This uniquely beautiful collection of outstanding icons with the majesty of the large group of the Deisiis tier offset by the miniature tapestry of the festival row would be enough to make any visit to the Kremlin memorable.

During the rebuilding of the Kremlin under Ivan III and his son, churches in a dilapidated condition such as the Cathedral of the Archangel Michael were rebuilt. The Italian, Alevisio Novi, who seems to have spent some time in Venice, rebuilt the cathedral in 1505–9. Although it bears five cupolas in accordance with the church canons of the time it differs essentially from other Russian churches in displaying distinctly Italian characteristics. Pilasters divide the entire length of the squared walls culminating in Corinthian capitals, a new element in Russian architecture. The most outstanding innovation in Venice at the time was the indented scalloped 'shell' which formed the motif of the gable. As can be seen at the Novodevichy Monastery and at the Vysoko Petrovsky Monastery, for more than a century Russian architects borrowed the ideas used in the Archangel Cathedral. The central dome was originally gilded and the four outside cupolas were then white – all are now painted silver. The lavish west door entrance into the cathedral is richly ornamented in the Italian Renaissance style.

The Archangel Michael is believed to be a protector of princes and the cathedral was used as the burial place of the Moscow grand princes from Ivan Kalita in 1349 until the capital was moved to St Petersburg in 1712–13. Thus Ivan III, Ivan the Terrible and his sons are buried here along with the first Romanovs, Mikhail Fyodorovich and Aleksei Mikhailovich. Boris Godunov is the only tsar before 1712 not to be buried in the cathedral – he was buried at the Troitse – Sergeyev Monastery

7 The bell-tower of Ivan Veliky in the Kremlin, by the Italian Marco Bono, 1505–08.

in Zagorsk – but to compensate for his absence Peter II, who died of smallpox at the age of sixteen while visiting Moscow in 1730, is buried here. Some years ago, the coffin of Ivan the Terrible was opened to allow archaeologists to examine his remains and an effigy was made of his head from his skull. It resembles remarkably closely existing portraits of the Tsar, most of which were done in the nineteenth century. The cathedral was used as a sort of shrine; here the grand princes and tsars came to pay their respects to their dead ancestors after their coronations or before setting out to do battle.

After the Archangel Cathedral was built every side of Cathedral Square displayed grand buildings but one. Therefore, between 1505 and 1508 the soaring column of the bell-tower of Ivan Veliky was raised on the site of the fourteenth-century church of Ivan 'of the Ladder' by yet another of the Italian architects, Marco Bono. The tall bell-tower with a chapel inside its lower part served to unite the ensemble of cupolas by providing the only upward lift. At first the white tower was two tiers lower than it is now but in 1600 Boris Godunov added the upper part as can be seen by the gilt inscription on the dark blue background around the top of the drum. The added height of the bell-tower was part of a grandiose plan by Godunov to build a huge church, the Church of the Resurrection, in place of the Assumption Cathedral but, fortunately for posterity, this part of his plan was never realized. Ivan Veliky, some 265 feet high, was used as the watch-tower of the Kremlin. For a time, after the Kremlin was reopened to the public in 1955 (it had been closed since Lenin's death), tourists were allowed to climb the steps to get a wonderful view of Moscow. The twenty-one bells of Ivan Veliky, silent since the Revolution, peeled again during the victory parade in Moscow in 1945.

Ivan III died in 1505 and was succeeded by his son Vasily III who completed his father's ambitious building programme in the Kremlin and who was responsible for the erection of many stone parish (*posad*) churches using the hard working Italian architects. The only one to survive is the Church of St Vladimir bez glavy (without domes) on Khokhlovsky Pereulok and Stary Sadekh streets. It was rebuilt about 1689 but the lower half and porch date from the original building. The lovely medieval arched porch is decorated with small columns embellished with melons and sheaves of wheat.

3 THE CITY AT THE END OF THE FIFTEENTH CENTURY

As it expanded its territory and its population increased Moscow outgrew the boundary imposed by the Kremlin walls and spread itself in a great arc around the Kremlin from the Moskva River on either side. However, settlement was concentrated to the east of the Kremlin and fifty years after the rebuilding of the Kremlin walls, massive thick stone walls commissioned by Vasily III before he died were built by the Italian Petrok Maly in 1534–38 to enclose the Great *Posad* or Settlement. It joined the Kremlin at the Moskva River to the south and at the Arsenal Tower where the Neglinnaya flowed to the north forming a sort of rectangle. The new fortress town was called Kitaigorod meaning not 'chinatown' as it would in modern Russian but 'defended city' or 'middle fortress' as the outer part of the city, Belgorod, was already heavily settled. Its walls were so broad that a carriage and pair of horses could drive along the top. They survived for the most part, although in dilapidated condition, until Soviet times when the fury of Metro building in the 1930s and 1950s led to their virtual disappearance. Remnants remain by the Rossiya Hotel on Kitaisky Proezd and between Sverdlov Square and Tretyakovsky Proezd.

8 Fragment of the Kitaigorod Wall, 1534–38.

During the sixteenth century a tentative step was made towards establishing close relations with western Europe, and for the first time there are traveller's tales by English observers, the first western Europeans to visit Muscovy after the Italians of Ivan the Great's reign, of how they found the strange land and people. By the end of the century, the printed word had come to Muscovy, the autoccphalous position of the Russian church had been recognized with the establishment of the position of the patriarchate, close relations with the English has been embarked upon, and the city, in spite of fire, raids and plague, had swollen its borders and twice extended its boundaries. Stone churches were no longer an unusual sight and an extravagant, even spectacular, architectural style with a closer relationship to indigenous wooden church architecture than to Byzantine models suddenly sprang up overwhelming the simple lines of the early Moscow style.

4 ST BASIL'S

The background to St Basil's

Ivan IV, Ivan Grozny (the Terrible), became legal ruler in 1533 at the age of three on the death of his father Vasily III. For over fifty years, until 1584, he dominated the country politically, economically and aesthetically. During his childhood violent and wily boyars vying for power around the child's throne conditioned him to be distrustful of those supposed to be closest to the Tsar's family. Creeping in and out of the dark low passages of the Kremlin palace in their long caftans the boyars so brilliantly portrayed in Eisenstein's film *Ivan the Terrible* listened for rumours and watched for opportunities to enhance their power. In later years Ivan was to reduce drastically the ability of the boyars to interfere in affairs of state. In 1547 at the age of seventeen he had himself crowned Tsar, the first Russian monarch to use the title formally. The coronation of Ivan was marred by the outbreak of an unusually severe fire which reduced much of Moscow to ashes. The event touched the young Tsar deeply and he made use of the newly constructed *Lobnoe Mesto*, the rostrum on Red Square near St Basil's, to address and reassure the populace after the fire. Ivan also chose his first wife at this time, a happy choice it seems for his reign can be roughly divided into two halves, the first, more stable period lasting until 1560 at which time his wife, Anastasiya, died suddenly, perhaps, as Ivan immediately suspected, of poisoning. After that time the irrationality and senseless cruelty for which he is mainly remembered became the hallmark of his reign.

Early in his reign Ivan determined to take Kazan, a strategic city on the Volga 900 kilometres east of Moscow and the nearest stronghold of the now disunited Golden Horde. With the help of a Danish engineer who laid explosives in a tunnel built under the Kazan Kremlin and succeeded in blowing it up, the city was captured on the feast of *Pokrova*, the Intercession of the Virgin, one of the most important religious festivals in the Russian church. Late in the summer of 1552 Moscow greeted the victorious troops with wild celebrations and the jubilant ringing of its many bells. It was the first time Muscovy had demonstrated its newly won strength by actually regaining territory from its old enemy. Although Tartar attacks continued to take place from time to time, the conquest of Kazan signalled the ultimate demise of the Tartars and is considered with the Battle of Kulikovo one of the most splendid victories in Russian history. To commemorate it the young Ivan decided to build a joyous church of thanksgiving, a permanent reminder of the glorious event, not in the boyar-infested Kremlin as his ancestors would have done but in Red Square, the commercial centre of Moscow, where people of all walks of life gathered daily. For this reason the extraordinary features of the Pokrova Cathedral, more familiarly known as St Basil's, were devised and built. Its form was the ultimate in which architecture could develop in that direction and the style was modified in the following century along simpler, more elegant lines.

Although 'Red Square' is the modern translation of Krasny Ploshchad the original meaning of *Krasnaya* would be more accurately given as 'beautiful'. *Krasny* still means 'fine' if used in certain contexts. The square came into being at the end of the fifteenth century when the new walls and towers of the Kremlin were being built and was known at first as Trinity Square after a wooden church which originally stood on the site of St Basil's. In 1493 Ivan III ordered the mass of houses, stalls and churches that were huddled close to the safety of the Kremlin walls to be dismantled and a space cleared of about 200 metres to protect the Kremlin from the ever-ominous threat of fire. In 1508 a large moat was dug along the eastern wall of the Kremlin approximately 35 metres wide and 3 to 4 metres deep fed by the Neglinnaya River which passed along the western side of the Kremlin. The moat was surrounded by a short wall with battlements or 'teeth', a smaller version of the main Kremlin wall. Wooden bridges, rebuilt in stone in the seventeenth century, were erected over the moat at the main entrances to the Kremlin. The square in the sixteenth century ended abruptly near the Spassky Gate where a sharp ravine plunged down to the Moskva River and where there is still a steep incline. The wooden church of the Trinity stood at this high place surrounded by a small graveyard where the body of the holy fool, St Basil the Blessed, was buried.

The origins of the unexpected design of St Basil's, which is so unlike the early Moscow churches, probably lie in the peculiar characteristics of Russian wooden architecture which had developed in the north perhaps as long ago as pre-Christian times. Wood was a natural, freely available material in the north-west and for centuries Russians had been building their *izba* (small wooden cottages), their bathhouses, their palaces, forts, bridges and churches in wood. What is so remarkable is that they were able to achieve great variety of design and decorative detail using only the humble axe. Not even a nail penetrated the grooved and fitted pieces of wood. Their houses were extremely simple in design, single chambers, a basic cube, to which other rooms might be added, similar to the log cabins of early America and Canada. The genius of the carpenters lay in the variations they were able to execute on this basic design, like open staircases, ogee-shaped *bochki* or gables, carved decorations at the ends of the gables and around the window frames – the *nalichniki* – which are still a delightful object in Russian villages today. Wood was so flexible that it could be fashioned very quickly into any form – curves, squares or angles. It was versatile in that it was easily and quickly repaired after damage done by the frequent fires. To this day there are many churches called St Ilya or St Nikolai 'which was built in one day'. Another important attribute of wood was that it provided a warmer dwelling than masonry. All these advantages helped to compensate for its greatest disadvantage, that of combustibility. In a little book by Giles Fletcher, Ambassador of Queen Elizabeth to Russia in 1588–89, the use of wood in Russian cities is described as follows:

The streates of their cities and townes instead of pauing, are planked with firre trees, plained and layed euen close to one to the other. They are fastened together with dentes or notches at euery corner, and so clasped fast together. Betwixt the trees or timber they thrust in mosse (whereof they gather plentie in their woods) to keepe out the ayre. Euery house hathe a paire of staiers that lead vp into the chambers out of the yards or streat after the Scottish manner. This building seemeth farre better for their countrie, then that of stone and bricke: as being colder and more dampish then their woodden houses, specially of firre, that is a dry and warme wood. Whereof the prouidence of God hath giuen them such store, as that you may build a faire house for twenty or thirtie rubbels or little more, where wood is most scant. The greatest inconuenience of their woodden building is the aptnes for firing, which happeneth very oft and in very fearful sort, by reason of the drinesse and fatnesse of the fire, that being once fired, burneth like a torch, and is hardly quenched till all be burnt vp.

Built with logs of standard length placed horizontally, churches were generally of three types: the *kletskiye* or square with the steep pitched roof; the octagonal pyramid building finished with an ogee or onion gable; and the church of a number of cubes one on top of the other, the higher one smaller than the lower, with a roof of eight sloping sides and finished by an onion cupola on a round neck. The octagonal pyramid church is probably indigenously Russian. It is depicted on icons as early as the thirteenth century. The shape of the octagonal church allowed for greater space inside than the cube churches as the logs were usually of standard lengths. Sometimes a square chancel and ante-room joined the octagon. Unlike stone churches where there are no seating arrangements, wooden churches, like the peasant's *izba*, usually had a stove in the middle and benches along the walls. Extremely tall churches were built based on the cube or octagon systems, some as high as 70 metres.

The oldest wooden churches which have survived to our time are no earlier than the fifteenth and sixteenth centuries but unlike buildings of masonry the style of wooden architecture did not change over the centuries and later examples, particularly in the north where many conservative Old Believers settled after the schism in the 1650s, are based on ancient models. Some of the more remarkable of the wooden churches can still be seen in the Lake Onega district, Kargopol, and at Archangelsk. Kizhi, an island in the boundless expanse of Lake Onega, is the location of several early churches and houses and is the site of the great Church of the Transfiguration (1714), the ultimate in wooden architecture. With twenty-two cupolas placed in tiered layers rising to the point of the topmost dome it belongs organically to its background strongly resembling the shape of the tall pines around it. The nearby church at Kondopoga, the extremely tall *kletsky* or cube-based church with its octagonal peaked roof reflected in the water of the lake is also a superb example of its type. A few of the more interesting wooden churches in the countryside near Moscow include those of the village of Dushenovo (1670), Gnilushchy (1774), Veretyevo (1778), Peski (eighteenth century), Kosino (1673), Voskresenskoe (1705), and Vasilevskoe (1689).

In the early sixteenth century the unique silhouette and decorative features of the octagonal pyramid churches were successfully translated into masonry. Two such stone churches, both built by royal decree, which are the precursors of St Basil's, are still standing only one quarter of a mile apart in south Moscow at Dyakovo and Kolomenskoe. They heralded a new style of church at a time when building in stone was becoming more common, a pyramid or tent-shaped style which was to fill the Russian landscape side by side with the more dignified onion-domed cube churches until the mid-seventeenth century when the Patriarch Nikon sternly ordered the return to the Greek-style Byzantine church and the end of the gabled pyramids.

The first of these churches to be built in Russia is the Vosnesenskaya Church (Ascension) at Kolomenskoe, the summer estate of the tsars from the times of Dmitry Donskoi in the fourteenth century. Seen through the arch of the seventeenth-century gate the church presents a spectacular view. Rising from a

9 Voznesenskaya (Ascension) Church at Kolomenskoe, *c.* 1532. The first of the pyramid churches to be built of stone instead of wood.

polygonal base in the shape of a Greek cross enlarged by the surrounding gallery, it towers upwards like a slim tent, a true tower church finished by the flourish of a small uppermost cupola. It is indeed the inheritor of the tall wooden churches with many *kokoshniki* gable devices, a roofed but open gallery surrounding the base, a high undercroft probably used for storing valuables, three entrances approached from

10 Sobor Vasiliya Blazhennovo (St Basil's Cathedral), 1555–60. Built by Barma and Postnik for Ivan the Terrible to honour the Russian victory over the Tartars at Kazan.

three flights of stairs. It is a most beautiful building, the immensely thick walls of the base supporting the slim octagonal form of the tall tower, the transition from one to the other made by corner buttresses from which *kokoshniki* reach up to the octagon. The decorative features, particularly the sharply pointed gables, are also to be found in St Basil's. The extremely narrow interior is lit from the tall thin windows placed regularly on two tiers of the base and the widest section of the tower. The inner part of the octagon tower is not obstructed and when it was used as a church the congregation could see up into its soaring, mysterious darkness. Its situation high on the banks of the Moskva River overlooking what were once water meadows but are now the industrial jumble of a large city must have been admired in the past for on the river's side is the tsar's throne. It is said that Ivan the Terrible liked to spend his birthdays at Kolomenskoe. Kolomenskoe is now used as a park for Muscovites and around this lovely church bathers and picnickers shout and play in summer and skiers and children with sleighs slide over the snow in winter.

At Dyakovo across the ravine is a most curious church, a transitional building between the styles of wooden architecture and the later pyramid-shaped churches like the Church of the Ascension next-door. It is not certain which church was built first. The Church of Ivan Predtechy (St John the Baptist) at Dyakovo was probably built about 1547 by Ivan IV in honour of his coronation and the birth of his first son, Dmitry. It was built on a high sub-basement or undercroft, an octagon with four octagonal chapels. Later the chapels were joined to each other by an exterior wall making a passageway on three sides, the fourth being the apse. It is very different from any earlier stone church both in its design and in its rich use of decorative motifs, particularly the sharp gables of the central octagon and the four chapels, and the curious multi-shafted drum and the cap-shaped cupola. Many of these motifs were copied in the design of St Basil's.

Pyramid-shaped churches of this date are extremely rare in Moscow but there is one other, the Preobrazhenskaya (Church of the Transfiguration) at Ostrov, erected in around 1550, just before St Basil's was built, in what was formerly a royal village only a few miles south of Moscow. It is simpler than the church at Dyakovo, a cube where the *kokoshniki* climbing to the base of the octagonal tower are met by sharp arrows, the whole ascending to the onion-shaped cupola. The pure whiteness of the stone adds to the beauty of the building although it is somewhat masked in front by the 1830 bell-tower. Like the other churches, it too is situated high up with a commanding position over the surrounding countryside.

The building of St Basil's
In Red Square the two Russian architects, Barma and Postnik, worked from 1555 to 1560 on the site of the old Trinity Church to create a more elaborate form of the new style of Russian architecture, a church worthy of the victory of Kazan. Although the exterior betrayed borrowings from the churches at Kolomenskoe and Dyakovo it was

a different sort of church from that known in Muscovy hitherto. Ivan decided that the church should have eight separate chapels, seven grouped around a central altar, to illustrate the eight attempts to take Kazan. But the architects insisted that for the sake of balance nine chapels would be necessary, eight grouped symmetrically around the ninth. The separate churches of alternating height, four large and four small, were united by a gallery, at first open but subsequently enclosed, as were the staircases to the north and south. The two porches were added in the seventeenth century and small pyramid-shaped towers were then placed at their entrances.

Although one's first impression is of a hodge-podge of shapes and colours, two main *leitmotifs* dominate the cathedral and eventually one becomes aware of great harmony. The first is that of the round arches which occur in great variety from the arcades at the cathedral's base to the dynamic gables at its upper levels. The second is the use of octagonal shapes in the supporting foundation of the church and the bases of the separate chapels. The acute gables delineating the chapels reflect the overall pyramid shape of the central church. The extraordinary variety of the colours, surface patterns (chevrons etc.) and mouldings of the cupolas are reminiscent of the textures and colours of Tartar carpets and materials, one of the few examples of their influence on Russian art. Inside, St Basil's is almost suffocating; the constraint of the little chapels is unpleasant and one gets the impression that the exterior view of the cathedral from the square was more important than its interior.

The central, Pokrov, chapel was painted in 1784, and the other frescoes date from the nineteenth century. In 1812 Napoleon failed in his attempt to blow up the cathedral but it was severely looted by his troops. (It is sometimes said that Napoleon used the cathedral as a stable but this is hard to believe in view of the stairs and narrowness of the rooms.) The cemetery that surrounded the cathedral was removed in 1817 after the damage inflicted by the French.

St Basil's dominates Red Square from every direction. Its many cupolas give variety to the look of the whole when viewed from different angles and are a caricature of the grander, more sedate golden onion shapes rising from the western side of the Kremlin. It stood, on completion, midway between the Kremlin and the more recent commercial settlement of Kitaigorod at a place where a system of radial streets met, symbolic of Ivan the Terrible's detestation of the Kremlin and its scheming boyars. Today it is a glorious symbol of all that is mysterious and misleading about Russia. Its symmetry is not easy to detect nor its glory immediately apparent; it seems at first to be a garish clashing mixture of dissonant colours and shapes. Foreigners are unfamiliar with its stylistic devices and it needs careful study to discern the intrinsic harmony, the clever design, the beauty of the streamlined, contrasting gable shapes. No other church of such magnificence was built after St Basil's during Ivan IV's long reign because of the unsettled nature of political and social life during most of that time. Like Ivan himself St Basil's is unique and yet, also like him, is archetypical of all that is Russian. But the way it narrows the exit

11 Sobor Vasiliya Blazhennovo (St Basil's Cathedral), 1555–1560. A detail of one of the towers.

from Red Square for the twice-yearly military parades irritated Stalin. According to a story current in Moscow, Stalin wanted to tear down St Basil's to allow his soldiers to leave the square *en masse* but a famous architect was so horrified he threatened to cut his throat on the steps of the cathedral if the great leader went ahead with his plan.

The true name of St Basil's is Pokrova shto na rvu, the 'Intercession of the Virgin by the moat', to commemorate the fact that Kazan was taken on the day of that festival. However, it is commonly known by the name of the holy fool, St Vasily the

Blessed or St Basil's. The story of the *yurodovy* (holy fool) Vasily is intimately connected with the cathedral. He was born in 1489 within the boundaries of present-day Moscow, a poor lad apprenticed to a bootmaker. At the age of sixteen he began making remarkable prophecies and eventually gave up the apprenticeship to start a life of holy wandering dressed in rags and draped with chains, a peculiar Russian custom. These 'holy fools' were much revered by the common people and many, like Rasputin centuries later, rose to positions of great influence. He came to the notice of the young Tsar, Ivan IV, in 1547 when he foretold the terrible fire Moscow was to suffer that year. Ivan even visited the *yurodovy* with the Tsaritsa in 1552 when he lay dying and at his death ordered that he be buried in the Trinity Church cemetery. When the new cathedral was built Vasily was reinterred in the lower walls and in 1588 Tsar Fyodor Ivanovich had a small chapel built over the grave, the tenth and smallest of the cathedral's cupolas. It is said that not only the patriarch but the tsar himself attended services here on the annual festival of Vasily's death, 2 August.

5 TENUOUS CONTACTS WITH THE ENGLISH

The emergence of Muscovy as a nation-state greatly encouraged mercantile commerce and the changeover to a money economy. Surprisingly, in 1560 Moscow was one of the largest cities in Europe with a population roughly estimated at over 150,000; it was even larger than London which in 1564 had a population slightly less (London had suffered considerably from plague). The many, proliferating monasteries had become wealthy and provided some of the better estate management but the state held a monopoly on grain and on goods produced for export like furs, timber, wax, honey, tallow, flax and hemp, the same items as were exported during Kievan Rus some five centuries earlier.

Although in the fifteenth century Moscow had had sporadic contact with developments in western Europe through the arrival of the Italian architects and Ivan the Great's marriage to Sophia Paleologue, it remained on the whole isolated and cut off from the main course of events taking place there, in particular the change of thought and attitude of the Renaissance period. However, with the increase in population and the removal of the Tartar overlords from its lands, in the sixteenth century Moscow began to emerge from its lonely isolation vis-à-vis Europe. In 1553 the inimitable Englishman, Richard Chancellor, commissioned by the Company of Merchant Adventurers to find the north-eastern passage to Cathay, sailed to the mouth of the Dvina in the *Eduard Bonaventure* and thence travelled with a small party to Moscow. There they were well received by the Tsar, who gave Chancellor a letter stating that he would grant the English merchants the right to trade freely throughout Muscovy. As he had had virtually no contact with European nations up to this time except through the ambassador of the Holy Roman Emperor, Ivan was anxious to obtain military supplies and other industrial products for his various military exploits. England, on the other hand, was anxious for new markets for its manufactured goods. Accordingly Chancellor gave up the idea of finding a passage to Cathay and returned to London in 1554 with the message from Ivan for the English rulers, Philip and Mary. The Muscovy Company was thereupon established by royal charter. In 1555 Chancellor returned to Russia and the agreement to trade was formally drawn up, the Tsar even granting the right of exemption from Russian law to representatives of the company in Muscovy. The English enjoyed this monopoly of trade for nearly a century.

Chancellor's impressions of Russia were written down by his friend Clement Adams and recorded in Hakluyt's *Principal Navigations, Voyages, Traffics and Discoveries*. He found immense wealth in Moscow and was impressed by the large area governed from there.

Our men say, that in bigness it is as great as the Citie of London with the suburbs thereof. There are many and great buildings in it, but for beautie and faireness nothing comparable to ours. There are many Townes and Villages also but built out of order, and with no stone such as ours are: the walles of their houses are of shingle boords. There is hard by the Citie a very faire Castle (Kremlin) strong, and furnished with artillerie, whereunto the Citie is joyned directly towards the North, with a bricke wall; the walles also of the Castle are built with bricks and are in breadth or thicknesse eighteen foote. This Castle hath on the one side a drie ditch, on the other side the river Moscua, whereby it is made almost inexpugnable.

During the second of Chancellor's visits, the agents of the Muscovy Company were granted a comfortable house by the courtesy of the Tsar in Kitaigorod just outside the Kremlin. This house, the Angliskoe Podvore, was simply requisitioned from its original inhabitants and given to the English. It was located on the Varvarka (now Ulitsa Razina) next door to the Romanov estate and had considerable grounds around it. Recently, during the preparations for the construction of the Rossiya Hotel, many buildings of the so-called *zaryady* (behind the rows of shops on Red Square) were removed. Among these was the Foreign Languages Library located in what appeared to be a nineteenth-century house. The architects found in the basement of the former Library traces of a medieval house, possibly as early as fifteenth-century, and after some painstaking research it was decided that it was indeed the Angliskoe Podvore, the first foreign embassy in Moscow. Slowly and carefully the house is undergoing restoration. Its red brick walls with their square indentations, restrained window decorations and high pitched roof once again adorn Kitaigorod.

The Romanov palace, which in the sixteenth century was next-door to the English merchants, is still standing, the way now obstructed by the Church of St Maxim the Greek, its bell tower, and the buildings of the Znamensky Monastery (of the Sign), all seventeenth-century. Nikita Romanov was the senior boyar in the time of Ivan the Terrible. His sister was the Tsar's first wife; his son became the patriarch Filaret; and his grandson became the first Romanov tsar, Mikhail Fyodorovich. In the seventeenth century when the Romanovs moved to their residence in the Kremlin, the palace became part of the property of the new Znamensky Monastery and was used as the residence of the abbot. It was 'restored' in the mid-nineteenth century at the request of Nicholas I in honour of his ancestors. The Russian architect F. F. Richter actually rebuilt it more in the prevailing eclectic style, a modern adaptation of old Russian motifs, than in the style of the sixteenth century. However, the basement is from the original structure and the interior has been retained as an accurate and delightful museum of furnishings and furniture of the sixteenth and seventeenth centuries. (Before the revolution it was known as the Romanov museum.) It is said that during the not infrequent raids of the dreaded black-hooded vigilantes of Ivan the Terrible (the *Oprichniki*) on the Romanov household, the family fled to the relative safety of the English establishment. In return, during the terrible fire of 1571 when the English house was badly damaged and some of its occupants burnt to death, the Romanovs assisted their neighbours. The English also taught Greek and Latin to the children of the boyars including the future tsar, Mikhail.

In this way the first real steps to recover the position in relation to the west that Rus had enjoyed in the time of Kiev's greatness were taken by Ivan the Terrible towards the English. Although a small foreign community composed mostly of Germans and Italians had existed in Moscow before the arrival of the English, it was greatly swollen by these merchants and their clerks who set up establishments in Novgorod, Vologda and other cities as well as the capital. Specialized English workers were encouraged to settle in Moscow and included doctors, shipbuilders, a goldsmith, an apothecary, and even a midwife sent by Elizabeth to assist the Tsaritsa in childbirth (which in the event she was not allowed to do). Increasing numbers of English and Scottish mercenaries also found their way to Moscow, including many who had been in service in Livonia. One of the tangible results of the close relations between Tudor England and the Russia of Ivan the Terrible are the many fine examples of Tudor silver sent to Ivan as gifts by Mary and Elizabeth. They are now on display in the Kremlin armoury, while examples have been rare in England since much of the old silver was melted down in the Civil War. Ivan the Terrible, for all his xenophobia and paranoia, was pro-English in his policies and was regarded as such by the suspicious, conservative boyars. When he died the English Ambassador, Sir Jerome Bowes, was given the news 'Your English Tsar is dead.' Afterwards, there was even a short-lived anti-English reaction that was quickly ended by Boris Godunov. Yet Russo-English relations were not always completely cordial. In 1567 Ivan sent a message to Elizabeth asking for asylum should he be forced to flee Moscow and for a mutual alliance against warring enemies; he had in mind his struggles with Poland and Livonia. Elizabeth readily granted the right to asylum but was more circumspect about becoming involved in the Tsar's military adventures. The Tsar was completely serious about his request for asylum; he kept a ship at Vologda in constant readiness for flight. A further strain was imposed by Ivan's wish to marry Elizabeth's cousin, Lady Mary Hastings. Lady Mary was not so inclined, particularly as the Tsar was already married to his fifth wife and the tales she had heard of the Tsar from the Muscovy Company agents would also have deterred her. The suit dragged on for many years, as the Tsar was disinclined to lose heart.

6 THE RISE OF BORIS GODUNOV

Although no Russian tsar has been exactly benevolent – even Nicholas II did not oppose the pogroms against the Jews at the beginning of this century – Ivan was certainly the most bloody. The most 'terrible' part of his long reign probably began with the death of his beloved wife, Anastasiya in 1560. It was exacerbated by an incident in 1553 when Ivan fell ill and, believing himself to be dying, asked the boyars to acknowledge his infant son, Dmitry, as his successor and the Tsaritsa as regent. Several refused, thereby further kindling Ivan's deep distrust, and when Anastasiya died in 1560 he immediately suspected poisoning. His always volatile anger and latent sadism came to a head when his most talented and trusted general, Kurbsky, fled to Lithuania after losing a battle against the Poles. Kurbsky's family were murdered on the Tsar's orders and Ivan abandoned Moscow. He moved to Alexandrovskaya Sloboda, a country estate owned by the grand princes since his father's day, about 125 kilometres north of the capital.*

Ivan threatened abdication but representations from the Moscow populace persuaded him to remain as tsar. On his return he divided the country into two parts: the *Oprichnina*, to come under his personal rule, comprising about half the territory of Muscovy; and the *Zemshchina*, ruled as before by the Council of Boyars. The *Oprichnina* were responsible for signs of treason in the *Zemshchina* and eventually, comprising a band of about 6,000 men, became terrorizers for terror's sake. They wore black constumes decorated only by a dog's head and a broom which symbolized devotion to the Tsar and the sweeping-away of treason. Atrocities reached a peak with the dreadful, unwarranted sacking of Novgorod in 1570 under the personal direction of the Tsar. Over 60,000 people were killed and the town was devastated. In 1571, by a sort of poetic revenge, Moscow, which was already suffering from the plague, was ravaged by a terrible Tartar raid during which the city was fired and many of the inhabitants taken for slaves. Ivan again abandoned Moscow, not returning for two years.

In spite of this negative side, there were some remarkable achievements during Ivan's reign. Not only did he win back Kazan, he also took Astrakhan temporarily from the Tartars, the first penetration of Siberia occurred during his reign, the first Zemsky Sobor, a sort of primitive national assembly, was convened in 1566, and in

---

*There are still churches, bell-towers and a refectory dating from his stay there. It became a monastery in the seventeenth century but unfortunately is not accessible to foreigners today.

1564 the first printing press was brought to Moscow and the first book printed, the *Acts of the Apostles* for which the printer was literally chased out of Moscow by the righteously indignant population, spurred on by the church.

Ironically Ivan died in 1584 from natural causes. His death led to the accession of his mentally enfeebled son, Fyodor Ivanovich, aged 27. All Ivan's other heirs had met death in one form or another including his favourite, his eldest son Ivan (his first son, Dmitry, had died in infancy). The young man died at the hands of his own father during a quarrel after his father had punished his pregnant wife for being too lightly clad. In anger, Ivan struck his son over the head with an iron staff he always carried and the young man died almost immediately. Ivan deeply regretted his action but it was too late. A famous painting of the incident by Repin hangs in the Tretyakov Gallery, the dying Ivan in the arms of his penitent father. The result was the accession of Fyodor to the throne confirming the Russian tradition that a strong tsar alternates with a weak one.

Boris Godunov, who had risen to prominence through the *Oprichnina*, was a member of the council which had been appointed by Ivan the Terrible to assist his son to rule. Godunov, no doubt helped by the fact that his sister, Irina, was the wife of Fyodor, managed to oust the other councillors and became regent for the fourteen years of Fyodor's reign. Godunov was of Mongol origin. His Tartar ancestors had taken service with the Grand Prince in the fourteenth century and he was a member of the junior branch of a leading boyar family. Unable to read or write, he was nevertheless an astute politician skilled in the ways of intrigue and content to continue the policies of Ivan the Terrible.

With the death of Fyodor in 1598 the line of the Rurikids which had provided rulers for Rus since the ninth century ended. The Zemsky Sobor met to choose a successor. With the new patriarch, Job, at its head and controlled by Godunov's men the choice naturally fell on the former regent. Boris at first modestly refused the honour and retired to Novodevichy Monastery, but crowds of people whipped up by his agents surrounded the monastery and persuaded the seemingly reluctant noble on the steps of Smolensk Cathedral to accept the throne. Pushkin's play and Moussorgsky's opera *Boris Godunov* shows this election scene most graphically. Although Boris was a politically adroit administrator – he had even sent thirty young Russians to study abroad (only two came back) – various problems beset his reign that he was not able to overcome. Famine became widespread and heavy taxes caused mass unrest and desertion of the villages and farms. Many fled to join the free cossacks in the Russian border country to the south.

A more persistent cause of unrest during Godunov's short rule was the deep-rooted and long-standing rumour that he was involved in the murder of the younger son of Ivan the Terrible. In 1591 the nine-year-old Prince Dmitry had been murdered in the town of Uglich where he was living as reigning prince with his mother and her family. The citizens of Uglich in a frenzy slew Godunov's agents and it was never properly established even by the official commission what had really happened. The doubt about those responsible for the boy's death led to the belief that he had not died at all and early in the seventeenth century it was rumoured that Dmitry had escaped to Poland. Thus commenced the *Smutnoe Vremya* or 'Time of Troubles' during which no less than three False Dmitrys claimed the Russian throne. Godunov died opportunely a few months before the first False Dmitry, probably a priest from the Chudov Monastery in the Kremlin, entered Moscow with the support of Polish troops and some of the populace. Godunov was first buried in a monastery on Ulitsa Zhdanova for unknown paupers and persons who died in the street but later his body and those of his family were taken to the Troitse-Sergeyev Monastery for reinterment.

After a year the first False Dmitry fell in the revolt led by Shuisky, the leading boyar, who became tsar of a by now disunited Muscovy. In 1610 he was deposed when Polish troops entered the city and occupied the Kremlin. A national uprising in 1612 finally expelled the Poles and a year later a special council chose Mikhail Romanov as tsar, the first of a new dynasty. This marked the formal end of the Time of Troubles.

The buildings of Moscow in the last half of the sixteenth century
The architecture of Moscow from the last half of the sixteenth century to the first quarter of the seventeenth is not enlivened by anything comparable to the originality and splendour of St Basil's. The troubled and uncertain times of the latter part of Ivan the Terrible's reign and the subsequent insuperable problems that beset Boris Godunov followed by the Time of Troubles and the Polish invasion of Moscow caused a decline in icon painting and strict adherence to traditional forms in the few stone buildings that were erected. Yet there were some adaptations of the old style. Nothing as glorious as St Basil's or the Church of the Ascension at Kolomenskoe was built yet some beautifully detailed stone churches appeared that enhance Moscow and its environs still.

Godunov was an astute politician and a clever negotiator who had risen above the senior boyars through cultivating the unpredictable whims of Ivan the Terrible, and in many respects his policies were a continuation of Ivan's. He had also, however, a fine artistic sense, evident in the several churches built under his patronage. At his estate at Vyazyomy about 40 kilometres from Moscow near the Golitsyn Station he built a graceful white stone church with some unusual features. In outward appearance it is not unlike the Church of the Transfiguration at Ostrov. It has two chapels to the north and south of the main body of the church springing from a raised terrace, largely roofed, and supported on a vault. There are five main cupolas on the central cube of the church and two adorning the side reminiscent of the fifteenth-century style. The Renaissance details of the Archangel Cathedral in the Kremlin

12 Archangelsky Sobor (Cathedral of the Archangel Michael), by Alevisio Novo, 1505–09. The royal burying-place. Note the Italian Renaissance details. (See pages 32–3.)

are discernible here in the profile of the cornices, the shells which complete the tripartite bays of the walls, and the decorations around the drums.

Several of these so-called 'Godunov' churches with their fine attention to detail are still extant in Moscow. One of these is the church at Khoroshevo on the river within greater Moscow just left of the main road to Serebryanny Bor. It was built in 1598 as part of an estate actually belonging to Godunov himself. Externally, it

13 St Nikita shto za Yauzy, end of the sixteenth century. Details betray the influence of the Boris Godunov style.

resembles the Old Cathedral of the Donskoi Monastery with its central cubic mass and rows of *kokoshniki*, now partially hidden by the later roof. It, too, has two side chapels to the south and north flanking the chancel each with its own cupola. Originally, an open terrace surrounded the church on three sides. Again the influence of Italian Renaissance architecture is seen here in the fine cornices, the elegant pilasters and arches of the walls and panels. An interesting feature of this church was the use of coloured glazed pottery in the round hollows of the *kokoshniki*, the predecessor of the extensive use of coloured tiles in the following century.

Much farther away, to the east of the Kremlin and high above the confluence of the Yauza and Moskva Rivers is another church, St Nikita shto za Yauzy (beyond the Yauza), the main body of which was erected in the time of Boris Godunov. This church, a sort of guardian high upon a hill, once commanded a striking view of the eastern part of the city to the domes of the Kremlin. Even now its approach is up a steep hill, Shvivaya Gorka, but its unique view has been completely obliterated by the soaring mass of one of Stalin's 'wedding cake' structures built just after the war. That this little church has survived at all is one of the miracles of Soviet restoration. In *The First Circle* Solzhenitsyn describes it as being a heap of ruins in 1948 whereas in 1922 it had been considered by the girl-friend of one of his characters as the most beautiful place in all of Moscow. It was restored or rather rebuilt in 1958–60 and to find it so perfect and unexpected, hidden away from the main roads, is like discovering buried treasure. The existing building still bears a plaque stating that the church was

51

built in 1595 by the merchant Savva Yemelyanov. The gentle semi-circular *zakomar-kokoshniki* (both decorative and functional) meet the small cap-shaped cupola and the fine detail of the walls and cornices are evidence that it was built in the reign of Boris Godunov. However, it is known that a much earlier church existed on this site and the undercroft, terrace and apse-ended chancel would seem to date from at least the beginning of the sixteenth century. The terrace and portal on the Moskva River side are its best features. Although a seventeenth-century addition, the bell tower blends well with the rest of the church, but the southern chapel, also a later addition, serves only to confuse. It is now used to house the products of the film company Diafilm.

Not far from St Nikita is another church of the late sixteenth century, Zachatiya

14 Zachatiya Anny shto v uglu (Church of the Immaculate Conception of St Anne in the corner), end of fifteenth century. The 'corner' referred to in the full title is that of the former walls of Kitaigorod. Rebuilt after a fire at the end of the sixteenth century.

Anny shto v uglu (the Immaculate Conception of St Anne in the corner). It stood in a corner of Kitaigorod where the walls turned at right angles from the river to the north. Now it stands in the grounds of the modern and massive Rossiya Hotel, a little incongruous among the uncompromising straight lines and terraces of the hotel. It was originally built in the late fifteenth century but it was badly burned in the terrible fire of 1547 and was almost totally rebuilt fifty years later in a more old-fashioned style than other churches of the time. The more frequent use of brick in the latter part of the century meant that the walls and roofing are entirely of that material. Here, as in the Spassky Cathedral of the Andronikov, the triple bayed and gabled wall reflect the vaulting of the interior. In recent years it has been used as a nursery school.

15 Zachatiya Anny shto v uglu (Church of the Immaculate Conception of St Anne in the corner). In the background is a power station of the 1920s.

About twenty years after the death of Boris Godunov the first tsar of the new dynasty, Mikhail Fyodorovich, built a church to commemorate the rout of the Polish invaders and the end of the Time of Troubles. Although intended to signal the beginning of a new era the design of the Pokrova (Intercession of the Virgin) v Rubtsove closely adheres to the basic elements of architecture of the late sixteenth century. It was built in 1619–26 on a part of the former Romanov estate on the Yauza River slightly east of the then boundaries of Moscow. It has many familiar features – a high undercroft or terrace, division of the walls into three bays, two side chapels with independent cupolas, tiers of *kokoshniki* and vaulting crossed to support the central cupola. However, it is more leaden and heavy than the churches of Godunov's time and it is difficult to feel its celebratory purpose.

City walls and monasteries

During the reign of the mentally deficient Fyodor Ivanovich and the regency of Godunov white stone walls were built around the third outgrowth of the city, Belgorod. It is the natural radial extension of the city around the Kremlin and Kitaigorod but is prevented from forming a complete circle by the barrier of the Moskva River to the east and to the west. Belgorod was such an integral part of Moscow by the fourteenth century that, after raids from the unruly citizens of Tver to the north and Lithuanians to the north-west, high earthen ramparts were erected protected by a moat along the path of the future walls. In the fifteenth century boyars and other high ranking people began to build second homes, suburban villas, in addition to their Kremlin residences in the western parts of Belgorod. They thus forced the artisans and trading settlements to move to the edge of the district beyond the protective ramparts. The eastern part of Belgorod was heavily wooded for much longer than the western side as is clear from the descriptive names of many of the churches there: 'under the firs', 'in the thicket', etc. However, by the late fifteenth century it too boasted a lay-out of streets and lanes, part of which has survived to the present, and several trading and artisan settlements. In the 1490s Ivan the Third cleared the woods from the high area forming a triangle between present-day Bogdan Khmelnitsky Street to the Yauza River and the Solyanka and established part of the Kremlin market gardens there; he also built a country residence in the midst of the gardens. In 1565 Ivan the Terrible built his Oprichny Dvor between today's Kalinin Prospekt, Hertsen Street and Prospekt Marksa, and the pace of colonization of Belgorod quickened after that.

The name Belgorod may have derived from the new whitewashed brick walls – *belyi* means white – but it probably refers to the exemption from land tax enjoyed by the boyars and nobility who formed the bulk of the population of Belgorod in the sixteenth and seventeenth centuries. In exchange they were under obligation to provide service to the tsar at his convenience. Those sectors of the population – artisans, traders and small farmers – who were not obliged to give continuous service, were said to live on 'black' land and were therefore required to pay the land tax. The phrase *belomestnye* cossacks was in use until the Revolution to denote cossacks in the service of the state who were granted exemption from payment or land tax.

The direct cause of the decision to build walls around Belgorod was the terrible ruin caused by the raid in 1571 by the forces of the Crimean khan, Devlet-Girei. Earthen ramparts were also erected for the same reason around Zemlyany Gorod or 'Skorodom', the next concentric populated ring around the nucleus of Moscow that followed the line of today's Garden Ring Road. Belgorod's thick brick walls were built between 1586 and 1593 under the direction of Fyodor Kon, the engineer of the Dulo Tower of the Simonov Monastery at Moscow and the strong walls and towers of Smolensk. The walls were ten kilometres in circumference and four to five metres thick. (These dimensions were discovered when the foundations were excavated during the building of the metro in the 1930s, the walls themselves having been demolished at the end of the eighteenth century.)

Vulnerability to Tartar raids led to improvements in the fortifications of existing monasteries and the building of new ones in areas most susceptible to attack. The monasteries were not entirely oases of devotional calm: they were also semi-fortresses guarding the outposts of Moscow and as such their defences were constantly under review. The boundaries of Muscovy had been so vastly extended in the previous century that monasteries as far away as the Troitse-Sergeyev in Zagorsk, about eighty kilometres north of Moscow and at Beloozero, several hundred kilometres away were considered to be instrumental in the city's defence and were given stone walls in the place of wooden ones.

The Novodevichy Convent (New Convent of the Maidens) was founded in 1524 in honour of the return of Smolensk to Russian control in 1514. The new cathedral erected a year later was named after the icon, the Virgin of Smolensk, which, like the Vladimir Virgin, had a long and chequered history ultimately finding a home in Smolensk.

Since its foundation Novodevichy has been the pre-eminent monastery-convent in Moscow. Many tsartitsas and tsarevnas have sought shelter within its walls. The convent was witness to the major struggle betweeen Peter the Great and his politically minded sister, Sophia, at the end of the seventeenth century. Today, of all the monasteries and convents in Moscow it is only at Novodevichy and Donskoi that there are functioning churches and at Novodevichy the official offices of the Patriarch and the Moscow Metropolitan are located. The total effect of the ensemble of Novodevichy buildings and walls, spires and crenellated towers, is stunning; there the best architects of the sixteenth to eighteenth centuries have left their finest work. The cemetery attached to it is, after the Kremlin wall and the space behind the mausoleum, the most prestigious in Moscow. Here are buried all the leading writers and artists of the nineteenth century and here too are Stalin's first

16 Novodevichy Convent (New Convent of the Maidens), sixteenth and seventeenth centuries. The most splendid of Moscow's circle of defence monasteries.

wife, Allilueva and, somewhat sadly, Khrushchev, who surely deserved a place in the Kremlin wall along with the old Bolsheviks, Stalin, and people like John Reed, Inessa Armand and the cosmonauts.

The Smolensk Cathedral is very similar in form to the Assumption Cathedral in the Kremlin. That it should have taken only two years to build compared with five years for the Assumption Cathedral suggests that the Russians by this time had mastered the superior building techniques introduced by Fioraventi. Although its exterior is very similar to the Assumption Cathedral the proportions are slightly different: the full-blown cupolas stand closer together and their general appearance

is more slender. The most striking difference is the use of a sub-basement or undercroft, the device used in wooden churches and in the Annunciation Cathedral in the Kremlin and which became widespread in Moscow in the course of the sixteenth century.

Inside, the frescoes which are contemporary with the buildings are of great interest, especially the huge vividly coloured figures of Russian saints on the pillars. The gilded iconostasis was the work of Mikhailov in the late seventeenth century and most of its icons also date from that time. The cathedral is not a functioning church.

The small church of St Ambrose in the south-west corner of the monastery, now no longer used for religious services, is the only other building of the monastery contemporary with the cathedral.

In 1593, two years after the founding of the Donskoi Monastery in south Moscow, the first stone cathedral in the monastery was erected. This is the Old Cathedral, a small unimposing church when compared with the more impressive New Cathedral built in the following century. It is totally unlike the grand cathedrals which adorn monasteries like Novodevichy and more closely resembles the modest parish churches that abounded in Moscow at this time. As very few parish churches of the sixteenth century have survived it is doubly interesting to study the features of the Old Cathedral. It is small and intimate, its form the traditional solid cube rising by three layers of *kokoshniki* to meet the elegant drum and cupola, the whole effect similar to that of the Church of the Transfiguration at Ostrov. As with early churches, the walls are divided into three bays separated by pilasters surmounted by elegant cornices, a sign of the new popularity of the classical order in the reign of Boris Godunov. At one time the interior was covered with frescoes depicting the

17 The Dulo Tower of the Simonov Monastery, sixteenth century. The most fortified of all the defence monasteries.

Tsar. Although they were added in the seventeenth century the side chapels, 'refectory' (the name given by Russians to the anteroom of a church because in ancient times it was used as a dining-room – the correct architectural term is narthex), and bell-tower blend particularly well. This charming red and white church is functioning still as a place of worship.

The most formidable of all the Moscow monasteries was the Simonov located high above the Moskva River a few miles south-east of the Kremlin beyond the boundary of the Zemlyany Gorod. It was the most exposed to the Tartars and was truly the sentinel of the city. It was famous as a religious centre and its zealous missionaries helped to found the Kirilo-Belozersk monastery on the Beloozero far to the north and provided many metropolitans and patriarchs of Moscow. An important and rich monastery, it has immensely thick walls united by five round and polygonal towers and three gates, and until the Revolution it had six churches, the oldest, the Church of the Assumption, built in 1405. In 1934 all the churches were summarily blown up in one day of explosions described by Vladimir Soloukhin in his book *Pisma iz Russkovo Muzeya*. The churches and walls have therefore mostly reverted to dust but the south wall facing the river is still largely standing and three of the towers remain, the Dulo, the Solevaya and the Kuznechnaya. This was one of the few monasteries that were fortified with stone walls and towers in the sixteenth century to protect it from the fierce Tartar raids. The Dulo Tower at the south-east corner is particularly impressive. The effect of the heavy lower part of the tower is broken by the use of incised pilasters on its many-sided surface. The windows are in three layers at staggered intervals, with only the upper level decorated in the pointed style of the sixteenth century. It is thought that Fyodor Kon, who designed the Belgorod walls and the walls of the city of Smolensk, was also responsible for this tower. The upper part of it, the typical pyramid steeple familiar from Kolomenskoe, was added in the seventeenth century when the towers of the Kremlin walls received similar stone additions. The pyramid steeple gives the tower its characteristic silhouette, a great elegance that the lower half alone would lack.

Thus, by the beginning of the seventeenth century, after the period of anarchy following upon the end of the Rurikid dynasty, Moscow was poised for a period of great expansion. The circular organization of the city around the boundary of the Kremlin was well established, the outlines of Belgorod firmly laid in stone and those of Zemlyany Gorod by ramparts and ditches. Beyond this the monasteries formed a ring of strong points guarding the city. Although it was almost entirely a city of wooden buildings, white limestone churches were no longer a feature of the Kremlin alone and had become familiar in nearly every district. Experience in building in stone was a valuable training ground for the more complex churches that were to follow. The foundations for the brilliant blossoming of art and architecture that took place in the seventeenth century were clearly laid in the developments and achievements of the more turbulent sixteenth.

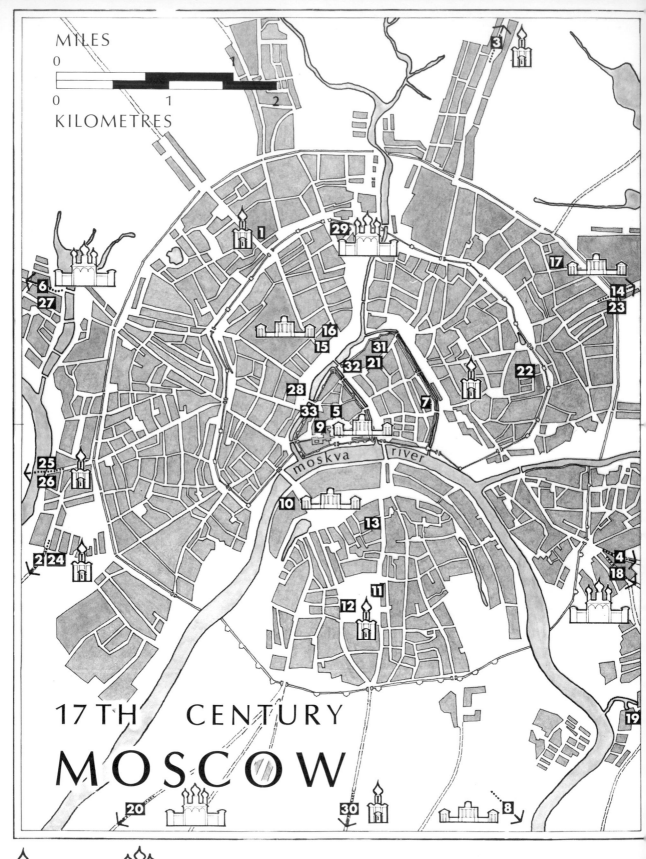

MILES

0   1

0   1   2

KILOMETRES

moskva river

17TH CENTURY

MOSCOW

 Cathedral/ Church/ Chapel

 Convent/ Monastery

 Palace/ Estate/ Mansion/House

 Apartment/ Hotel

 Railway station

2 Moscow in the Seventeenth Century

The seventeenth century was for Moscow a period of great contrasts. The beginning of the century was clouded by the Time of Troubles, by famine, and by the Polish occupation. With the acceptance of a new dynasty in 1613 a rapid recovery took place and in the eighty years that followed Moscow, still a medieval, enclosed city with an almost entirely illiterate population and an economy strictly regulated by guilds and senior merchants, experienced a re-awakening in the field of architecture and a revival of icon painting unequalled at any later date. This is the last period of the aloofness of Moscow from western thought and influence; in the course of the century this isolation began, little by little, to break down until with Peter the Great at the end of the century it was unceremoniously swept away with a crudeness that could only result in deep antagonisms. With Peter's decision to transfer the capital to St Petersburg in 1712 the fortunes of Moscow fell dramatically.

The energy involved in rebuilding the city devastated by two years of Polish occupation and ten years of virtual anarchy is paralleled only by the great effort to restore Moscow after the invasion in 1812 by the French under Napoleon and the terrible fire that followed. The number of seventeenth-century stone buildings that still exist in Moscow is amazing in view of the vicissitudes they have undergone including extensive eighteenth-century rebuilding under Catherine the Great, the consuming fires of 1737 and 1812 (not to mention innumerable smaller fires), the lack of appreciation of medieval architecture until the late nineteenth century, and, finally, the destruction of old buildings in the twentieth century during the 'reconstruction' of Moscow. In spite of these upheavals, over fifty completely restored churches, palaces and other secular buildings of the seventeenth century still lend colour to Moscow's drab streets, and of the secular buildings alone, over a hundred still await restoration. Of course there is nothing like the number of churches which clustered everywhere in the seventeenth century when travellers, amazed at the sight, spoke of over two thousand churches within the present

1 Rozhdestvo Bogoroditsy shto v Putnikakh, 1649–52   2 Troitsa v Troitskom-Golenishchevo, 1647   3 Pokrova v Medvedkovo, first quarter of the 17th century   4 Church at Veshnyaky, 1646   5 Patriarch's Palace and Church of the Twelve Apostles, Kremlin 1645–55 and 1680   6 Monastery of New Jerusalem, 1658–1685   7 Troitsa v Nikitnikakh, 1635–53   8 Great Wooden Palace at Kolomenskoe, 1667   9 The Terem palace, Kremlin, 1635–6   10 The Kirillov Palace and Church, 1656–7   11 St Nikolai shto v Pyzhakh, 1657–70   12 St Gregory Neokesariiskovo, 1667–9   13 Voskreseniye v Kadashakh, 1687   14 The Royal Estate at Izmailovo, 1679–89   15 Golitsyn Palace, 1696   16 Troekurov Palace, 1696   17 The Volkov (Yusupov) Mansion, end of the 17th century   18 Simonov Monastery Refectory, 1677–80   19 Krutitskoe Podvore, 1694, and Uspensky Church, 1685   20 'New Cathedral' of the Donskoi Monastery, 1684–98   21 Slavono-Greek-Latin Academy at the Zaikonospassky Monastery   22 Troitsa Church in Khokhlovsky Lane, 1696   23 Lefort Palace 1697–9   24 Pokrova Gate Church at Novodevichy Convent, 1683–8   25 Spas Church at Ubory, 1694–6   26 Pokrova Church at Fili, 1693–4   27 Troitse in Troitsko-Lykovo, 1698–1703   28 Znameniya Church at Sheremetiev, 1704   29 Vysoko-Petrovsky Monastery, latter part of the 17th century   30 Znameniya Church at Dubrovitsy, 1690–1704   31 Pechatny Dvor (behind the Synod Printing House)   32 Monetny Dvor, 1697   33 Poteshny Dvorets Kremlin, 1653. Altered in the 19th century.

18 A view of seventeenth-century cupolas on Ulitsa Razina (formerly the Varvarka) in Kitaigorod.

Sadovaya Ring Road. Although wood was still the most common building material, more and more buildings during the course of the century – not only churches but also palaces and administrative and industrial buildings – were made of stone. It is possible, therefore, to use existing examples to get some idea of Moscow in the seventeenth century and to trace the development from the comparatively restrained churches at the end of the sixteenth century to the extraordinary, vividly coloured churches of the second half of the seventeenth century and their final culmination in the exquisite elegance of the *Naryshkin* or soaring Moscow baroque churches.

The long reign of Mikhail Fyodorovich ushered in nearly a century of comparatively stable administration and Russia made rapid recovery from the disintegration of the Time of Troubles. Although the timid and cautious Mikhail did not have a strong personality, the autocracy not only held sway but became even more entrenched during his reign. He managed to get his father released from a Polish prison and appointed him Patriarch. Mikhail then ruled with the close assistance of his father, both sharing in the title of 'Great Sovereign' and church and state became more closely identified than ever before. During his reign the landlord continued to gain more power over the peasant and runaway peasants and those who aided them were severely punished.

I TOWER CHURCHES

The first churches of the new reign such as the Pokrova (Intercession of the Virgin) v Rubtsove belonged to the late sixteenth-century style of architecture but quite soon innovations appeared that were to receive full expression in the course of the rule of the first two Romanovs. The pyramid tower, modelled on the shape introduced at Kolomenskoe, developed into two or even three towers. Sadly, there are very few of these tall churches left in Moscow today, some of the most outstanding examples having disappeared since 1917. At the same time the more simple cube churches with their full-blown onion domes were being augmented by the addition of anterooms, bell-towers, and roofs (see p. 71). The combination of different masses

19 Rozhdestvo Bogoroditsy shto v Putnikakh (Church of the Nativity of Our Lady), 1649–52. The last of the towered churches.

with different roof heights was made more complex by rich decorative detail and the almost lurid use of colour. Asymmetry, which became the hallmark of all that is now considered typically Russian in church and secular architecture, is a product of the seventeenth century. St Basil's in its appearance of irregularity is in fact strictly symmetrical and the Godunov churches with their two chapels on either side of the altar are similarly balanced in design. But in the seventeenth century additions to earlier churches resulted in a mixture of heights and shapes that, although exceedingly picturesque, are decidedly irregular.

The most outstanding of the pyramid-towered churches is the Rozhdestvo Bogoroditsy (Nativity of Our Lady) shto v Putnikakh built in 1649–52, a *troine* or triple-pyramid-towered church. It was built on the eve of the Patriarch's ban on the further building of pyramid-style churches and may therefore be the last major officially sponsored church in this style. An earlier church had been damaged in a fire of 1648 and there is written evidence that the priests of the church approached the Tsar with the support of the Patriarch for assistance in rebuilding it. His help amounted to 800 rubles, a considerable fortune in those days, given at two different periods probably because the original estimate was too low. The church stood in an important position just outside the Belgorod wall on the main route to Dmitrov and was meant to be viewed from the Belgorod gate. It was called 'v Putnikakh' because foreign emissaries (*putniki*, meaning 'travellers') were able to wash and rest in a special house located behind the church after their dusty trip to Moscow. This church is particularly interesting as it provides a transition to the more elaborate decoration of the middle and late seventeenth century.

The plan of the building is extremely confusing. The main body of the church and a chapel are placed at right angles to each other, with the taller bell-tower in the corner of the right angle, and a low 'refectory', or narthex, with pitched roof and tent-shaped porch filling the gap to make a rough square. The roofing and cupolas are of unequal height and size. The main body of the church is a cube, possibly older than the other sections, with the triple apse surmounted by three narrow, exceedingly elegant octagonal towers crowned by slim cupolas. The chapel connects to the main body of the church and is roofed with three rows of *kokoshniki* gables. Its more squat pyramid-shaped octagonal tower is pierced with windows intended to light the chapel below – later the interior of the cupola was blocked up. The 'refectory', whose ceiling was supported by a huge pier as in the Faceted Palace of the Kremlin, was altered in the 1880s and given classical features but has been restored in Soviet times. The bell-tower in the corner of the square is built over the *tainik* or secret room of the chapel. It is surmounted by an elaborate pyramid, heavier and taller than the other towers, with a commanding position over them.

The details of the wall of the main church are very simple, with no horizontal lines, whereas those of the chapel are much more complex and rich. *Lopatka*, or division of walls into three or four vertical parts, so familiar in earlier architecture, is missing here and the façade is divided by string courses into three divisions in which small columns articulate the walls vertically. There are five varieties of window. Although all have a pointed arch above and columns at the side, some have *kokoshniki* surmounts and some have steeply pitched pediments. It is one of the first churches in Moscow to use such richness and variety in the window surrounds and the effect is overwhelming. The gate of Belgorod may have been crowned with *dvoine* or twin pyramids and the roof of the church may have been deliberately so designed to reflect the silhouette of the gate.

Near the Moscow Film Studio in the Sparrow Hills is another triple-towered church, the Troitsa (Trinity) v Troitskom-Golenishchevo built in 1647, high over the valley of a little river, the Setun, which empties into the Moskva opposite Novodevichy Convent. Two of the towers flank a central, higher one. Its symmetry, restrained window decorations and the fact that the windows are set well into the walls, are reminiscent of sixteenth-century fortress buildings like the Dulo Tower at the Simonov Monastery. The total effect of the church is somewhat lugubrious, for the central tower is too small and squat for the mass of the church which is unduly broad at the base. Ironically, the church originally served as the chapel of the Patriarch's summer palace and was built only a few years before this style of architecture was outlawed by the edicts of Patriarch Nikon himself (it was commissioned by Nikon's predecessor).

Of the *dvoine* or twin-pyramid-towered churches in Moscow there are now none left. The most beautiful of the single-towered churches after the Ascension Church at Kolomenskoe is the Pokrova (Intercession of the Virgin) at Medvedkovo, north of the Permanent Economic Exhibition but within the boundary of greater Moscow. It was built in the first quarter of the seventeenth century by Prince Pozharsky, the hero who had gathered together all the northern towns to defeat the Poles in Moscow. Its high, refined, octagonal tower rests upon a cube which was once surrounded by an open gallery on three sides, further emphasizing the tall silhouette of the tower. The bell-tower and internal decorations derive from the nineteenth century.

There remains only one more of the pyramid-shaped churches and its history illustrates the abrupt end of their predominance. Built by the wealthy boyar, Sheremetiev, in 1646, it lies just outside the outer ring road, at the suburban railway station, Veshnyaky, which is on the Kazan railway line. Raised high on its undercroft, it still retains the original open gallery and is similar to the church at Medvedkovo although its detail are more modest. A few years after it was built the owners decided to add two chapels on either side of the altar. The Patriarch, by now the famous Nikon, whose permission was solicited, ordained in 1655 that the 'heads on those chapels should be round and not peaked'.

2 PATRIARCH NIKON

Nikon, the most famous patriarch in Russian history, held this high office for only six years from 1652 to 1658. He was the son of a peasant but as a young priest he caught the attention of the fervently devout tsar, Aleksei Mikhailovich. As a result he was given the important post of Archbishop of Novgorod. The close personal relationship between Nikon and Aleksei meant that on the death of Patriarch Iosif in 1652 Nikon became Patriarch at the relatively young age of forty-seven. This strong-minded, intolerant man became head of the Russian Orthodox Church at the very time when momentous decisions were being made. It was an unfortunate coincidence. For all that it saw the blossoming of the arts of medieval Russia, the seventeenth century was a time of deep social unrest and discontent. There was complete subservience to the interests of the state which spread its tentacles over every aspect of commercial and social life. Any new, industrial enterprise, such as the iron works at Tula established by a Dutchman, was a state enterprise; the population was carefully organized into various strata ascending in a pyramid to the tsar and trade functioned closely under state control.

Into this tightly organized society came the unwelcome tide of a more questioning attitude to the practices of the Orthodox religion as it was conducted in Muscovy. Russians completely accepted the customs of their faith – extremely long services, the use of barely understood Church Slavonic, the importance of elaborate and magnificent ritual. However, the printing press had come to Moscow in the sixteenth century and religious books had begun to appear in some numbers. Constantinople had fallen and Moscow had become the bastion of the Orthodox religion. Because of the missionary zeal of the Jesuits pressing from the west, Orthodox priests from the Academy in Kiev were more self-conscious of their religion than their semi-literate brethren in Moscow. In the first half of the seventeenth century they came to the city in some numbers to escape increasing Polish persecution. They were horrified to find deep ignorance of religious matters in Moscow, particularly with regard to certain deviations from the Greek original that were being perpetrated in the newly printed religious books. Visiting Greek prelates also began to cavil at these discrepancies and suggested that the books be corrected.

Meanwhile Nikon had succeeded in establishing an unusually close relationship with the Tsar, a relationship exceeded only by the father-son accord of Patriarch Philaret and Tsar Mikhail. He had even persuaded Aleksei to acknowledge publicly that the power of the Church was superior to secular power and Nikon, like Philaret, also shared with the Tsar the title of *Veliky Gosudar* or Great Sovereign. Although he had earlier opposed the correction of the books and ritual, Nikon suddenly changed and became its most ardent champion. Under his leadership several Church councils were convened to study the issues. The most important in 1654 was attended by many luminaries of the Orthodox Church from other lands. The triteness of their deliberations is evident from the major debate over the spelling of Jesus – which in Church Slavonic was 'Isus' instead of the Greek 'Isius' – and over the number of fingers to be used in crossing oneself – the Greeks used three fingers whereas it was the Russian custom to use only two.

Nikon agreed with the Greek prelates and energetically set about the task of re-establishing the purity of the Greek tradition. But the field of his activity extended over a broader area than the purely theological. He attacked recent 'western' trends in icon painting and even destroyed and burnt offending works of art. He discovered that the architecture of Russian churches had been tainted by an indigenous development of purely Russian origin, the *shatrovy* or pyramid-shaped towers, built in stone in the sixteenth and seventeenth centuries but known from time immemorial in Russian wooden architecture. In 1653 Nikon unceremoniously banned the further building of churches in the 'worldly' pyramid style. He bluntly ordered the return to Byzantine church architecture, the Greek cross (four arms of equal length), with one, three, or preferably five, cupolas. He advised that the Cathedral of the Assumption in the Kremlin should be the model for future churches but 'not transformed to suit the artist's own ideas. . . . In observance of the rules of the Holy Apostles and the Fathers the Lord's church should have five cupolas and not resemble a tent. . . . [It] should be one-, or three-, or five-domed, but henceforth do not build tent-shaped churches . . . neither should the cupolas have the shape of a tent.'

Nikon also struck out against the 'worldly' custom of decorating churches externally in a 'patterned' style. It is interesting that the ban on pyramid-shaped churches was not so extreme as to cause the destruction of any existing churches; at least no such action is recorded. Of course the attack on church architecture must be seen in the context of the general revision of church books and customs, and was a very minor event in the whole turmoil. Indeed, the ban on tall towers on the central body of the church did not mean that they were to be entirely excluded elsewhere. Bell-towers in the seventeenth century and later, like those of the Novodevichy and Troitse-Sergeyev monasteries were freely built in this style, and the towers of the Kremlin porches, gates and bridge entrances were all given stone pyramid-shaped finials in the latter half of the century, which they still bear.

The effect of Nikon's reforms, which had the full sanction of the Tsar, was a tremendous shock to the Russian people. Illiterate and uncouth, their blind devotion to the forms of their religion made them antagonistic to any attempt, no matter how small, to change it from above. They had entirely missed out on the probing ideas of the Renaissance, Reformation and Counter-reformation, but now for the first time Russians were obliged to think about religious matters, to take sides, to awaken an intellectual consciousness that had long lain dormant. Nikon's unremitting insistence and arrogant manner naturally threw up its martyrs like the priest Avvakum who was ultimately burned at the stake. As the Tsar became aware of the opposition caused by the reforms and of Nikon's abuse of his power in putting down the rebellious dissenters, relations between them cooled. In 1658 Nikon retired to a site where he was building the Monastery of New Jersalem at what is now Istra and waited for the Tsar to beg for his return to Moscow. He waited in vain. It was not until eight years later that the stalemate was finally resolved and a move was made to depose him at a special council held in the Chudov (Miracle) Monastery in the Kremlin. Nikon was banished to the Feropontov monastery far away on the White Lake. At the accession of Fyodor he was pardoned but died on the journey back to Moscow. His reforms remained in force, however, in spite of the fervent opposition of such groups as the monks of the Solovetsk Monastery near Archangelsk who refused to give in and withstood a siege of eight years before being overwhelmed. The opposition groups became known as the *Raskolniki* (schismatics) of Old

20 The 'Skit' or chapel-residence of the Patriarch Nikon at the New Jerusalem Monastery, 1658.

Believers. Over the centuries they were to suffer bouts of severe persecution but they have managed to survive and can still be found in parts of Moscow.

Nikon's personal buildings

Nikon's strongly expressed views on the necessity for plain exteriors and on interiors enlivened only by religious paintings were put into practice in the three-storied Patriarch's Palace (the fourth was added in 1691) in the Kremlin. It contains the Church of the Twelve Apostles which his predecessor commissioned but the design of which Nikon is mainly responsible for. The large palace and church were built between 1645 and 1655 and much rebuilt in 1680 but Nikon's influence can clearly be seen. The plain exterior is decorated only by a narrow blind arcade girdling the building, similar to the friezes in Vladimir-Suzdal architecture. The church has five symmetrical cupolas, the roof supported by four piers. The carefully organized building was very different from the contemporary charmingly picturesque but utterly haphazard palaces of the senior nobility and the Tsar. The central

Krestovaya hall of the palace is a grand room, 20 by 14 metres, and is the first hall of such a large size to be built in Russia without the support of a central column. It rivalled if not surpassed the grandeur of the Tsar's Faceted Palace which was the official audience chamber. The Tsar and foreign ambassadors were received in the Krestovaya Palata and church councils and banquets were held there. Nikon had a series of covered passageways built connecting the palace to the Tsar's apartments and the Chudov Monastery. Traces of these still exist along the upper part of the northern wall. The entrance into the palace is in contrast to the lavish portal of the Tsar's palace. It is articulated by small doric columns which support a rectangular pediment, an innovation in Moscow which illustrates the growing influence on Russian architecture of western Europe where use of the classical order was by then widespread. The windows of the hall were placed regularly along the length of the wall giving even lighting to the large room inside.

It would have been sacrilegious to site a holy altar over rooms where people carried on normal business and everyday life and therefore churches on upper levels had to be built over other churches, or archways, or else, like the Poteshny (Pleasaunce) Palace nearby, with the altar jutting over the street. The cathedral is therefore situated over an archway leading into Cathedral Square. It has a splendid iconostasis of the same date as the palace which was transferred from the nearby Chudov Monastery when the latter was dismantled in the 1930s.

A splendid description of the palace at its house-warming in December 1655 was given by Archbishop Paul of Aleppo, son of Macarius, the Patriarch of Antioch, who had been invited to Moscow to attend the councils. The banquet was preceded by the presentation to Nikon of the traditional gifts of icons, bread and salt. The feast went on from morning to night, the Tsar and company drinking the health of the Patriarch and placing the empty cups upside down on their heads. Singers ceaselessly chanted, new dishes were continually being proffered, and the *Life of the Saints* was read to the company as they feasted. Paul described the Krestovaya Palata on the day of the feast thus:

The architecture . . . surprises the mind with its extraordinary height, length and breadth. Its greatest beauty is an exceedingly wide cupola, without any pillars in the centre; all around which he has made rows of steps. The pavement remains in the middle, shining like a lake, to which nothing but water is wanting. . . . He has also adorned this hall with beautiful tapestry of a variety of colours. This apartment has its immense windows (glazed with panes of beautiful crystal, prettily ornamented with various flowers . . .) looking on the one side towards the Cathedral [the Assumption] and on the other side towards the court of the patriarchal palace. He has furnished it with a large stove of handsome tiles standing near the door. . . . In a word these buildings are an object of wonder to everyone; for scarcely in the royal palaces is there anything to equal them.

21 Uspenie v Goncharakh (Church of the Assumption), in the potters' district, 1654. An example of a local church of the seventeenth century.

The second group of buildings erected by Nikon is rather more surprising. On the Istra River, some 60 kilometres to the west of Moscow, the arch-enemy of the 'worldly' pyramid-towered churches proceeded, with supreme irony, to erect the largest pyramid-towered church ever built in Muscovy. The apparent contradiction has never been satisfactorily explained but presumably the shape of the church was dictated by his intention to build a monastery on the model of the Church of the Sepulchre at the Monastery of the Caves in Jerusalem. The centre-piece of the Monastery of New Jerusalem was a huge church built in the shape of a widely based tower pointed at the top. Begun in 1658 it was finally completed in 1685 long after Nikon had fallen from power and been banished to the Feropontov Monastery. At first the wildly ambitious Nikon had wanted to include 365 chapels in the church, one for every day of the year, but he was persuaded to abandon this idea. The finished structure was very complex and the diameter of the tower so great that the architects had difficulties with roof supports and the upper part suddenly cracked in 1723.

Nikon, the antagonist of 'patterned' churches, literally plastered the interior with coloured tiles. The portal, window-frames, cornices, roofing of the tower, and even the iconostasis were made of blue, green, brown and white tiles. The damage to the roof in 1723 and two serious fires led, in 1748, to extensive repairs being carried out under the direction of the great baroque architect of St Petersburg, Bartolommeo Rastrelli, assisted by the Moscow architect, Karl Blank. The new tower was built of wood rather than masonry and baroque sculptured details were added to the interior decoration and iconostasis. However, the basic design of the church remained unaltered and some of the original tiles were used in the redecoration. In 1941 the German Army, repulsed at the very gates of Moscow, blew up the church and other buildings in the monastery before they retreated. It is now under restoration. In the woods nearby is the little *skit* or house with private chapel, Nikon's home during the long years he waited in vain for a summons back to the halls of power in Moscow. It is charmingly sited among the trees and waters of the little tributary of the Istra called, appropriately, the Jordan.

3 ASYMMETRY IN ARCHITECTURE

Side by side with the pyramid-style churches the cube churches, the true descendants of Byzantine architecture, were developing into the most extravagant and colourful buildings ever to be built in Russia, surpassed only by St Basil's. These many sectional asymmetrical, highly decorated and vividly coloured churches with differing roof levels gave a total effect of immense gaiety and even today lend colour and variety to Moscow's peeling, drab streets. Their particular characteristics are the elaborate exterior sculpture and brick-work around the windows (*nalichniki*) with the upper part over the windows sometimes shaped like a *kokoshnik* gable, sometimes in semi-circles and triangles and other more complicated forms. The walls around the window and doors are often decorated with engaged columns of brightly coloured bricks. The tops of each storey of wall were decorated with entablatures and pierced parapets so that the upper part of every section stands out in outline giving a bold delineation to the next level. Sometimes the frieze consisted of squares within squares in which carved figures or coloured tiles were set. It must be admitted that the incredible variety and richness of these decorations robbed the churches of the simplicity of form which was the essential element of the previous centuries. Yet these colourful churches and the few extant palaces of similar design display a joy and vivacity which were short-lived, soon to be quelled by the sobriety of the eighteenth-century classical style.

The most characteristic example of this wild disregard for absolute uniformity and love of rich adornment is the Troitsa v Nikitnikakh, the Church of the Trinity on Nikitnikov Pereulok off Ipatievsky Pereulok in Kitaigorod near Ulitsa Razina. It is known locally as the Church of the Georgian Virgin from an icon that once hung there. Completely submerged by tall buildings and the narrowness of the lane, it is a shock to come across the vividly red and white conglomeration of pyramid-towered porch, full-blown cupolas, richly scuptured window decorations and oddly protruding sections all joined together to form a gay and striking building, its size more like that of a cathedral than of a simple parish church. In fact it was the private chapel of a very important citizen, Nikitnikov, a wealthy merchant and leading member of the most influential guild, the *gost*, of which the Tsar was also a member. This was the guild of about thirty most favoured merchants, entrepreneurs who had unlimited rights of importation and were exempted from payment of custom dues. They also enjoyed the freedom of unlimited travel within Russia and abroad, an important concession at a time when serfs were unable even to leave their landlords and the artisans and small traders of the various settlements in Moscow were forbidden to move even to another part of the city. As the leading member of the *gost* guild Nikitnikov helped shape the Tsar's economic policies by acting as a sort of senior financial adviser. In spite of his wealth and power Nikitnikov, not being of boyarial descent, was barred from making his home inside the Kremlin walls. So in 1635–53 he built a palace and magnificent church here, in Kitaigorod, not far from the Kremlin. The palace disappeared long ago and the church is crowded by modern buildings mushrooming higher and higher on every side. Yet when it was built it dominated this part of Kitaigorod, rising majestically above the little single-storey wooden houses and palaces and could be seen from a long way off.

Like the Putnikakh Church it has a basic nucleus surrounded by a number of additional chambers, chapels, porch, staircase and passageway and a secret room for storing valuables. The deep soft red of the exterior walls contrasts with the white sculpture of the window decorations, the cornices and fine *kokoshniki* and the drums of the cupolas. The high, wide sub-basement or undercroft was an important part of

22 Troitsa v Nikitnikakh (Trinity Church of the Nikitnikov Family), 1635–53. A rare example of the private church of an influential medieval merchant.

a wealthy merchant's private church in which he would place his most valuable goods, safe under the protection of the altar from greedy thieves. The interior frescoes and iconostasis are still magnificent. The severe dark faces are by the hand of Simon Ushakov, considered to be the last of the great icon painters in Russia during the revival in icon painting after the hiatus of the Time of Troubles. Possibly influenced by Dutch and Flemish painting of the early sixteenth century, he paid great attention to detail and there is more naturalism in his art than in previous religious painting. Yet he still painted formal figures placed in preordained positions in order to express the simple abstract tenets of the medieval Russian Church.

23 Troitsa v Nikitnikakh (Trinity Church of the Nikitnikov Family), 1635–53.

Ushakov lived around the corner from the Nikitnikov family at 12 Ipatievsky Pereulok where his much rebuilt house still stands.

The royal palaces

Secular architecture was also developing along the same lines as the exuberant churches. In the seventeenth century for the first time it became common for the nobility who lived in the inner parts of Moscow, Kitaigorod and Belgorod, to build their houses out of masonry. They considered the stone mansions to be the more prestigious of their residences but they really preferred to live in the comfortable wooden ramshackle chambers of their ancestors. Surprisingly, there are over a hundred listed secular buildings of the seventeenth century still to be seen in Moscow. Most were former monk's cells or offices connected to the numerous monasteries but in addition to these there are many private palaces or town mansions disguised as bits and pieces of cellars or wings of later houses. There are, as well, a few almost complete examples of the complex establishment or estate of a Russian nobleman of the time.

As is to be expected, the most magnificent palaces were those built by the Tsar himself. Most of the older parts of the Kremlin palace were built in the 1630s, although some of the chapels are much older, and indeed one dates from 1393. Even after the completion of the great Kremlin palace the tsars, like the nobility, still preferred to live in wooden structures for their warmth and comfort. In 1667 what was probably the last great wooden palace was built at Kolomenskoe by Tsar Aleksei. It may have been built in a fit of nostalgia for the date is rather late for such an irregular plan dotted with bulbous domes, galleries and tent-shaped porches and contrasts greatly with the almost contemporary palace at Izmailovo. After the court had transferred to St Petersburg in 1712 it fell into disuse and its dilapidated shell was finally pulled down in the late eighteenth century on the orders of Catherine II. However, also at her insistence, a model was made of the splendid structure, as foreign to eighteenth-century eyes as it is to our own, which is still on view in the former service quarters of the palace at Kolomenskoe. Unlike the churches of the time it was entirely without a central nucleus, but consisted of a collection of many small wooden houses all connected to each other with gables, huge bulbous domes, pyramid-shaped roofs, *bochki*, and carved woodwork. The chambers were placed around various courtyards and galleries sited at various angles so that it appears that the mass of the buildings turns and shifts, making for a confusing external view. It is difficult to imagine how anyone would have found his way about the interior without a compass. Within this combination of angles, shapes, roofs and stairs, there are the chambers of the Tsar, his wife and their children and, on the lower floors, the service quarters. The white stone Kazan cathedral, which was connected by a gallery to the Tsaritsa's part of the palace, still stands and is still used as a church. Built in 1660, it is a classic mid-seventeenth-century church with its five cupolas, peaked porch, once

24 Kazan Cathedral at Kolomenskoe, 1660. The royal chapel attached to the former wooden palace.

open gallery, vaulted undercroft, pyramid-shaped bell-tower and carved window decorations.

The flexibility of wood made it possible to build the palace at Kolomenskoe by simply adding one chamber to another, joining them by galleries and corridors. The Kremlin palace, often referred to as the Terem, (which more specifically means an upper room where the women lived), was an attempt to translate the architecture of the wooden mansions into stone to provide more permanent and luxurious quarters for the royal family.

Although most of the palace was built in 1635–36 by the Russians Antip Konstantinov and Larion Ushakov, the design of the chambers is much earlier. Under Ivan III and his son Vasily III the Grand Prince's palace had been greatly extended and rebuilt, mostly in wood, as part of their grand rebuilding project. Many fires since then necessitated the extensive rebuilding of the palace in the seventeenth century but parts of it had survived from an earlier era. At that time buildings were not designed as a single block, but floors were placed one on top of the other in a receding succession of stories separated by cornices like a stepped or tiered pyramid. Like the wooden houses, chambers were placed next to each other in a long line and were usually entered from the neighbouring room or from arcaded galleries.

The Terem consists of five levels. The two lower levels were first built in the fourteenth and sixteenth centuries respectively (they received new façades in the nineteenth). The three upper levels were added by the first Romanovs in the seventeenth century. The first storey was used for artisan workshops for the preparation of all the cloth, armour, utensils and other items needed in the heavily populated Kremlin. After the artisans moved to the new capital in St Petersburg, the rooms were used to house the Tsar's suite during his visits to Moscow. The third storey with its low vaulted ceilings and deeply inset windows served in the seventeenth century for various administrative functions and those closest to the Tsar resided here. Later it was used to store state papers and formed apartments for part of the court on the Tsar's visits to Moscow. The fourth and fifth stories are the most exciting and interesting parts; the rooms of state and the Tsar's personal apartments were located there. Nothing remains of the royal women's quarters other than their chapel and the Golden Chamber of the Tsaritsas.

Because of the removal of the Red Staircase in Palace Square in recent times, the entry to the Terem Palace today is through the nineteenth-century Kremlin Great Palace to St Vladimir's Hall and thence up the open staircase in an inner courtyard to the Golden Porch, through the famous Golden Grille, across Upper Saviour Square and into the Tsar's apartments on one side and the Upper Saviour Cathedral on the other. The Golden Grille has delicate filigree ironwork of legendary beasts, one of the finest things in the Terem. Similar ironwork is found on the doors of the Church of the Trinity v Nikitnikakh executed about the same time. Pagan symbols continued to appear in Russian decorative art as late as the twentieth century in peasant embroidery, painted distaffs (*prialki*) and sleigh paintings.

Of the ancient royal ceremonial and private rooms to the left of the Golden Grille, the first room, low-vaulted with a splendid tiled stove, is the anteroom where boyars would gather to wait for the Tsar. The second room leading out of the anteroom is the Cross or Reception Chamber where the Tsar would grant audiences to the boyars, particularly during Holy Week. The third room is the throne room, a sort of study where only the boyar closest to the tsar was received. The middle window, known as the Petition Window, is where a box hung down to the courtyard for people to put in their written requests. It became known as the 'Longtime Box' owing to the lack of attention the petitions received. (The phrase 'to put into the Longtime Box' is still used in modern Russian to mean 'to put off till Doomsday'.) The fourth room, like the others leading out of the preceding room, is the Tsar's bedchamber. The 'Freuline' corridor named after the maids of honour has a lovely stone floor and passes alongside all five of the Tsar's chambers. Here the ancient tradition was observed whereby selected virgins from boyar and noble families gathered together to be subjected to the scrutiny of the Tsar, who came to choose one as his bride. He would march up and down the line of girls three times and then grasp the embroidered cloth of the girl of his choice. During the reign of Ivan the Terrible such parades were held more than once.

A staircase from the Throne Room leads to the Upper Terem where a large nursery surrounded on all sides by a balcony was built in 1637 for the children of Tsar Mikhail Fyodorovich. The upper, peach-coloured storey is colourfully visible a long way down the river but seems to disappear as one gets nearer the Kremlin. A frieze of coloured tiles encircles this upper tier. These upper fourth and fifth stories are more characteristic of the seventeenth century with their irregular positioning and elaborate window-surrounds of lavish stone carvings of plants and flowers originally brightly painted. It has been suggested that the seventeenth-century love of decoration on the façades and interiors of houses originated with the Terem Palace.

On the right of the main staircase and the Golden Grille is the Upper Saviour Cathedral Behind the Golden Grille, the domestic chapel of the tsars built in 1635–6. It is the most important of a group of four chapels, three small and cramped, built above and beside one another in a higgledy-piggledy fashion all sharing one roof topped by eleven gay gilded onion domes with brightly tiled drums visible from Cathedral Square.

The Golden Chamber of the Tsaritsas was first built in the sixteenth century and is the best preserved and, next to the Faceted Palace, the oldest of the secular part of the palace. Here the Tsaritsa received visiting dignitaries and congratulations from the Tsar and the Patriarch on feast days and 'name days' (festival days of the saint after which the Tsaritsa was named). It is said that Tsaritsa Irina, wife of Tsar Fyodor Ivanovich, received here the Patriarch of Constantinople, Jeremy, in 1589 during his stay in Russia to help in the appointment of the first Russian patriarch. A huge single arch supports the Upper Saviour Church above. Three asymmetrical windows on the eastern wall look out between the Faceted Palace and the Church of the Deposition of the Robe onto Cathedral Square.

The oldest structure in the Kremlin is the remaining part of the Church of the Raising of Lazarus built in 1393. The church had been bricked up in the eighteenth century and was rediscovered only during the building of the Kremlin Great Palace in 1838–49. Restoration work in 1924 revealed the west portal. It now acts as the crypt of the Church of the Nativity of the Virgin built in 1514 by Alevisio Novi which adjoins the Terem Palace to the west. Massive columns of stone blocks carry arches supporting a vault and act as a strong foil to the decorated west portal.

In the seventeenth century the Metropolitan of Krutitsky and Kolomna (the title still denotes the most senior metropolitan in the Russian Church) was forced to vacate his Kremlin home in favour of the recently established patriarchate. Where the Moskva River makes a sudden, sharp turn in eastern Moscow he built a splendid group of buildings comprising a church and palace which almost rivalled those of the Tsar. Behind a high stone wall were the private chapel, the Uspensky (Assumption) built in 1685 with the customary five cupolas, a palace of two stories and a high raised gallery joining church to palace. An enclosed stone walkway or *teremok* connected the palace to a summer residence on the edge of the steep bank. In 1694 the *teremok* was faced with the most delightful green, yellow and brown painted tiles. The effect of the roofed, arcaded gallery with heavy stout columns leading from the severe church to the attractive colours and gay design of the tiled façade of the *teremok* is quite astonishing. Here the metropolitans would pause to admire the superb view of Moscow (now obscured by tall buildings). In Catherine the Great's reign the sumptuous palace of the metropolitans was confiscated for the use of the state and became part of a soldiers' barracks. It even served as a prison – the writer Herzen was held briefly in one of the buildings in 1834. Lately the buildings abutting onto the *teremok* have been relieved of their tenants and work has begun in earnest to restore the palace and whole complex of buildings to their seventeenth-century grandeur. However, through the arches of the *teremok* a soldier can still be seen rifle at the ready guarding the barracks behind which now house Red Army soldiers.

---

25 Krutitskoe Podvore (Residence of the Metropolitan), 1694. The only completely tiled building in Moscow.

Three churches of Zamoskvareche

There are three outstanding churches of the middle and second half of the seventeenth century still extant in Zamoskvareche (across the river), the southern part of old Moscow facing the Kremlin. All are under the protection of the state. The church of St Nikolai shto v Pyzhakh dating from 1657 was built in the Streletskaya Sloboda, the main colony of the armed soldiers-traders-artisans, by order of one of their officers, Pyzhov. The *streltsy* lived in various colonies scattered throughout Moscow, usually composed of between 500 and 1,000 persons. Some of these colonies were concentrated at the boundaries of Moscow, on the Zemlyanoi Val (Garden Ring Road), while others were on Manezh Square and opposite the Kremlin's Borovitsky Gate. But most of the *streltsy* lived in Zamoskvareche, the area closest to the Tartars, the main danger. In 1681, seventeen years before the great *streltsy* rebellion, there were more than 22,000 of these part-time soldiers. They must have been a colourful sight, armed with muskets and pikes and dressed in long caftans with turned down collars quite distinct from the caftans of the nobility, fastened with loops and toggles, and their fur-trimmed cloth caps indicating by the colours their particular regiment. Zamoskvareche at the time was dotted with swamps and fields and only sparsely inhabited (the canal that is there today was not dug until the nineteenth century). The *streltsy* settlement with its wall and gates resembled a small fortress.

The church is all that has survived of the soldier's colony. It is a rather old-fashioned church, a good example of the principle of 'patterned' architecture. It has five well-proportioned, round, full-blown cupolas, the windows are framed by small columns and a small *kokoshnik* gable over the upper part, the broad cornice of the central cube is overlaid with decorative detail and the doorway is likewise richly embroidered. The apse is in three parts containing three chapels of which, unusually, the two outer ones do not bear cupolas.

Not far away, on Bolshaya Polyanka, is the church of St Gregory Neokesariiskovo (New Caeserea) built by Ivan Kusnechik and Karp Guba in 1667–69. The five cupolas sit astride the roof drawing attention to the marvellous frieze of variously coloured tiles. The tile maker, Polubes, was the designer of the many tiles at the Monastery of New Jerusalem but when Patriarch Nikon fell from power and work on the monastery ceased in 1666, he came to Moscow and turned his attention to this parish church. The fantastic flower design reminded people of peacock feathers and the church became known as the 'Peacock's Eye'. The ironwork is also of a high order.

Also nearby is the Voskreseniye v Kadashakh, the Church of the Resurrection in the Second Kadashevsky Pereulok, built by the employees of the state enterprise for cloth manufacture. This church, somewhat rebuilt in the nineteenth century, shows some signs of the incipient change to baroque elements in Russian architecture. The *kokoshniki* have disappeared and are replaced by a crenellated parapet. Height is

26 St Nikolai shto v Pyzhakh (Church of St Nicholas built by Pyzhov). Built in 1657–70 in the area across the river from the Kremlin.

emphasized by the very sharp silhouette, the tall slim drums carrying the elegant cupolas which, with the elaborate design of the window decorations, force the eye upwards.

The typical town estate of the seventeenth century

Although most secular seventeenth-century architecture outside the Kremlin still standing in Moscow is obscured by later additions, there is one remarkably complete example of a town estate of the upper levels of society built around mid-century. It consists of a palace and church which hold pride of place, surrounded by servant's quarters, service buildings, gardens and a small orchard. It is on the Bersenyevsky Embankment under the brooding grey mass of a tall block of government flats built in the 1930s. How strange for these officials to look out of their bedroom windows down onto the gay contours and richly decorated façade of the Church of St Nikolai and the palace of the *Dumny Dyak*, Averky Kirillov! A *Dumny Dyak* was a member of the Tsar's council, a very influential person. Kirillov, among other things, was in charge of the Tsar's market gardens that at this time occupied most of the land on the island to the east of his estate. The church and house were built in 1656–7. Kirillov died in 1689 at the hands of the *streltsy* and his grave is near the church.

The exterior of the church is gay with coloured brick tiles and stone carvings. These harmonize with similar decorative features in the house. They were once joined by an open-sided vaulted passageway. The roofing of the church uses the system of stepped vaulting leaving large hollows for windows and doors. The house was much changed by the addition of a Dutch gable at the entrance on the north side in the early eighteenth century, possibly designed by Ivan Petrovich Zarudny, but the south elevation retains purely seventeenth-century features like the immensely attractive open porch held up by stout columns. The church and house both share elaborately designed windows with engaged columns and entablature, a characteristic porch with columns like fat pitchers, and red brick squares with carved stone details inset with coloured tiles.

4 WESTERN INFLUENCE ON ARCHITECTURE

Information about developments in Europe was gradually infiltrating Moscow and influencing its institutions and its architecture. It came from Poland, filtered via Belorussia through the Ukraine, to which Moscow had drawn closer in the seventeenth century, and thence to Moscow.

The Ukraine and Muscovy

The Ukraine had been in and out of Russian hands since the reign of Ivan the Terrible's father, Vasily III, but during the Time of Troubles had again become part of the Polish-Lithuanian union. Except for brief periods, the peoples of Kiev and the south had been cut off from their brothers in Moscow and the north-west since the time the Tartar hordes had conquered their lands. Although there are basic similarities, they had developed different patterns of speech, dress, culture and architecture.

Meanwhile, on the southern borders of the Russian and the Polish empires, in the lower reaches of the Don, Dnieper and Ural Rivers, a growing horde of escaped serfs and a motley assortment of adventurers had formed themselves into a kind of military brotherhood, the famous cossacks. By the seventeenth century the cossack numbers had been swollen by the large number of fugitives who had run away during the Time of Troubles and by many from the troubled sections of the Ukraine where religious intolerance had caused serfs to leave the estates. The cossacks had become a formidable force. They were the cowboys of the Russian border areas capable of fighting on any side that was advantageous to them – Turk, Russian or Polish. They were also able to threaten Muscovy with a serious revolt, the rebellion of Stepan Razin that only ended in 1671 after the whole of the lower Volga area had been sacked and burnt.

Nevertheless, religious persecution by the Poles aroused in the cossacks latent patriotic feelings towards the Orthodox Church and by the middle of the seventeenth century they were increasingly turning towards Muscovy for help in ridding themselves of Polish sovereignty. Although at first hesitant about engaging in a war with Poland, Tsar Aleksei could no longer ignore blood ties and in 1654 the conflict began. By 1667 Russian successes led to the armistice of Andrussovo under which the left bank of the Dnieper remained with Moscow and Kiev, on the right bank, was ceded by the Poles initially for two years but subsequently on a permanent basis. Although Moscow had agreed that if the outcome of the war were favourable the Ukraine would remain semi-autonomous, this promise was never fulfilled.

After the war many Ukrainians came to Moscow. The impact of their arrival was enormous. Already Ukrainian priests from the Academy in Kiev had arrived in some numbers to escape Polish persecution and to help with the correction of the books. Those that stayed had a decisive influence on the establishment of the first institutions of learning in the mainly illiterate city. Although a century earlier a Church council had strongly recommended the establishment of schools, it was not until 1649 that objections to subjects like Latin were overruled and a school was opened in the Andreevsky Monastery by Fedor Rtishchev under the tutelage of the Kievan monks. By 1687 a school was opened on the lines of the Kiev Academy but also devoted to the study of Greek, the Slavono-Greek-Latin Academy in the Zaikonospassky Monastery in Kitaigorod (25th October Street). It was not a school in the liberal tradition but an intolerant medieval establishment which became the arbiter in all religious matters. Michael Florinsky comments: 'the intellectual treasures of seventeenth-century Russia were hardly more than a pale reflection of European Scholasticism of the twelfth and thirteenth centuries' (*Russia: A History and Interpretation*, New York 1959). Still, the school did help to break down the appalling barrier of illiteracy and pave the way for the reforms of the eighteenth century.

Ukrainian and Belorussian innovations were evident not only in tentative efforts to introduce education but also in the forms and devices of architecture. Already the hegemony of the purely Russian national form, the pyramid-shaped church, was being eroded, and with the spread of ideas brought from Poland by the Ukrainian colonists the corruption was assured. In many churches the Ukrainian plan of three cupolas placed from west to east, completely opposite to the Muscovy north-south siting of cupolas, was adopted. Where there were five cupolas, the Ukrainian custom was to place them not one at each corner with one at the centre but at each arm of the Greek cross plan, i.e. midway along the walls of the cube. The New Cathedral of the Donskoi Monastery, built between 1684 and 1698 illustrates this system. Internally, the iconostasis underwent a great change in that it became no longer purely a frame for supporting icons but a greatly embellished work of art rich with carvings, an architectural device in its own right. Similarly, the more florid patterns of Ukrainian churches were introduced into Moscow church architecture, particularly by such artists as Zarudny (St John the Warrior and the Menshikov Tower).

The Ukrainian colonists settled in the still picturesque eastern part of Belgorod where today's traffic barely penetrates and where there is an unusual number of buildings from the seventeenth century owing to the minimal damage suffered here in the 1812 fire. Roughly, the area stretches between Novaya Ploshchad and the boulevards, and Bogdan Khmelnitsky Street and the Solyanka. Until 1953 Bogdan Khmelnitsky Street was known as the Maroseika or colloquially as Little Russia which was also the name for the Ukraine. As Bogdan Khmelnitsky was one of the principal cossack leaders the modern name has retained the Ukrainian flavour. One of the small streets that leads to the heart of the Ukrainian quarter is Khokhlovsky Pereulok. The Russians also referred to the Ukrainians as *khokhli* because of their elaborate headdress (*khokhol* means crest). The Trinity Church on the corner was built in 1696 in the Ukrainian baroque style and was the main place of worship for the *khokhli*.

The foreigners' colony – Nemetskaya Sloboda
Foreign influence, not just that imbibed through the Ukraine but directly from western Europe, was gradually making itself felt in many aspects of Russian life. One of the chief sources of this influence was the presence of many western Europeans in Moscow. The expansion of Muscovy and the competition among European states for its lucrative trade had inevitably meant that the English could not indefinitely maintain the trade monopoly granted them a century earlier by Ivan the Terrible. After the Time of Troubles the number of foreigners living in Moscow grew to such an extent that the Englishmen of Giles Fletcher's day would have been astonished to find so many rivals. Thus, when relations with Britain were broken off in 1649, ostensibly because of the beheading of Charles I, the interests of the Dutch and Germans were probably as much to blame as the Tsar's abhorrence of regicide.

The first foreigners' colony formed in the sixteenth century was wiped out and its inhabitants dispersed during the occupation of Moscow by the Poles between 1610 and 1612. Under the first Romanov tsar, Mikhail Fyodorovich, foreigners were allowed to live where they chose and most settled in the streets to the north of Bogdan Khmelnitsky Street, especially favouring Armyansky Pereulok, where

27 Novy Sobor (New Cathedral) of the Donskoi Monastery, 1684–98.

Artamon Matveyev, the Tsar's adviser and head of the Posolsky Prikaz (foreign office), lived with his Scottish wife. By 1658 foreigners owned fifty-eight houses in the district.

The effect of increasingly large numbers of foreigners was very unsettling. Not only were there Ukrainians, Armenians, Georgians and Greeks with whom, in a small way, the Muscovites had been familiar for centuries, but also western Europeans different in dress, manner and customs, much wealthier than the Muscovites, and worshipping at different churches. Russians were by nature deeply suspicious of foreigners. For example, no priest or monk was allowed to speak with a foreigner 'on any occasion whatsoever'. It is said that on one of his grand processions through the streets the Patriarch noticed that some people did not remove their caps nor cross themselves at the sight of the crosses and holy icons. He found out later that they were foreigners dressed in Russian costume. Henceforth foreigners were told that they must dress in their own national garb. The foreigners not only irritated by their lack of reverence for Russian customs of obeisance, but they persisted in building their 'prayer houses' wherever they settled. As more and more foreigners moved into the area around Armyansky Pereulok the income from the principal churches like St Kozma and St Damian on Ulitsa Bogdana Khmelnitskovo, fell dramatically and the clergy complained to the Tsar. Mikhail Fyodorovich ordered the demolition of the foreigners' prayer houses and put a stop to the steady increase in the number of foreigners moving into the area. The next tsar, Aleksei Mikhailovich, was influenced by Patriarch Nikon in 1652 to order the eviction of all westerners from the central parts of Moscow and their removal to a special settlement on the Yauza. The site of the former settlement under Ivan the Terrible, this was now overgrown, empty and desolate and some miles from the Kremlin beyond the boundary of the ramparts of Zemlyany Gorod.

It was assumed that the removal of foreigners from central Moscow would prevent further 'contamination' (Tsar Mikhail used to wash his hands symbolically after receiving foreign ambassadors). This was not to be so; the siting of the settlement was conveniently near to the old palace at Preobrazhenskoe where Peter the Great spent most of his childhood. Soloviev, the great pre-revolutionary Russian historian, described the irony of the situation: 'They singled out the foreigners, moved them to a special suburb. It seemed as if Rus had shut itself off from the 'Germans' but it only seemed so. Rus had set out moving from east to west, and the west in its representative, Nemetskaya Sloboda, thrust her onto the path she must take, and soon old Moscow knelt down before her own suburb as once upon a time old Rostov knelt before its subordinate village Vladimir: soon Nemetskaya Sloboda enticed the tsar and court from the Kremlin and gave them new palaces. Nemetskaya Sloboda was a step in the direction of Petersburg just as Vladimir was a step in the direction of Moscow.'

A few rich merchants and the Tsar's doctor, Samuel Collins, were permitted to continue living in Kitaigorod and Belgorod but most foreigners were to be confined to the walled village with its Russian sentries. It was soon known as 'Nemetskaya Sloboda' or the German Settlement. *Nemets* is Russian for 'German'; it derives from *nemoi* meaning 'dumb', implying that a people unable to speak the Russian tongue are incapable of any speech. Eventually it came to mean all foreigners. There are many parallels between the walled foreigner's settlement of the seventeenth century and the rigidly guarded special blocks of flat where Moscow's foreign residents are obliged to live today.

In Nemetskaya Sloboda the foreigners accepted their lot and began to make it one of the most attractive parts of Moscow. They built firm, solid houses along straight lines with little gardens better appointed than most Russian homes. By 1665 there were 204 houses in the colony although thirty years later the streets were still not paved, not even with wood, and the mud of spring and autumn must have been a trial. The upper classes built large, richly appointed houses while the craftsmen built simpler, smaller houses, usually of wood. The straight and parallel streets were later

28 Nemetskaya Sloboda (Foreigners' Colony), with the palace of Franz Lefort, 1697–98.

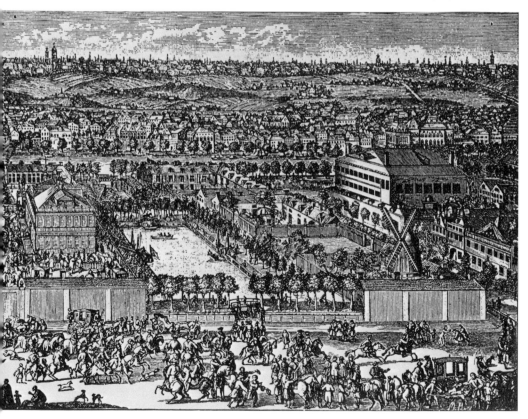

copied in the soldier's settlement across the Yauza River founded by Peter in the early eighteenth century and in the streets around the Meshchanskaya. The Russian-Polish war and the ending in Europe in 1648 of the Thirty Years' War meant that many soldier-adventurers came from foreign lands to serve in the Russian armed forces and in 1665 this group owned three quarters of all the houses. Dutch and Hamburg merchants complained in 1658 that the feasts and drinking of the military and their many duels disrupted the life of the colony. Although the colony was subject to Russian law and was kept under strict surveillance until 1695 when their seclusion was ended by Peter the Great, they enjoyed a large measure of self-government and built their own churches and schools unhampered. Overall responsibility was with the Posolsky Prikaz. The whole area of the settlement accounted for one fifth of the total area of Moscow. Moscow has now swollen and grown beyond the old foreigner's ghetto but a few buildings that date from the seventeenth century can still be found. One such building on Starokirochnyi Pereulok is the little house said to have belonged to Anna Mons, the daughter of a Swiss jeweller, with whom Peter the Great had his first love affair. On Second Bauman Street is another building originally built as a palace for Peter's favourite, Franz Lefort, a Swiss adventurer, and which later passed into the Tsar's possession. Eighteenth-century additions have much altered the building.

Thus, western influence was reaching Moscow in two ways, via Poland through the recent Ukrainian colonists, and more directly from western Europeans themselves grouped together in the extensive foreigner's colony. After the 1654–67 war with Poland the upper ranks of the Russian nobility began copying what they had seen in Poland by importing furniture, acquiring clocks and secular paintings and even displaying statues (forbidden in the Russian Church). Some went so far as to change their traditional caftan for foreign dress. Inside the churches, the iconostasis reflected a more worldly attitude. Its paintings were no longer the cardinal fact of the screen, but instead the frame had become more important than the icons.

The beginnings of regularity in architecture

Architecture changed very much between the middle and end of the seventeenth century. In the 1650s it was distinguished by a picturesque and complicated composition, exceptionally varied, with maximum saturation of architectural details in brick and coloured tiles worked on walls like a colourful carpet (for example, Krutitsky Teremok). By the end of the century the composition is simpler and more clear-cut, use of strict symmetry reappears in the façades, and the employment of standardized details in stone which clearly stand out against the red background of the brick walls has become widespread. Also by this time windows and doors have become larger, each storey is separately identified, and a peculiarly Russian interpretation of the classical order has become fashionable. The estate at Izmailovo shows some of these developments.

On an island surrounded by two small rivers east of Moscow and now within the boundaries of Greater Moscow Tsar Aleksei built at Izmailovo a very different kind of estate from the one at Kolomenskoe or the royal palace in the Kremlin. Although already in Moscow the homes of the upper gentry were beginning to boast gardens, Izmailovo was the beginning of regularity in the planning of great estates, the first hint of the formal parks of the eighteenth century. The estate consisted of the palace at the centre on an island surrounded by ponds and canals built around a square connected by galleries to the Pokrovsky Cathedral built in 1679. The palace itself had a stone basement over which wooden rooms were placed but in 1765 it suffered the same fate as the Kolomenskoe palace and was dismantled. In the nineteenth century two wings were added to either side of the cathedral and the whole complex of buildings became a poor house. Like Kolomenskoe, the huge park attached to the estate and the remaining buildings are now part of a public park much used by skiers in winter and walkers in summer.

Although the cathedral was modelled on the much earlier church at Alexandrovskaya Sloboda north of Moscow, it still bears characteristics of its era in the tall brick window-frames executed in a chain pattern and the decorative tiles covering the upper parts of the walls. The glowering Mostovaya or Bridge Tower (1671) with its heavy proportions once stood at the end of the bridge to Izmailovsky Island.

Perhaps the most interesting building at Izmailovo is the gate at the entrance to the estate. Built in 1682 by Terenty Makarov, it was to be the prototype for such entrance gates at monasteries in Moscow such as the Vysoko-Petrovsky and Andronikov. They were built in strict axial composition and were the first to boast three entrances, a main one at the centre flanked by smaller entrances on either side. The main entrance was emphasized by coupled columns and a great pyramid tower over the central axis. An open walled terrace with a carved stone balustrade surmounted the two side arches. This was the first use of symmetry in the building of gates, the first time coupled columns were employed in such a way and also the first time such a fine archivolt (i.e., the tracing of the arch) was incorporated. A small church, Iosafas Tsarevich, built in 1688–9 with elements of the Ukrainian style, has not survived; it was removed in this century.

The private palaces were also undergoing changes. In the last quarter of the seventeenth century the wooden houses of the boyars and upper ranks of the nobility were being replaced with larger and more formal stone houses bearing a clear-cut division of the façade into two or three floors. They usually had a large courtyard and a covered passageway to a private church. A stone gate bearing an octagonal pyramid tower, like the one at Izmailovo, would lead into the main or *krasny* courtyard where the house had its principal entrance. The most magnificent and rich of these new houses was that of Vasily Golitsyn, probably the best educated and most intelligent Russian of the late seventeenth century. During the time in which Sophia, Peter the

Great's half-sister, was Regent, from 1682 to 1689, he became her lover and exerted enormous influence. When she fell from power he suffered banishment and exile at the hands of Peter. Ironically, he was probably the Russian closest in spirit at that time to the many reforms introduced by Peter.

The Golitsyn Palace had fifty-three separate rooms. Living, kitchen and storage rooms were located on the ground floor, the more formal rooms on the first floor. The great dining room was lit by forty-six windows in two tiers. The wooden ceiling was covered with painted canvas and the walls of each room hung with coloured materials, foreign wallpaper and stamped leather. Coloured tiled stoves, oriental rugs and carved, wooden furniture completed the rich interior. At first a third wooden floor existed.

The historian V. I. Klyuchevsky wrote of the Golitsyn Palace:

In his large Moscow house, everything was organized according to European tastes: in the large halls on the walls between the windows hung great mirrors; paintings, portraits of Russian and foreign lords and German geographical maps in gold frames hung on the walls; on the ceilings the planetary system was depicted; the many beautifully fashioned clocks and thermometers completed the decoration of the rooms. The roof of the house was made of copper leaf, the window and door surrounds were of stone carvings. In V. V. Golitsyn's house the most educated men of his time, speaking in several foreign tongues, met together from . . . Jesuits to . . . the avant garde of Russian society.

After the Revolution Soviet restorers rediscovered the Golitsyn Palace just off Okhotny Ryad and the smaller Troekurov Palace next-door of the same date, both in a dilapidated state, and embarked on a plan to restore them to their original beauty.

29 Palace of the boyar Troekurov, mid-seventeenth century.

Igor Grabar, the head of the restoration office, considered the Golitsyn Palace one of the most historically interesting buildings in central Moscow, particularly in view of the fact that few seventeenth-century private dwellings survived intact. He even published a plan in 1925 to turn the whole area with the Golitsyn and Troekurov Palaces, the nearby Hall of Columns and the Pyatnitskaya Church into a grassed and tree-lined square, removing all the other unimportant buildings. But in 1932 the newly restored palace and the church fell prey to the rapacious appetite of the bulldozer. At that time Grabar had prudently resigned and no-one dared to protest; the era of the Great Terror had begun and everyone was falling silent.

The Troekurov Palace, however, hidden by the massive stone of the new Council of Ministers building next-door, was spared. Between it and the Hall of Columns is a narrow driveway at the end of which, inside the dark courtyard vastly overshadowed by high-rise buildings all around, is the delightful façade of the peach and white Troekurov Palace, now used as the Glinka Museum. The boyar Troekurov was the leader of the *streltsy*, the mercenaries, in the late seventeenth century.

The palace has been carefully restored several times in the last fifty years. It was built on three floors, the ground floor for domestic services and the first and second for the use of the boyar and his family. The first-floor window decorations and cornices are typical of the mid-seventeenth century but the more elaborate ones of the upper floor show that it was added some fifty years later. It seems that the palace was originally built as a collection of free-standing chambers, each with its own roof, joined by galleries and passages. In the 1680s a second floor was added to the separate chambers, making the whole into one building. The side of the house with the main entrance once had an open gallery and staircase, as can be seen from the marks on the wall. Inside, the square rooms with high vaulted ceilings remind one of Russian wooden architecture.

A third late-seventeenth-century palace is the Volkov Mansion. After 1727 it was owned by the Yusupov family, on Bolshoi Kharitoniev Pereulok, near the Garden Ring Road and the former Krasnye Vorota (Red Gate). Although much changed in the nineteenth century when it was 'restored', it is still most attractive with the chess-board roof of varying heights, the modestly decorated ground floor used for the domestic needs of the house, the first floor designed for the living-rooms and reception chambers with giant columns and carved composite capitals. Inside there is a large vaulted hall 14 metres long with a painted ceiling of portraits of the Yusupov family. Although built at the end of the seventeenth century, it is not in one single block like the Golitsyn and Troekurov houses but is composed of a mixture of various chambers linked by galleries in the old style of multi-cellular architecture. The external staircase leads to the formal first floor and a sort of tower-like addition forms the second floor. The columns and capitals of the exterior show the influence of Moscow baroque in spite of the building's old-fashioned style. It is now used by the Academy of Agriculture, rather uncomfortably, as it is under the care of the state

30 Volkov or Yusupov Mansion, late seventeenth century. One of the few private palaces surviving from this period.

and may not be altered.

During the second half of the seventeenth century a great building programme was inaugurated in the monasteries, so many of which were affected only a few years later by Peter the Great's decision to curtail their activities. Richly decorated refectory palaces were built. The refectory was no longer part of the church but had separated to become an important building in its own right with its own chapel at the end of the long hall. The best refectories of the period are those at the Troitse-Sergeyev Monastery at Zagorsk (1685–92) and the lovely Dutch and Polish fronted refectory at the Simonov Monastery (1677–80), unfortunately now used to house part of the Likhachev Automobile Factory. The refectories, like the palaces of the time, bore two tiers of windows, had spacious halls, open exterior galleries, with a main staircase, and made use of some elements of the classical order in the indulgent abundance of their decoration.

Moscow or Naryshkin baroque

The Ukrainian-Belorussian-Polish influence in architecture eventually expressed itself in a peculiar form of baroque known as Moscow or Naryshkin baroque after its greatest patron (the maternal uncle of Peter the Great). The baroque style which had risen with the Counter-reformation in Italy travelled slowly to Moscow via Poland, Belorussia and the Ukraine. This is the first time Russian architecture can be said to have joined the mainstream of architectural development in the west. Although churches such as St Basil's have features in common with early Renaissance buildings in Italy, especially in the ground-plan, and churches such as the Archangelsky in the Kremlin have Renaissance details such as lunettes, the total view of Russian architecture prior to the end of the seventeenth century is of a predominantly individual, national style. Now, with the appearance of Moscow baroque it began to lose the peculiar characteristics that made it unique. However, Moscow baroque is no pale imitation of western models and was expressed in a distinctly national way, coming as it did through the sieve of Ukrainian-Belorussian experience. The abolition of the pyramid-towered church in 1653 left a void in Russian architectural development uneasily filled by the cube churches with their gables and five cupolas. With the emergence of the Ukrainian style, which reintroduced the octagonal form, there occurred some interesting restatements of familiar shapes. Ukrainian influence is also detectable in the upward thrust of the buildings achieved by the use of layering, rising from an octagonal form on a square base to form a sort of tower. The gate-tower church of the Novodevichy Convent, the Pokrova (Intercession of the Virgin), built in 1683–88, was constructed in this manner, with two octagons, one resting on the other and topped by three cupolas. The second gate-tower church at Novodevichy, the Preobrazhenskaya (Transfiguration), was also deeply influenced by the new ideas and is decorated inside and out with religious sculptures lending the church a Catholic appearance.

31 St Philip, late seventeenth century, together with a view of the Arbat.

These churches of receding tiers began to be built in great numbers in the last ten years of the century. The astonishing fact about them is the return they signal to the pyramid form so decisively rejected forty years earlier (except in the far north where they were still being built). The new yet familiar form was lavishly embellished with the carvings, window-frames and balustrades of the Italian Mannerist School and so was utterly different in execution from the purity of the earlier pyramid churches such as the Ascension Church at Kolomenskoe. Yet the total effect is again that of a pyramid, although encrusted with baubles.

32 Church at Troparevo, 1693. Moscow or Naryshkin baroque in a village.

In Moscow the new architecture blossomed in the reign of Fyodor Alekseyevich and regency of Sophia in the last quarter of the century under the sponsorship of the influential Naryshkin family, the family of the Tsaritsa, Peter the Great's mother. The churches were usually built as part of an estate. Their diminishing tiers ending in a single cupola did not occupy a large area, and the compactness of the churches and their fine silhouette was not to be marred by locating a bell-tower nearby – by 1691 bells were being incorporated into the upper part of the tower and churches in this style became known as 'churches-under-the-bells'. The best of the baroque churches still extant in Moscow are the Spas (Saviour) in Ubory, (1694–96); the Pokrova (Intercession of the Virgin) in Fili (1693–4); the Troitsa (Trinity) in Troitsko-Lykovo (1698–1703); and the lovely Sheremetiev Znameniya Church (the Church of the Sign) near the old University in Belgorod.

Before considering the towered churches further it is important to realize that the cube churches, elongated by the addition of the entranceway, also exhibited more controlled features at the end of the century. Indeed, the Naryshkin family demonstrated this themselves when they had the monastery rebuilt that they used as the resting-place of the family and regarded almost as a personal possession: the

34 Refectory Church at the Vysoko–Petrovsky Monastery, 1697.

33 *Opposite* Gate of the Zachatievsky Monastery of the Immaculate Conception, 1696.

35 Cathedral of the Bogoyavlensky (Epiphany) Monastery, 1693–6. Moscow baroque.

Vysoko-Petrovsky (Upper Peter) Monastery on the Petrovka. Part of the inner circle of monasteries originally built for the defence of the city, it was rebuilt towards the end of the seventeenth century. The large central church dating from 1686, Bogolyubskaya Bogomatery in the centre of the monastery, is not of particular interest, but the two-storey monks' cells dating from the 1680s and the refectory opposite illustrate the increasing use of Renaissance architectural vocabulary and regular design. Because the cells form the boundary of the monastery and are placed right on the street, the lower floor is almost bare of windows and was used for storage and domestic offices. The upper floor, however, has splendid groups of four windows separated by coupled columns and decorated in the rich style of Moscow baroque, a sharp contrast with the bare walls below. On the inner side of the building, towards the main part of the monastery, is a fine open gallery running along the first floor connecting the cells to the refectory opposite, which is a more elegant building than the central church. The galleries formerly connected the cells to all the important buildings of the monastery. The tall elegant bell-tower rising over the main gateway on the Petrovka, also built at the same time in the baroque style, punctuates the monastery vertically.

The loveliest of the towered churches is the Pokrova at Fili. Around the base is a superb open gallery on three sides shouldered from the ground by arches, giving the tall building a broad support. The basic plan of the church consists of four semi-circular chapels projecting from the sides of a square. Each chapel is surmounted by a drum and cupola. Rising from the central body of the building are three octagonal tiers. The uppermost, the drum, bears an elegant cupola over which the tall Greek cross with the half-moon at its foot stands triumphant. Other features of this church which make it different from earlier seventeenth-century churches are an observance of strict symmetry in the plan and façade; richly carved pediments known in Russia as 'cockscombs' because of their decorative nature which complete the various levels of the building; large and spacious door and window openings; a moderate use of columns and absence of leafy capitals; and, finally, an elegant silhouette. The walls are very thick – two metres – to allow for an internal staircase within the walls to reach the bells hanging in the second tier. Inside, a high balcony forms the choir and provides a place for the estate-owner and his family. But it is really the shape of the building more than its decorations that makes it a work of art – effective though the white stone carving is against the red background of the church.

The ultimate in Moscow baroque is expressed in the Znameniya Church (the Church of the Sign) at Dubrovitsy just south of Moscow built by Prince B. A. Golitsyn, tutor to Peter the Great, in 1690–1704. A near relative was the powerful Vasily Vasilevich Golitsyn, the lover of Sophia. This extraordinary church is almost secular in its design with its many sculptures, surmounted by a gilded iron crown very similar to the crown used in Russian marriage ceremonies, and finished with a tiny, inconspicuous cupola, and covered with Latin inscriptions. It is baroque gone mad; and it does not seem to have been copied in other buildings. The church is now in a dilapidated state in its isolated position, subject to vandals and pilferers. The palace which was originally built with the church was much rebuilt in the nineteenth century and is now used as a rest-home.

In conclusion the architecture of the end of the seventeenth century was utterly different from earlier buildings with their exceptional use of colour and form, and proliferation of architectural detail in brick and coloured tiles. Strict symmetry and a simpler composition had begun to predominate. The same effect was repeated everywhere, and white stone carvings like lace stand out clearly against the red background of a brick wall. Larger windows and doors were built and space was more clearly defined by the separation of buildings into floors. Secular buildings of stone, not just palaces but public buildings, also were erected at this time. They are all one- or two-storied buildings, the older ones bearing porches and the later ones boasting columns and pediments over the windows. Existing examples include the wonderful Pechatny Dvor (Printing House) which was almost entirely burnt in the 1812 fire but was cleverly restored; the Monetny Dvor (Mint); and the Poteshny Dvorets (Pleasaunce Palace) in the Kremlin.

5 THE CITY AT THE END OF THE SEVENTEENTH CENTURY

Moscow was the archetypal Russian town of the seventeenth century. Its nucleus was the Kremlin, the fortified, administrative and religious centre, with the palace of the prince, his chanceries, cathedrals, prisons, state granary and warehouses for powder and cannon, located in a high place surrounded by a moat and rivers. The second circle of settlement, as in other towns, was the *posad* or suburb (Kitaigorod and Belgorod) where the townspeople had their houses, the *gostiny dvor* or merchants' place of business, the market, the administrative office of the *posad*, the chancery of the council of elders, the 'washing house' or baths, and the state enterprise which sold products like wine and vodka. The third line of settlement was the *sloboda* or colonies of small traders and artisans. All roads led to the Kremlin where the population could seek refuge in time of attack. The larger monasteries and landowners kept 'siege' houses in the Kremlin and used them only during times of trouble. Even peasants from the surrounding countryside with their wives and children brought their animals to the Kremlin for protection. By the seventeenth century the city had grown so large that the Kremlin could no longer provide a haven for the entire population and the protective walls were extended to Kitaigorod and Belgorod and to the ramparts and wooden walls of Zemlyanygorod.

The population of Moscow at the end of the seventeenth century was about 150,000, the same as it had been in the mid-sixteenth century when the English traders had first arrived. The Time of Troubles, when the population fell to 80,000, and the lengthy Polish-Livonian wars had helped to deplete it and prevent it from increasing. It was composed of boyars, black and white clergy, clerks, servants of the rich, soldiers, foreigners and the *sloboda* or settlements of various trades and crafts who formed the majority. At the top of the hierarchy were the *gost*, including people like the wealthy merchant Nikitnikov. They were very privileged people who could hawk their trade anywhere and had such concessions as the right to heat their houses and bath-houses in summer, denied to the rest of the population because of the danger of fire. Next to the *gost* were the *gostinoi sotni* and *sukonnye sotni*, which were rather like the senior guilds in England at the time. The members of these *sotni* had many privileges and were not obliged as other craftsmen were to live in a particular area. *Sotni* means 'hundreds', which is the name for similar guilds in England in medieval times; in 1649 in the *gostinoi sotni* there were 158 families. Below the hundreds were a number of senior trade and small industrial managers, and below this the multitude of petty traders and artisans of various professions organized into settlements.

The settlements were divided into five groups as follows:

1. Palace and state employees accounted for fifty-one settlements. They provided all the services and food necessary for the upper classes.

2. The military population, the *streltsy*, accounted for thirty-three settlements. They also pursued various crafts.

3. Employees of the monasteries, the patriarchate and metropolitan households comprised twenty-six settlements.

4. Foreigners were grouped in eight settlements.

5. The 'black hundreds', artisans and small manufacturers accounted for twenty-five settlements.

The names of the settlements referred to their trade or chief occupation and some Moscow streets still bear these names, viz.: Kuznetskaya (Smith), Myasnitskaya (Butcher), Goncharnaya (Potter), Plotnichnaya (Turner). None of the settlements were located in the Kremlin, only one was in Kitaigorod and there were only twenty-one in Belgorod. The great mass were in Zemlyanygorod and Zamoskvareche and they were known as *chernye slobody* or 'black settlements' because they paid land taxes. The settlements were separated from each other by large empty areas at first occupied by gardens and orchards, hills and swamps, but later filled in by people not belonging to any particular settlement.

In addition to the settlements, Moscow was divided into districts, at first twelve and then seventeen, in the charge of designated members of the nobility whose duty it was to keep order, decide minor law cases, and take fire protection measures. The Kremlin always formed one district, and Kitaigorod, the original Bolshoi Posad or Great Settlement, was also usually administered as one district. Although the boundaries of the districts changed frequently, Belgorod was usually divided into four and Zemlyanygorod into seven.

The Kitaigorod district was considered the most important as here were the trading stalls, the warehouses and cellars, the *gostiny dvor* for visiting merchants. It was usually in the charge of an experienced man like a courtier, with a *dyak* or senior clerk, other clerks and a dozen or so of the *streltsy* at his command appointed by the *rasryadny prikaz*. Each district and colony had its church. As they were less susceptible to fire those built of stone were used to store records of the local population and descriptions of where they lived as there was little naming of streets or numbering of houses until the first half of the nineteenth century.

In each settlement a *mirsky soviet* of elected elders and their assistants directed the local government of the group under the watchful eye of the nobleman who was in charge of the larger district. Meetings of the *mirsky soviet* on the pattern of the village *mir* were held in the 'brotherly house' or the entrance hall of the local church.

The habits and appearances of Muscovites and their city were admirably set down by Adam Olearius, a secretary to the Embassy of the Duke of Holstein to the Tsar between 1633 and 1649. This book was first printed in German but was quickly translated into French, Dutch and Italian and, in 1662, into English. After Giles Fletcher, it is the first travel book about Muscovy to have been published in English. His impressions seem to be fairly objective and if his attitude to Russian customs seems overlaid with horror, their manners had likewise impressed other travellers from western Europe and Byzantium.

Olearius admired the resilience of the Russians in rebuilding their mutilated city after the Tartar raids and the Time of Troubles: 'The Tartars of Krim and Precop burnt it in the year 1571 and the Poles set it afire in the year 1611 so that there was nothing left of it but the Castle; and yet now there are numbered in it above 40,000 houses and it is out of all controversy one of the greatest Cities in Europe.' He noted that in the city as a whole there were over two thousand churches, monasteries and chapels and that the Kremlin alone had two monasteries and fifty churches and chapels. (Today there are no monastery buildings in the Kremlin and at the most generous count only eleven churches and chapels, none of them functioning as places of worship.)

Olearius described the market in Kitaigorod, and its rows of traders' stalls, with each trade represented in its own section or 'row'. Many lords, princes and superior merchants had their homes in Kitaigorod. He noted that the homes of gentlemen and some lords and boyars are located in Tsargorod or Belgorod as well as the royal foundry for making cannon and the royal stables.

Olearius thought the Muscovites were corpulent, fat and strong, and the women well-proportioned but with dreadfully painted faces. Of the men he said 'they much esteem great beards as also great bellies', particularly the merchants. Men wore broadshirts not quite covering the thigh, large breeches over which a caftan fell to the knees, and over that a long coat. The sleeves of the caftan were so long they had to be folded back. All classes wore caps rather than hats; men of position wore very high caps of fur while the common people's caps were more coarse. The country people had wretched coarse clothing and shoes of bark. Olearius noted that the Russian fashion in dress was not subject to whims and did not change.

Olearius found the Muscovites very ignorant: 'there cannot be anything more barbarous than that people'. He thought their manners particularly offensive. They cheated and lied continuously and engaged in endless quarrelling, railing like fish-wives. They yawned, belched and stretched anywhere, which Olearius found especially disgusting because of the large amounts of garlic and onions they ate. There is 'no place in the world where drunkenness is more common', among women as well as men. Tobacco was once widespread but in 1634 it was forbidden because of the risk of fire and anyone found guilty of using or selling tobacco was liable to have his nostrils slit or be whipped.

Although a few Russians were beginning to write about Muscovy, most of the observations in the seventeenth century were by foreigners. The last view of Moscow in this period is an immensely readable treatise on *The Present State of Russia* by the personal physician for nine years to Tsar Aleksei Mikhailovich, Dr Samuel Collins. As Dr Collins was in a privileged position, he was not obliged to live in the foreigner's colony but could dwell in the superior environs of Kitaigorod, and as the Tsar's physician he held an important place at court. He seems to have interested himself deeply in Russian customs, history and way of life and he records his impressions most vividly.

Like Olearius, he was surprised by the depths of ignorance found in Moscow. 'For the people are very jealous and suspect those who ask them any questions concering their Policy, or Religion, they being wholly devoted to their own Ignorance, and Education; (which is altogether illiterate and rude, both in Civil and Ecclesiastical Affairs) look upon Learning as a Monster, and fear it no less than a Ship of Wildfire. . . .' Collins described the severity with which women were treated by their husbands, there being no penalty if a man should beat his wife to death, whereas if a woman killed her husband she was buried in the ground up to the neck until she died, 'which is soon done in winter'.

Finally, Dr Collins caught something of the indisputable flavour of Russia in that he devoted a whole chapter to a description of caviar, with an account of its origins and how it is made, and another to the varieties of mushroom which were 'very remarkable for their shape and qualities.'

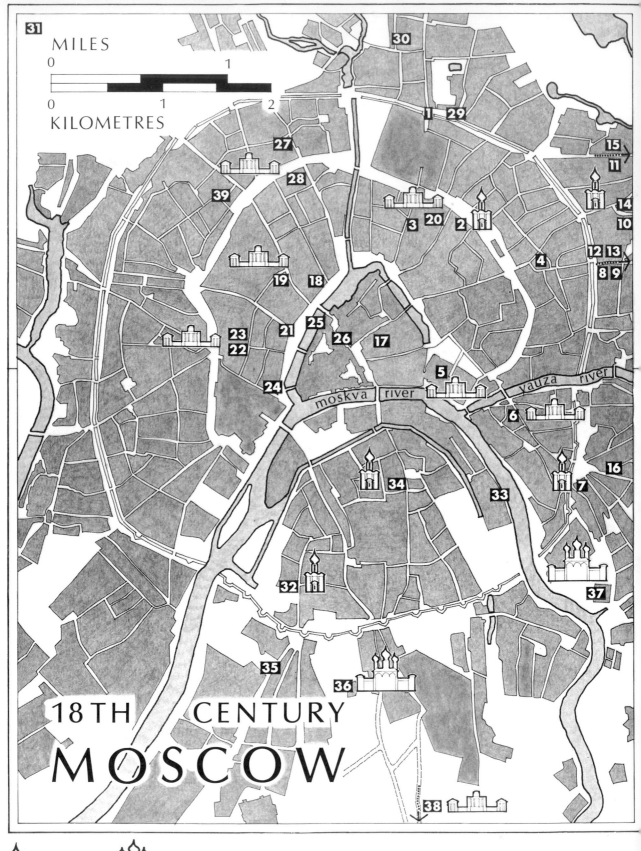

18TH CENTURY
MOSCOW

MILES
0   1

0   1   2
KILOMETRES

moskva river

yauza river

 Cathedral/ Church/ Chapel

 Convent/ Monastery

 Palace/ Estate/ Mansion/House

 Apartment/ Hotel

 Railway station

3 The Eighteenth Century: Decline, Stagnation, Rebirth

The seventeenth century had ended with a young, volatile, talented tsar on the throne determined to change everything; even the name of Muscovy was altered to Rossiya to convey a new, enlarged concept of the state. As a result of Peter the Great's eagerness to emulate the achievements of western Europe, Russia altered beyond recognition, both visually and intrinsically at least as far as the upper classes were concerned. The nobility and gentry were no longer allowed to wear beards (the hallmark of a medieval Muscovite) and their long flowing caftans and high fur-trimmed caps were banned in 1698 as part of the imperial order that only western dress could be worn. There was much opposition to these reforms and some preferred to pay the heavy fines rather than obey. Yet these decrees affected only a tiny minority. The labouring peasantry, forming some 90 per cent of the population, were not obliged to shave off their beards or dispose of their smocks. Far from improving in the course of this century famed for the introduction of the enlightened age into Russia, their lot was to sink back even further into the morass of poverty and ignorance. An increasing incidence of absentee landlordism led to a deterioration in farm management. The plight of the peasantry was made the more poignant by the obvious contrast between themselves and their masters' changed appearance and attitudes in accepting foreign dress, foreign manners and, as the century wore on, foreign tongues, first German and then French. Medieval Muscovy, for all its obvious faults, was at least a union of its people all more or less equally rough and uncouth, all wrapped up in the Russian Church, none, not even the tsars, enjoying comforts greatly superior to the *izba*-dwellers. But the abrupt jerk from the dark ages to the enlightenment of eighteenth-century Europe, a process that had taken three centuries to achieve in Paris and Rome, only served further to alienate the gentry from the masses. Although these abrupt changes must have seemed, at first, to have been artificial encumbrances, a sort of passing fashion, the division between the upper classes and the people continued unabated till 1917.

---

1 Sukharev Tower, 1692–1701 (now demolished)   2 Church of the Archangel Gabriel (Menshikov Tower) 1705–07, rebuilt in 1780   3 Rostopchin House, first half of the 18th century   4 Apraksin House, 1760s   5 Foundling Home, 1764–70 6 Batashov House, now a hospital, end of 18th century   7 St Martin the Confessor, 1782–93   8 Dvortsovy Most, 1779–81   9 Razumovsky House, now the Institute of Physical Culture, 1790–93   10 Demidov House, 1779–91 11 Musin-Pushkin House, end of the 18th century   12 The Military Hospital, 1798–1802   13 The Catherine Palace, 1773–96   14 St Nikita the Martyr, 1751   15 Preobrazhenskoe Cemetery, Old Believers   16 Rogozhskoe Cemetery, Old Believers   17 Gostiny Dvor, 1790–1805   18 The Dolgoruky House, latter Nobles' Club, now House of Unions, 1784 19 Chernyshevsky House, now Mossoviet, 1782–84, almost totally rebuilt in the 1940s   20 Yushkov House, 1780s 21 The University Old Buildings and Chapel, 1786–93   22 Talyzin House, now the Museum of Russian Architecture, 1787   23 Sheremetiev House, 1780   24 Pashkov House, now Old Building of the Lenin Library, 1784–6   25 The Arsenal, 1701–36   26 The Senate, 1776–87   27 The Gagarin House or Catherine Hospital, 1786–90   28 The Gubin House, 1780s   29 The Sheremetiev Hospital, now Skliforovsky Institute, 1794–1807   30 Church of Filip the Metropolitan, 1777–88   31 Petrovsky Zamok, the Peter Palace, 1775–82   32 Ioanna Voina, St John the Warrior, 1709–13   33 Kriegskommissariat, 1778–80   34 St Klimenta, 1740s–1770s   35 Golitsyn Hospital, 1796–1801   36 Gate Bell-tower of the Donskoi Monastery, 1730–1750   37 Bell-tower of the Novospassky Convent, 1759–62   38 Tsaritsyno, 1775–97   39 The English Club, 1780

Peter hated Moscow with a hatred for the city of his birth that seemed at times to be obsessive, and in his reign Moscow was despised and eventually abandoned. Following his return from abroad in 1698, he punished the rebellious *streltsy* in one of the worst massacres in Russian history, after which he refused to live in the fusty overdecorated chambers of the old Kremlin palaces and restlessly moved about. At first he preferred to hold court in the less formal atmosphere of the run-down palace at Preobrazhenskoe on the east bank of the Yauza River where he had spent his childhood. It was conveniently close to his favourite part of Moscow, the orderly foreigner's colony which he had often visited as a boy, and finally he moved there altogether. That was where his friends lived: the Scot, General Gordon; the Swiss, Franz Lefort; and his mistress Anna Mons.

Peter's policies provide a dramatic turning-point in Russian history whichever way they are considered. The war with Sweden went on intermittently from 1700 to 1722 and, if the wars against Turkey and Persia are included, there were only two years of peace during his long reign. Although they started badly the Swedish wars resulted in the decisive defeat of Charles XII first at Poltavo and later in other battles and proved that Russia could be a formidable military power on the European scene. A century later the retreat of Napoleon decisively sealed this development. The taxes imposed on the people to pay for the increasingly expensive wars were more burdensome than in any other regime. Military expenditure at times consumed 80 per cent of the total revenues. A special department was set up to invent new taxes and everything taxable was taxed, even such things as the storage of ice for the summer, watermelons, and marriages of non-Christian people. A tax already existed on households, but as the number of households was declining it was decided to tax all male 'souls', even old men and young male children. Considerable new revenue accrued to the state in this way. Thus, at the end of Peter's reign the great mass of the people were not only alienated by the strange non-Russian customs of the court and gentry but were obliged to bear a tax burden that had become intolerable.

The gain from Sweden of some worthless marshes on the Baltic at the mouth of the Neva River gave Peter the opportunity not only to leave the detested Moscow, with its paralyzing traditions and conservatism, but also to realize what had long been a dream of the tsars: an outlet to the sea for the land-locked country. His vision of a palatial capital on the Baltic, six hundred and fifty kilometres north of Moscow on marshy, uninviting land, was eventually accomplished owing to his great energy, resourcefulness and ruthlessness. The geographic position of St Petersburg was a disadvantage, the climate unpleasant and inhospitable, yet in Peter's lifetime great engineers and architects laid the foundations and built the first simple but impressive buildings some of which, like the cathedral and fortress of Sts Peter and Paul, are still standing. Nevertheless St Petersburg always suffered from its position out on a limb to the north of the vast country, in contrast to Moscow which was placed squarely at the centre of the communications network. The three-year siege of Leningrad in the last war when thousands died of starvation and cold was the most recent demonstration of the basic vulnerability of the new capital.

With Peter's attention focused on the Baltic, Moscow's demise seemed final. In the words of Pushkin from *The Bronze Horseman*, 'Old Moscow was put in the shade by the younger capital like a purple-clad dowager by a new Tsaritsa.' Certainly for the first third of the century the former capital was utterly neglected and allowed to fall into ruin. From 1714 to 1728 all building in stone was forbidden in Moscow in order to channel the stone and masons to the new capital. The arts of building which had been handed down from father to son were literally forgotten. Yet the death of Peter brought to the throne new emperors and strong empresses, not so poisoned by hatred of the old capital, and slowly Moscow began to revive and dress herself in the new fashion of the western baroque manner until, by the time of Catherine the Great, the rebirth was complete.

1   PETRINE MOSCOW

In spite of the Tsar's antipathy to Moscow, the years up to 1712–13 when the capital was transferred to St Petersburg were so active with the implementation of Peter's reforms and the erection of new buildings associated with them that there is a distinctive period known as Petrine Moscow. Klyuchevsky, the greatest Russian historian, said of the Tsar: 'if Peter was not engaged in battle, then, without fail, he was occupied in building'. Peter's practical sense, his interest in introducing educational institutions like those he had seen in western Europe, his involvement of the state in more and more industrial and social activities, and his deep interest in reorganizing the military along more modern lines meant that he devoted great energy to the building of secular establishments such as schools, hospitals, theatres, museums, libraries and buildings of military significance like arsenals and shipyards. Although a few of these still lay their shadow over Moscow's streets most have disappeared, including perhaps the greatest loss, the Sukharev Tower, which was demolished only fifty years ago.

Whereas in the seventeenth century and earlier all buildings, whatever their use, tended to resemble one another in most details, these new buildings were formed more according to their function and required different and more efficient building techniques. The old methods were critically reviewed. The architect was no longer a master builder who had served a long apprenticeship and acquired his knowledge of building empirically, but a learned man, precisely educated in formal institutions, familiar with mechanics, physics, mathematics and the recently translated classical theory of architectural order and design. *The Rules of the Five Orders*, the text by the Italian architect Vignola on the principles of architecture, was published three times in Peter's reign, in 1709, 1712 and 1722. Building materials became more versatile and more easily available; lime, bricks of a standard size, cement, stone, marble and glass were used and plaster gradually became more common. Improved techniques of glass-making meant that windows could be numerous and large, and interiors were transformed into lighter, more airy spaces. Strict orders were issued on how to lay foundations and build walls, on the use of non-inflammable material even for the traditional cottages, the *izba*, where an effort was made to change over to clay instead of wood. Naturally, these changes were made slowly and were more apparent in the new St Petersburg than in Moscow. It was not until 1716 that Russian students, Peter's famous 'pensioners', were sent abroad to study architecture, and it was not until the early 1730s that their new knowledge began to make itself felt.

Although a purely western baroque triumphal arch, festooned with carved flowers and fruit, was placed at the southern end of the new Kamenny Most or Stone Bridge to honour the taking of Azov in 1696, and similar wooden arches were built for the victories over the Swedes in 1709 and 1721, Moscow or Naryshkin baroque was continuing to display vitality in the Moscow of this period. For a time the features of Moscow baroque, such as the receding tiers, the use of half-columns to complete corners, and the ribbed shape of the cupola, triumphed over the innovatory, westernized baroque style from St Petersburg, but eventually it began to give way and its original character altered irretrievably. However, the persistence of the two parallel branches of the same style give Petrine baroque a special stamp.

The Sukharev Tower

The Sukharev Tower, which was built in 1692–1701 under the supervision of Mikhail Ivanovich Cheglokov, was one of the first monumental stone buildings of an entirely secular nature. Although it is no longer standing, its demise was so recent as to have remained in the memories of many Russians and its style and function were so typical of the new 'Rossiya' that it deserves a place here.

The tower was not designed to be a fortress; the danger of imminent invasion particularly from the north and east had passed. It consisted of three floors; the first formed the arched exit from the city and served as a gate, the second contained the guard-rooms, and the third was used to house Peter's newly established Mathematical and Navigational School. A four-storied central tower 64 metres high with a clock and state coat-of-arms completed the building, making it the tallest in Moscow after the Ivan Veliky bell-tower in the Kremlin. At the four corners of the base of the tower slim, pointed neo-Gothic turrets like minarets rose upwards and helped to soften the abruptness of the change from horizontal to the vertical. Nevertheless, the tower still appeared clumsy and badly proportioned. Unlike the seventeenth-century houses, its walls were clearly divided into floors and the windows were enhanced by fine architraves similar in style to Moscow baroque. An attractive, typically Muscovite, wide exterior staircase led to a gallery on the first floor and surrounded the building.

The school was the grandest part of Peter's ambitious plan to introduce education on the western model. At his coronation, there were only two theological academies and one school, the Moscow Academy, in the entire country. In 1714 Peter issued a decree ordering the establishment of two mathematical schools in each province and the selection of pupils by provincial authorities, but twenty years later the whole scheme had collapsed.

By 1712 there were over 500 pupils at the academy. Most of the teachers were foreigners, including two Englishmen, Andrew Farvarson and Stephen Gwen. The importance of the school is in some ways comparable to the role of the Greenwich Observatory in seventeenth-century England. The astronomer Yakob Bruce built the first observatory in Russia in the tower and the first Russian sea charts were made in the school. By 1829, no longer used as a school, the second floor was turned into an iron reservoir to hold water brought from Mytishchi north of the city to Moscow, the first piped water for the new fountains, pools and public taps. After the Revolution, the tower was carefully cleaned and repainted and the Moscow Communal Museum opened there early in 1926. By 1934 state interest in protecting old buildings had lapsed and it was decided to pull down the tower, ostensibly to allow a freer flow of traffic through the square, although Moscow in the early 1930s was hardly suffering from traffic jams. So disappeared what was popularly known as 'the bride of Ivan Veliky and the sister of the Menshikov Tower'.

The Arsenal

A severe fire in 1701 destroyed nearly all the wooden buildings in the north part of the Kremlin and in November of that year the Tsar ordered all those that survived to be pulled down to make way for a new armoury to be called initially Tseikhauz and later the Arsenal. It was to serve as an armoury for weapons and military equipment and also as a military museum, and was part of Peter's plan to reorganize the military into an effective fighting force on the western model to replace the unreliable *streltsy*. He also built a large barracks, a hospital and a church for the new regiments in Lefortovo across the Yauza River from the new court. The Arsenal was one of the largest buildings in Russia when it was first built. The architects were probably the Saxon Kristofer Konrad and the Russians D. Ivanov and M. Choglokov. The building is in the form of a trapezoid, with two sharp and two obtuse angles at the four corners. This odd shape was dictated by the requirements of the site along a long expanse of the western Kremlin wall and the shorter corner space, and it is a mark of its fine planning that the odd shape is not more obvious. In the summer of 1706 work on the building was postponed because of the exigencies of the Swedish war and was resumed only sixteen years later. It was still covered with scaffolding in 1731 when the Empress Anna Ivanovna moved into the Annenhof next-door, the lovely wooden palace built for her by Rastrelli. The Empress abhorred the dirt of the unfinished building and ordered it to be completed forthwith. It finally was finished in 1736. Bad luck followed the new building as only a year later it was damaged in another severe fire. However, Prince Ukhtomsky, Moscow's primary architect of the mid-eighteenth century, directed its restoration in 1754, and although he changed the façade slightly, he was careful not to alter the original design.

Paired windows separated by bare walls give particular power to the long, low building – a power intrinsic also in the thickness of the walls and expanse of its chambers and mansard roofing. The strong horizontal lines emphasize the upward thrust of the Kremlin towers. Originally, it was covered with the same diamond pattern (diaper work) as the Faceted Palace and with cornices of the cockscomb type familiar in Moscow baroque. Its façade was made more severe when it was restored after the fire of 1737. The original main entrance on Senate Square has been preserved behind the later mid-eighteenth-century doorway and Peter's monogram is still visible with the Latin letters PP (Petrus Primus) intertwined with 1.

St John the Warrior

Ivan Petrovich Zarudny, one of the Ukrainian immigrants to Moscow after the Ukraine was incorporated into Muscovy in the mid-seventeenth century, was responsible for some of the best architecture of the early part of the eighteenth century. Before he began designing buildings, he was well known as a sculptor and painter and his buildings have a definite sculptural quality. In fact Zarudny's talent as a painter led to the commission for several iconostases, one of which, that designed for the Cathedral of Sts Peter and Paul in the fortress at St Petersburg, is still in its original place. He was also the architect of the Triumphal Arches built in 1709 in honour of the victory at Poltava over the Swedes and in 1721 to celebrate the Peace of Neustadt. The latter stood near the Kazan Cathedral on Red Square at the entrance to 25th October Street.

Ulitsa Dmitrova is one of the ancient main highways of Moscow leading south from the Kremlin. It is still a principal route today just as it was in the time of Peter the Great, but its turns and twists are presently undergoing the ruthless widening and straightening that modern planners consider so important. In the spring of 1709 the Moskva River flooded its banks to an unusual degree and when he was travelling along the flooded street the Tsar noticed a church entirely surrounded by water. He stopped and enquired its name. On being told it was Ivan Voina or St John the Warrior, he exclaimed, according to tradition, 'that is our patron saint. Inform the priest I would like to see a new, stone church on the highest point on this street. I will contribute towards it and will send a plan.' Responsibility for the plans of the new church was assigned to Zarudny. The site chosen as the Tsar had ordered was the highest elevation in the street and work began immediately on the building. It was completed in 1713 just before the ban on building was imposed.

This splendid church, still used, is truly transitional in that it combines elements of the old order, in an octagonal bell-tower and in its original faceted façade and receding pyramidical tiers, with innovations in the segmental gables on each side which allow for the large windows with their highly decorated architraves, in the small oval windows placed over the larger rectangular ones, and in the small volutes of the uppermost stage. Although the form of the church is still the pyramid shape like the typical 'octagonal on the square', the long line of the refectory joining the main part of the church to the bell-tower counteracts the verticality of the tower. Bazhenov, the most lyrical of the eighteenth-century architects, admired it very much and referred to it in the presence of Catherine II in his speech on the occasion of the ceremonial laying of the first foundation stone of the ill-fated Kremlin palace.

36 Ioanna Voina (Church of St John the Warrior), 1709–13. The church illustrates the transition from Moscow Baroque to a more western Petrine form.

The Menshikov Tower

Zarudny, the probable author of St John the Warrior, was definitely the architect of the most outstanding and beautiful building in Moscow dating from Peter's reign. It is the Church of the Archangel Gabriel built in 1705–7 just off Telegrafny Pereulok near Chistye Prudy (Clean Ponds) on the boulevard. Church architecture had now begun the solemn transition to more secular times. Whereas in the past it was the architecture of the church that influenced secular buildings and was assiduously copied, now the new state buildings began to influence the design and decorative features of the churches. The Church of the Archangel Gabriel is usually known as the Menshikov Tower after its original owner, A. D. Menshikov, an illiterate pieboy who rose to become Peter's closest confidant and adviser and the most powerful man in Russia. The church was built on Menshikov's estate in the eastern part of Moscow a little distance from the Kremlin and between it and the then fashionable suburb of Nemetskaya Sloboda.

Prince Menshikov wanted the church to be taller than any other building in Moscow and at first it was three metres higher than the Ivan Veliky bell-tower in the Kremlin. The idea of the magnificent tower probably arose after Menshikov was struck by Peter's regard for the new Sukharev Tower. Thus, in spite of Peter's general negative attitude to Moscow, his reign saw the skyline changed by two new tall spires.

The transfer of the government and capital to St Petersburg meant that Prince Menshikov left Moscow as well. However, in 1711 he appeared to be still concerned with completing the unfinished tower when he sent an English clock with half-hourly chimes to be attached to the highest tier. After that time he became deeply involved with the lavish building of the extensive palace at Oranienbaum outside St Petersburg and was less interested in his Moscow property. In 1723 the upper tier and tall wooden spire of the church caught fire after being struck by lightning and the lower roof-vaulting cracked. The clock was burned and the copper statue of the Archangel Gabriel holding the cross at the top of the spire was also destroyed. Rebuilding did not take place until 1780 and today's tower is quite different from the original. It is a whole tier lower, leaving only two octagonals on the square base, and the small spire that grows out of the elongated cupola does not approach the slender height of the original.

In profile the church is not unlike the Moscow baroque churches. The tower is placed squarely over the centre of the Greek cross. The most original and exciting aspect of the church is the design of the main façade on the west elevation. Its use of a giant volute as a buttress was unique in Russia. Although a foreign feature, Russians soon learned to love the form of the voluptuous volute, the strong curve and roll of the scroll, and after this time it began to appear frequently. Zarudny used it more dramatically than other architects, perhaps because he was also a gifted sculptor and painter. The segmental pediment, the modillions and oval windows of the main

37 The Menshikov Tower or the Church of the Archangel Gabriel, by I. P. Zarudny, 1705–07.

entrance are also new, western features on an essentially Russian design.

One unusual fact about the Menshikov Tower in Soviet Moscow is that not only is it, like St John's, still a functioning church in a city where only one in twenty of the church buildings are used for religious services, but next-door to it, in a nondescript nineteenth-century building, is a second functioning church. It is possible that the second church is the successor of a temporary church established during the lengthy building and rebuilding of the tower, which was repeatedly ordered to be closed, once even by Peter himself, but seems obstinately to have remained open.

2 ST PETERSBURG

About six hundred and fifty kilometres north of Moscow in the desolate region at the mouth of the Neva feverish activity was going on to realize Peter's dream of a glorious new capital. St Petersburg was to be entirely different in character and visual aspect from patriarchal Moscow, spread about in quaint disorder on its seven hills. In contrast to this was the new city rising above a flat swampy waste, neat and orderly with planned, regular streets and rigidly symmetrical houses. In spite of the hostility of the site, the marshes, water not deep enough to float the lightest vessels, frequent floods, unhealthy climate and long dark winters, the problems were tackled and to a great extent nature was conquered. The new city was to be planned, rational, a city of science and exactitude rather than the medieval jumble of leaning buildings, narrow lanes, dirt and ignorance that was Moscow.

Peter was intent on training Russians in the new arts and sciences of the west and in 1716 he sent twenty 'pensioners' to study abroad, among whom were eight architects who studied in France, Holland and Italy. The return of these architects trained in the western European manner led to the establishment of regular architectural schools in both St Petersburg and Moscow, although the Moscow school seems always to have been the more vigorous and individual. The existence of the two schools meant that the architectural genius of the two cities did not merge but grew disparately and the hallmark of Moscow buildings remained quite different from that of St Petersburg. The greatest personalities of the St Petersburg architects were invariably taken up by the court and worked outside the school putting it very much in the shade. In Moscow, on the other hand, there was a strong tradition of architectural families and the school managed to keep them all under its control. Moscow buildings in some ways had more character than those in St Petersburg where the regularity of the planning of the city, the straightness of the streets and canals, was reflected in the comfortless rectilinear lines of its architecture. Moscow still contains unexpected corners with enchanting details enhanced by the irregularity of the streets, the roundness of the cupolas, and the vistas obtained by the seven hills.

The growth of St Petersburg was stupendous; in 1703 a barren marsh, a century later it had overtaken Moscow in size of population, had become a world metropolis, and placed Russia at the centre of European affairs in the struggle against Napoleon. The architects of St Petersburg until the end of the century were predominantly foreign, and the prevailing international style became St Petersburg's style, only more so, for no other European city was such a haven for the gifted architects of the baroque and neo-classical periods. Court patronage was lavish, the commissions were very large, and the opportunity to design new creations in the near-empty city did not obtain elsewhere in Europe. At first Peter's taste was for a strong, stern architecture devoid of unnecessary excrescences, as in the Petropavlovsk and Kronstadt fortresses and the early palaces built by Tressini (Swiss), Schlüter (German), Michetti (Italian) and Zemstov (Russian). In 1716 Peter invited the French architect Leblond to formulate a general scheme. Houses were to be built according to one plan, a different house for each level of society. By the end of his reign the city was well established and with the building of the Admiralty was beginning to move from the islands to the mainland. A cold, impersonal, artificial city imposed by the great will of one powerful man.

Empresses and the reign of luxuriant decoration

After Peter's death there was a reaction against his policies. His successors were not so serious as he had been about the growth of his beloved new capital or, until the advent of Catherine, about extending reforms on the western model, nor were they so unsympathetic to the idea, if not of living permanently in Moscow, at least of residing there for long sojourns. The post-Petrine period is a fascinating one marked by long, stable feminine reigns punctuated by short periods of weak male rule. Twice women engineered successful palace revolutions against the legitimate male heirs. Frivolity and lavish court spending on entertainments and balls are also characteristic of the reigns up to Catherine's more serious regimen. The empresses enthusiastically ordered new palaces to add to the existing more austere royal residences. One outstanding architect, the Italian Count Bartolommeo Rastrelli, survived the reigns of two contesting empresses, Anna Ivanovna and Elizaveta Petrovna, and more than any other style his exuberant baroque catches the lightness and frivolity of the time.

Before he died Peter changed the rules of the succession, which hitherto had been the prerogative of the eldest male heir. Henceforth it was to be at the will of the Emperor, thus creating the conditions in which the palace revolutions were able to flourish. Many rulers, including Peter himself, neglected to name an heir before they died.

On Peter's death in 1726 his wife, the Empress Catherine I, an illiterate Lithuanian servant girl who had first shared the bed of Peter's favourite Prince Menshikov, became ruler for two years until she died in 1727. Although there had been women regents before her she was the first woman sovereign to rule Russia.

Menshikov insinuated himself into a commanding position during Catherine's reign. He maintained this when the grandson of Peter the Great, Peter Alekseyevich, whose father had been imprisoned on the orders of his illustrious grandfather and had mysteriously died, became Tsar at the age of eleven. The young ruler was soon betrothed to Menshikov's daughter and that gentleman's career as virtual head of government seemed to be assured. However, the boy unexpectedly fell out with his future father-in-law, broke his engagement, and ignominiously sent Menshikov into exile along with his daughter.

With the fall of Menshikov, the fortunes of old Muscovy painfully began to revive. The boy tsar came under the influence of the ancient and conservative Dolgoruky family, one of the old boyar clans, bitterly opposed to the reforms of Peter the Great. Under their urging the court was moved back to Moscow in January 1728 to prepare for the coronation, always held in the old capital, and six months later a number of important government departments followed. The Dolgorukys obtained the most important government posts. Under the pre-eminence of the Dolgoruky family many began to fear that St Petersburg was doomed. Their fears were further fuelled by the announcement of Peter's engagement to the seventeen-year-old daughter of Prince Aleksei Dolgoruky. However, on 19 January 1730, the day fixed for his wedding, the luckless bridegroom aged fourteen years and three months died of smallpox in the Lefort Palace.

As the young Peter like his grandfather before him had not named an heir, the Privy Council decided upon Anna Ivanovna, the widowed Duchess of Courland, the daughter of Ivan v, Peter the Great's co-tsar for a time. Believing Anna to be a benign, malleable person, the Privy Council attempted to limit her powers and even removed from her control the famous guards' regiments. This was the only attempt in Russian history specifically to limit a sovereign's powers and it was not successful. The nobility were not genuinely interested in representative government, the church and guards' regiments preferred an autocracy to oligarchy, and on 28 February 1730 in the Moscow Kremlin and before the nobility assembled for the coronation Anna tore up the document listing the conditions and abolished the Privy Council.

After Anna's coronation the court remained in Moscow for nearly two years. Then, protesting that she must govern 'in the spirit of Peter the Great', the court and government were returned to St Petersburg in the autumn of 1731. She ruled until 1740, a decade in which the government was entirely under the influence of her German advisers, in which the crude and barely educated Empress showed not the slightest interest in the arts of government but spent her energies in organizing absurd jokes, buffoonery, and amusements like the famous wedding of her jester, Prince Golitsyn, and a hideously ugly Kalmuck woman in the ice palace erected for the purpose on the River Neva. Over half the national income was spent by the court on these and similar amusements.

In spite of Anna's irresponsibility, it was she who found and commissioned the services of the outstanding decorative baroque architect of the St Petersburg period, Count Bartolommeo Francesco Rastrelli. He was the son of a court sculptor who came to Russia from Italy in 1716 and who created the famous busts of Peter 1 and Menshikov now in the Hermitage. Rastrelli's gifts were recognized early and he was sent from his adopted country to study abroad for five years, mostly in Paris. After returning to St Petersburg briefly in 1723 he again left to continue his studies, finally returning in 1730 just as Anna Ivanovna was offered the throne. His first work for the court was in Moscow, a small wooden palace in the Kremlin, built near the unfinished Arsenal. The wooden palace, known as Annenhof after its mistress, was moved in 1736 to the former foreigner's colony on the banks of the Yauza near the Lefort Palace, which was more congenial to the court than the Kremlin. The Kremlin was in great disrepair from such a long neglect and many of the palaces were completely uninhabitable. (Even during the coronation of the Empress Elizabeth in 1742 the Kremlin royal apartments were not properly repaired and rain dripped through the roofs.)

Along the narrow, winding Yauza, however, a new complex of fine, modern-style palaces was growing up. Rastrelli had built a second small wooden palace, the Summer Annenhof, in 1730 on the banks of the Yauza across the river from the Lefort Palace, and now added to it the Winter Annenhof, transported from the Kremlin. This gay baroque palace only survived until 1746 when it was burned to the ground. The gardens around it were also laid out by Rastrelli but they were damaged in a hurricane in 1905. There is still a park in this part of Moscow where the royal residence once was. In January 1732 Rastrelli followed the Empress from Moscow to St Petersburg. He then entered upon his most impressive creative period and is the architect of the most important buildings during the reigns of Anna Ivanovna, the infant Ivan VI and the Empress Elizabeth. He designed the Winter Palace in the centre of St Petersburg, redesigned Peterhof, and built the Smolny Institute and the Stroganof and Vorontsov Palaces. The inventiveness with which he used decoration and his extreme lightness and delicacy of touch betray the French influence of rococo, the ultimate development of baroque.

Although Rastrelli built several buildings in Moscow not a single palace survives unless one includes the Rostopchin House, number 14 Ulitsa Dzerzhinskovo, which some think may have been designed by him. The only definite trace of Rastrelli in Moscow is the great dome of the tower of the cathedral at the New Jerusalem Monastery some sixty kilometres to the west of Moscow. This was the monastery so grandly planned by the patriarch Nikon at the height of his power and so sadly vacated at his arrest. The tower had cracked and was in danger of falling. Elizabeth invited Rastrelli to make new plans. Karl Blank carried them out and the cathedral became more of a Roman baroque church than the Greek church envisaged by Nikon. It is perhaps overlain with detail on the interior which is more typical of Blank than Rastrelli, but the tall, sparkling iconostasis is definitely Rastrelli's work.

3 MOSCOW REAWAKENS: THE BAROQUE OF PRINCE UKHTOMSKY

To return to the Moscow of the third and fourth decades of the eighteenth century is to step from the gaiety and lightness of Rastrelli's palaces to the glum streets of the twice-abandoned city. Moscow's doldrums were deepened by the fact that the fourteen-year ban on building effectively paralyzed new construction for half a century. In a society where architects and builders did not study their trade at schools but passed on their knowledge from father to son the building techniques were soon forgotten. In any case, many of the most experienced builders and masons had emigrated to St Petersburg. When the ban was lifted, it took some considerable time before the know-how involved in the construction of strong, firm buildings was relearned.

In 1730 the Empress Anna decided to commission a small church, the Blagoveshchensky (Annunciation) na Zhitnom Dvore to be built against the Kremlin river wall beside the Nameless Tower at the spot where a miracle had been reported. It was so badly built that its foundations soon cracked and it had to be drastically repaired (this church was one of a number in the Kremlin that was removed in the 1930s). However, the Russian architects sent abroad to study were returning and, happily, some found their way to Moscow.

The first returned student to work in Moscow was Ivan Aleksandrovich Mordvinov. Initially he went to St Petersburg but came to Moscow in 1731 in connection with a scheme to draw up a general plan. A similar such plan was being prepared of St Petersburg and the St Petersburg Senate subsequently demanded that Mordvinov should return. However, Moscow jealously refused to let him go on the grounds that the only architects in Moscow were Mordvinov and his assistant while in St Petersburg there were at least five qualified architects. Mordvinov died in 1734 without completing the detailed map but his assistant, Ivan Fyodorovich Michurin, finished it in 1739. In the course of his work, Michurin carried out necessary repairs to old neglected buildings and built several new ones in a quiet, conservative style, none of which have survived. He was the true saviour of the old Moscow, the first Russian restorer of the tattered city. After the serious fire of 1737 he became even busier, listing damage to palaces, churches and public buildings and organizing their repair or rebuilding. He may have been the architect of the church Paraskeva Pyatnitskaya on Okhotny Ryad in central Moscow which was removed in 1934. After Michurin's detailed map was finished Moscow's frontiers were extended in 1742 to the Kamerkollezhsky boundary, taking its name from the customs and excise office. The new boundary, which doubled the size of the city as it had been within the Zemlyany Val, was purely a commercial one to control the flow of goods and was not defensive.

Other minor architects who came to Moscow after study abroad were Ivan

Kuzmich Korobov and Ivan Yakovlevich Blank. Blank found too many architects in St Petersburg competing for too few jobs but when he came to Moscow in 1742 to prepare for Elizabeth's coronation he found that the competition was less and decided to remain. His son was the better-known architect Karl Blank.

In 1742 the voluptuous and attractive Elizabeth, daugher of Peter the Great and Catherine I, seized the throne at the age of thirty-four from the infant Ivan VI, great-grandson of Ivan V. The baby had acceded to the throne on the death of his great-aunt Anna Ivanovna a few months previously. Elizabeth's *coup d'état* was assisted by the French Ambassador de la Chétardie (fortuitously Elizabeth had learned French as a young girl in the hope of marrying Louis XV). This marked the replacement of German by French in court circles. The *coup* was made possible by the enthusiasm of the guards' regiments for the attractive princess. The coronation was a uniquely splendid affair, superior even to the formalities of Anna's coronation twelve years earlier. It involved moving the court to Moscow in a river of 24,000 people which emptied St Petersburg of one quarter of its population. Elizabeth's reign lasted twenty years, and was the largely benevolent rule of a gay empress which saw a religious revival, the abolition of capital punishment and, less typically, the prudish separation of the sexes in the public baths.

The rebirth of Moscow begun by Mordvinov and Michurin was definitely established with the building, probably by Prince Dmitry Vasilievich Ukhtomsky, of the large Church of St Nikita the Martyr in 1751, on the former Staraya Basmannaya (now Ulitsa Karla Marksa), another of the principal routes to the foreigners' colony. Although it has hints of an earlier period, the decorations around the large windows, the columns supporting the pediments, and the overhanging cornices betray its baroque origins. With a simpler, more dynamic form the bell-tower is more typical of Ukhtomsky. Ukhtomsky, a student of Mordvinov who became the most influental architect of the middle of the century, is in some ways as important to Moscow as Rastrelli was to St Petersburg.

Prince Ukhtomsky inherited all of Michurin's apprentices when the latter left for Kiev in 1747 and formed them into a highly organized school. His twenty-eight pupils included the eminent architects of the succeeding generation such as Kokorinov, Bazhenov, Starov and Kazakov. He built up an impressive library including the latest books from abroad on classical architecture with the help of generous grants from the Moscow Senate. The Moscow school included literally all the architects working in Moscow in one way or another and was extremely important for the future of building in the city.

Ukhtomsky was an architect of the late baroque style, rather heavy in sculptural details, volume, and lush ornamentation, and although he was fond of colour he lacked the lightness that characterized Rastrelli's work. His first important successes were the Triumphal Gates designed with Blank (the elder) for the coronation of the Empress Elizabeth in 1742. As an indication of the sluggish development of Moscow architecture at this time, Ukhtomsky was still designing in the early style of Anna Ivanovna during the reign of Elizabeth when a more refined and elegant fashion prevailed. Ukhtomsky's Triumphal Gates (there were four for Elizabeth's coronation) were originally called *krasny*, or beautiful. Although it was built in wood for the coronation the principal gate was later rebuilt by the same architect in masonry in 1753. The stone gate stood at the junction of Staraya Basmannaya and Zemlyany Val at what is now Lermontovskaya Square well into the twentieth century but in 1928, like the Sukharev Tower, it was pulled down to free the square for expected traffic. Although considerably altered in the nineteenth century and painted in only two colours rather than the original polychrome, the gates retained many of their rich details and gilded sculpture. Muscovites still refer to Lermontovskaya Square as Krasnye Vorota and even guidebooks prefer the old name.

38 Krasnye Vorota ('Red' Gate), by Prince Ukhtomsky, 1753–57.

The middle of the eighteenth century marks the second period of tall bell-towers, and among Ukhtomsky's greatest achievements is the bell-tower of the Troitse-Sergeyev Monastery seventy kilometres north of Moscow. The tower has five tall tiers narrowing upwards and is one of the most elegant buildings of the monastery. It was to have had thirty gilded statues on allegorical themes but the monastery authorities protested against the display of so many secular symbols. At the same time a colleague of Ukhtomsky, Aleksei Yevlashev, built the gate bell-tower of the Donskoi Monastery out of red brick and white stone. The bell-tower of Novospassky Monastery was erected between 1759 and 1762 by Ivan Zherebtsov but of the architect's intended five tiers only four were actually built and its proportions suffer correspondingly. Ukhtomsky's greatest project was an Invalid Hospital, a huge edifice with a 75-metre-high cathedral and four wings, to have been situated near the Simonov Monastery on the eastern border of Moscow. Although it was never built, the grand idea of such a huge charitable institution was not forgotten and some thirty years later was realized in the building of the Foundling Home.

Two other buildings which are still standing in Moscow are characteristic of the architecture of the middle of the eighteenth century. Very few secular buildings are left from this period in Moscow but fortunately the Apraksin House at the Pokrovka Gate, Ulitsa Chernyshevskaya, perhaps the ultimate in decorative baroque in Moscow, is still standing. Originally built with a large, regular garden behind, placed squarely on the line of the street that was part of the major route to the royal palaces in the old foreigner's colony, encrusted with sculptured decoration, it was conceived as a palatial residence. The reception rooms overlooked the street but the large hall with tall windows faced the park. The emerald colour of the façade offset by the white pilasters, cornices and window architraves was typical of the middle of the eighteenth century. The second example of this period is the Klimenta (St Clement) Church in southern Moscow across the river from the Kremlin on Ulitsa Pyatnikskaya. It was probably begun about 1740 and completed in the 1770s but, as with the Apraksin House, the architect is not known. A tall, strong cube, surmounted by five powerful cupolas, heavily decorated, it still forms an important part of the silhouette of southern Moscow visible from the Kremlin. Its large size, clear division of the façade into lofty stories, rich decorations and the red background brought into relief by white decoration place it clearly at the beginning of the period of 'monumental' architecture in Moscow. It is related to the secular architecture of the time by the great gilded iconostasis of the interior, the gilded wrought iron of the exterior and the sculptural pediments.

Social and cultural changes

With the ending of the German influence at court and the decline in the activity of the secret police of Anna's reign, Russian culture began to blossom. The writer Tatishchev, who had served with Peter the Great on his Swedish campaigns, was the first to interest himself in Russian history. The genius Mikhail Lomonosov, a fisherman's son turned poet, scientist and philologist, transformed Russian into a literary language. Explorers penetrated Siberia, inventors flourished – even an early steam engine was made – and the Academy of Fine Arts was founded in St Petersburg. Ivan Ivanovich Shuvalov, one of Elizabeth's closest confidants and her chief adviser in the last years of her reign, persuaded the empress during a visit to Moscow in 1754 of the necessity of founding a university there. By April 1755 the University of Moscow began to function with Lomonosov at its head. It offered three faculties: law, medicine and philosophy (significantly there was no theology faculty). Lectures were available in both Russian and Latin and were open to students of all races, religions and social class. It was not until some years later, however, that the teaching and calibre of the students reached acceptable standards. Shuvalov was also instrumental in establishing two secondary schools in Moscow and similar schools in the provinces. Elizabeth's benevolence helped to foster the growth of the arts which were in any case stimulated by the close contact now existing with the west and the freedom to travel abroad. Upper-class Russians were beginning to look at their country with more critical eyes and the expansion of literature was soon to include some talented satirists.

With this boom in the arts other changes were occurring in Russia. Russia had gradually become a world power. She had become involved in wars with Prussia, Turkey and Sweden and had established close links with the countries of western Europe. Society was changing as the population of the cities rapidly expanded, fed by immigration from the countryside, and new towns were built. For the first time since the fourteenth century, trade became a respectable, desirable profession and after the nobility and the clergy merchants formed the 'third estate'.

The exploitation of the peasants remained a blot on the new enlightenment in Russia. Writers like Fonvizin and Novikov and, later, the satirist Radishchev, pointed out the dangers of the gap between the overwhelming majority of the population, tied to their landlords – some 97 per cent of the total – and the French-speaking westernized ladies and gentlemen of the upper classes whose way of life differed only slightly from their counterparts in Paris and Berlin (except that bonded serfdom had not existed in western Europe since the Middle Ages). The prescient Radishchev warned that this gap was to be the main obstacle to Russia's progress.

A reawakening of interest in the ideas and achievements of antiquity, coinciding with a diminution of the power of the Church, was widespread at this time throughout the western world, but in Russia, now firmly a part of western Europe, it was interpreted in its own way.

In architecture, earlier artistic principles were re-examined and great attention was paid to mastering the concepts of the architecture of ancient Greece and Rome. Thus the second half of the eighteenth century saw the birth of the movement to achieve a new 'classicism' in architecture. With it came a striving for monumental effects and a severity of form designed to symbolize the new ideals of citizenship, together with order in composition, nationalism, and a totality in town and city planning. The change did not come about abruptly but can be traced through the development of Catherine the Great's taste in architecture from a liking for the decorated and neo-Gothic style of Bazhenov, Veldten and Rinaldi to a preference for the stark simplicity of Quarenghi and the later Kazakov. By the end of the century and the beginning of the next it was possible to speak of a Russian classical school.

These developments in architectural theory were influenced by improvements in technology. More brick-works were built and brick sizes were at last becoming standardized. Glass and gypsum were becoming common and marble was in great demand. It was now possible to build the roofs of huge buildings, like the Kremlin Senate, of stone and brick (the span of the Senate roof was 24.7 metres, the largest in the world at the time). Cast iron had come into use for fencing, balconies and railings. The *izbas* were being replaced by houses of vertical boarding and the sizes of the rooms were therefore no longer so limited.

Government and public buildings were erected as never before. Society began to demand schools, hospitals, theatres, market buildings, poor-houses, even fire stations and, in Moscow, engineering works like the laying of water pipes and bridges. At this time the concept of a town as a consciously unified architectural design became popular. Houses were designed with continuous façades; building heights and widths of streets were strictly regulated. The cities acquired a delineated character entirely different from the muddle of medieval times. In the centres of the towns the large stone buildings belonging to the nobility and merchants dominated the large central square around which were also grouped administrative buildings and perhaps the Governor's residence. With the rebuilding of the ancient city of Tver which had been almost totally destroyed by fire in 1763 the opportunity came to put these principles into practice, and although damaged by German occupation in the Second World War it still illustrates town development in the eighteenth century. More than 400 towns were replanned in the last decade of the century and although most of these remained paper projects, the changes wrought on town landscapes can still be seen in such diverse places as Vladimir and Petrozavodsk.

The plague and cemeteries

The Black Death made its last visitation to Russia in 1771. Emergency measures were taken to move the many cemeteries clustering around every little church to beyond the city boundaries. This greatly changed the medieval character of Moscow. The plague had begun infiltrating southern Russia and Moldavia a year earlier after it had been carried there from infested areas of the Turkish front but no attempt was made in Moscow to impose restrictions on the flow of goods and food into the city. In November 1770 the disease broke out in the Sukonny Dvor, the large textile factory set up by Peter the Great, which employed over 3,000 workers. It was not until March 1771, after 130 had died, that the factory was closed and measures taken to try to inhibit the spread of the disease.

In September 21,400 died, in October 17,500, but by December deaths had fallen to 805. The rich fled to their country estates and gradually the life of the city began to break down. With no trade going in or out, food was scarce and there was mass unemployment. The disease was most ruthless in the poorer parts of the city. Of some 12,500 houses in Moscow in 1770, 3,000 were officially burnt after infected persons had died in them, but most of these were in Zemlyany Gorod, the poorest district. In the whole of Moscow and the Moscow Province over 200,000 people, or one third of the population, died of the plague in that terrible year.

All the cemeteries within the Kamerkollezhsky boundary of Moscow were removed. Seven new large cemeteries for the Orthodox were established to cope with the huge numbers of the dead. Most of these cemeteries still function today at Dorogomilovskoe, Miusskoe, Pyatnitskoe, Semyonovskoe, Kalitnikovskoe and Danilovskoe. In addition, a cemetery at Vvedenskoe for western Europeans, the Lutheran-Catholic cemetery, was built across the Yauza from the former foreigner's colony. Armenian, Jewish and Tartar cemeteries were also built. But perhaps the most interesting were the two cemeteries allocated to the Old Believers.

These were the cemeteries at Preobrazhenskoe and Rogozhskoe. Since their resistance to Nikon's changes in the previous century the Old Believers had been alternately hounded and tolerated by successive regimes, but with the advent of the plague they were now able to establish themselves as never before. Like Catherine the Empress, Orlov, who was in charge of Moscow's affairs during the emergency, was grateful to have the Old Believers look after their own followers, and turned a blind eye to the gradual development of large religious communities and the virtual re-establishment of the sects, particularly at Rogozhskoe. A long way out of the city, difficult of access even today, near the road to Vladimir, a strange world still exists at Rogozhskoe. As they had no bishop to consecrate new priests, the Old Believers were able to continue only as long as priests continued to flee to them from the established church. During Catherine's reign and those of Paul and Alexander this situation was tolerated but in the stricter atmosphere of the reign of Nicholas I it was forbidden. The Old Believers managed to hang on, even when their churches were closed in 1856, with the help of an expatriate community with its own bishop living in Austria. Finally, in 1905 the ban was lifted and the community allowed to continue its existence openly. At Rogozhskoe now there is a winter church of rather florid baroque, and a lovely summer church built by M. F. Kazakov, in which an amazing number of icons, well cared for, decorate every inch of wall space. It is the only example in Moscow of a functioning church complete with such a wonderful display of icons. The graveyard is also fascinating; here the scions of Moscow merchant class are buried, the most conservative of the population, who kept their old beliefs despite harassment.

4 CATHERINE AND THE GENIUS OF BAZHENOV

Elizabeth died on Christmas Day 1761 and Peter, her nephew, ascended the throne as Peter III. He thought of himself as a Holsteiner first and as a Russian only secondarily. Not surprisingly, he was extremely unpopular for his pro-German sentiments; he abruptly ended the war with Prussia when Russia was in the ascendant and invited Prussia to name its terms. Peter managed to antagonize the powerful guards' regiments by forcing them to dress in Prussian uniforms and he dismayed the Russian Church by confiscating its property and favouring Protestant practices. There was one measure, however, which won him unanimous approval from the upper classes. In complete opposition to the principle laid down by Peter the Great of state service for all, Peter III exempted the gentry from service to the state during times of peace. This measure more than any other caused the gentry to attain a position of importance they had never held before, and indirectly led to a general movement of the nobility back to Moscow.

However, Peter's reign lasted only six months; there was not even time to organize a coronation. On 28 June 1762 Catherine, his wife, like her illustrious aunt-by-marriage before her, deposed the male heir to the throne with the help of the five Orlov brothers, including her then lover Gregory Orlov and the important guards' regiments among whom the Orlov brothers wielded much influence. Although a princess of a minor German principality, born neither a Romanov nor a Russian, she was to prove one of the greatest monarchs of the Romanov house. Her deposed husband was imprisoned at his estate at Ropsha and died there shortly afterwards probably at the hands of Alexis Orlov. Thus Catherine, who liked to imagine herself as an enlightened monarch, began her reign by wresting the throne from her husband and, indirectly, bringing about his death.

Catherine's tastes and interests in law, history and foreign policy were decisive, but no more so than her flair for all the arts of which her consuming passions was for architecture. Ironically, despite the stupendous palaces she built, she herself led a simple, abstemious life, rising early, preparing her own fire, and working prodigiously at affairs of state. She was interested in every detail of her buildings and sometimes added changes to the plans in her own hand. It was her chief pleasure to spend hours discussing the details with her architects and it was important that her architects maintain a close and special relationship with her. The progression of her predilections for particular styles is fascinating to follow as it both mirrored the natural development occurring outside Russia while, at the same time, it appeared to be the sharpening and clarification of her own individual taste – from a more modified baroque to a passing fancy for neo-gothic to the more solid severity of neo-classical. Architectural style remained, as it had been for centuries, a court prerogative.

On attaining the throne Catherine was not attracted to the frivolous rococo of

Rastrelli which was alien to her more intellectual interests and habits of personal discipline. The ultimate development of the baroque style seemed in any case to have run its course. In the first fifteen years of her reign three major architects predominated: Rinaldi, Veldten and Bazhenov, with styles that belong to the period of late baroque tempered by classicism. Veldten and Rinaldi, with de la Mothe, rebuilt the Winter Palace in St Petersburg and added the Hermitage, the museum of the arts that was one of Catherine's greatest achievements. Her most beloved architect was probably Charles Cameron, a Scottish architect of Jacobite sympathies, a Palladian who like Adam was steeped in the neo-classical tradition. He came to Russia in 1779. He managed to add apartments to Tsarskoe Selo in the classical style that did not clash with the Renaissance line of the rest of the building. Although he did not lose favour with Catherine like the luckless Bazhenov, he was eventually supplanted by Quarenghi.

Vasily Ivanovich Bazhenov (1737–99) was the most original and talented of the court architects of the time and through chance came to Moscow where he played a decisive role in the development of the city. The son of a poor priest from the provinces, he eventually became one of the first pupils of the new Academy of Fine Arts of St Petersburg. In 1760 at the age of twenty-three he went to Paris where he stayed for two years at the Paris Academy. It is said that he would have won the Prix de Rome, the most coveted prize, but for the fact that he was not French. Before returning to St Petersburg in 1765 he spent two years in Rome. This highly educated, successful young architect, professor of two foreign academies and member of three, was welcomed back with open arms. Catherine was especially pleased to see him and immediately commissioned from him a palace for her son the Grand Prince Paul on Kamenny Ostrov. The palace bore a classical façade but more in the Palladian taste than purely Greek or Roman. Bazhenov also built the Arsenal in 1769 but gradually he began to lose favour, perhaps not so much with the court but among his peers, particularly at the Academy where there may have been jealousy over his successes.

In 1769 he moved to Moscow where he was to remain for most of the rest of his life, returning to St Petersburg only shortly before his death. Catherine had decided that the medieval buildings of the Kremlin needed to be given a more modern look as part of the projected total reconstruction of the centre of Moscow. Bazhenov was commissioned with the project of providing a new palace for the Kremlin that would involve the total rebuilding of the ancient nucleus of the old city. The task was tremendous, requiring great inventiveness and ingenuity to encompass all the existing Kremlin churches, palaces, monasteries and other buildings into one unified whole. The problem was further exacerbated by the difficult shape of the Kremlin – an irregular triangle – and the terrain with the high cliff fronting the river. Bazhenov solved these problems masterfully. Beginning in 1769 he spent some years building the model, now in the Museum of Architecture, which is all that is left to show his genius for overcoming particular architectural and engineering problems.

His ingenious solution would at the same time have been disastrous to the ancient ensemble of the Kremlin. The colossal palace was to have occupied the whole southern brow of the hill of the Kremlin on a high terrace facing the Moskva River. The Old Kremlin wall was to have been demolished. On the west side near the Borovitsky and Trinity Gates there was to have been a long wing, meeting the Arsenal, while on the eastern side a huge new oval square would act as the central pivot, joining all parts of the Kremlin by new roads and other squares.

The main façade of four floors rose from a terrace embellished with sculptures from which steps descended to the river. The third floor was to contain the huge throne room. Giant colonnades ran around the building on all sides providing the main point of interest. The old palaces and cathedrals were to be preserved, with Bazhenov's palace encircling them protectively.

This incredible scheme which, if built, would have been one of the largest palaces in the world, was actually begun in 1772 following a ceremonial opening in the presence of Catherine. Bazhenov commenced digging the huge foundations on the river side of the palace, tearing down part of the Kremlin wall along the south side and generally planning the solution to various engineering problems like the periodic flooding of the Moskva. Suddenly and completely unexpectedly, after three years when construction work was still at foundation level, Catherine turned against the grandiose project. She seemed to have lost interest in the plan, perhaps because the war with Turkey had been successfully concluded in 1774 and perhaps also because of the widespread social unrest which erupted in the Pugachev rebellion in 1775. At any rate, Bazhenov was abruptly removed from the Kremlin and given a new order, to build pavilions on Khodynka Pole to the north of Moscow, for the celebrations for the agreement of the Kuchuk-Kainardji Peace.

Tsaritsyno

His work on the Kremlin a vain effort, Bazhenov tidied up after himself, restored the dismantled wall and towers, filled in the excavations, and bolstered up the south wall of the Archangelsky Cathedral, which had cracked during the excavations, with buttresses still there to this day.

In 1775 the Empress purchased an estate near Moscow called Chernyi Gryaz (Black Mud) from the writer A. Kantemir and gave it the more appealing name Tsaritsyno. Here Bazhenov worked ten years building the main palace and many of the pavilions and fashioning the bridges over the streams to the lake. His brief included two palaces for Catherine and her son Paul, a Cavaliers' Korpus to house the royal suite, a Bread House for the servants and services, an Opera House, a figured bridge and a second bridge over the ravine, a clock-tower and stables. The style Catherine laid down was to be 'Moorish-Gothic', in line with the latest architectural fashion in western Europe. In 1785 Catherine came to view the nearly

39 Catherine the Great's unfinished estate at Tsaritsyno by Bazhenov and Kazakov, late eighteenth century.

completed buildings with their neo-gothic touches and red and white contrasting brick. She objected to the main palace which Bazhenov had designed as two equal parts linked by corridors, one for the Empress and one for the Grand Prince Paul, with whom she had poor relations. Her displeasure meant that the palace was destroyed and another architect, M. F. Kazakov, a young colleague of Bazhenov's, invited to rebuild it. Kazakov was not allowed to finish his work either, owing to the resumption of the war with Turkey and the drain on the royal treasury. In the nineteenth century a local factory borrowed some of the bricks and tiles for building materials and the cluster of buildings remains today a roofless ruin, a memorial to imperial whims.

Bazhenov must have been a bitterly disappointed man. His greatest schemes, on which he worked for twenty years, were not allowed to reach fruition and he repeatedly incurred the Empress's displeasure. Catherine's inexplicable changes of heart may have been partly owing to the fact that Bazhenov had become a leading member of the Freemason movement in Moscow.

The best Russian minds of the eighteenth century seem to have associated themselves with the Masonic movement; in 1785 even the great historian, Karamzin, became a member. After the Pugachev uprising in 1772–75, Catherine came to regard the secrecy of the Masonic movement as dangerous to the state, possibly as the chief danger. She went to great lengths to attack the Masons. In 1786 she even wrote three successful comedies in which the Masons were the chief butt of her attacks. In the same year Masonic charities in the form of schools and hospitals were removed from the Masons' control and Masonic publishing activities fell under suspicion.

Meanwhile, although he was invited to serve on the board set up to build yet another palace for Catherine, a huge edifice on the left bank of the Yauza, Bazhenov began to withdraw from active life, gave up his students and turned more and more to mysticism. He lost his state salary, finally was forced to sell his Moscow house, and lived privately amid a fine collection of paintings on his wife's estate in the country, occasionally receiving private commissions.

The Pashkov House

One of Bazhenov's private commissions was for an imposing house on a promontory facing the west side of the Kremlin near the Borovitsky Gate. It is still one of the most noble buildings in Moscow, made more imposing by its situation, and grand in its execution of the late baroque style. The Pashkov House, now used as the Old Building of the Lenin Library and before the Revolution as the repository of the Rumyantsev Collection, is the cardinal private noble house in Moscow of this period. It is still distinctly baroque with its rich façade, its statues, the stone urns ornamenting the skyline and its general impression of opulence. Yet the use of the flat order of giant pilasters speaks most decisively of the transitional position of this grand building, a bridge between baroque and neo-classicism. It was probably built between 1784 and 1786 and it is now definitely ascribed to Bazhenov. It was commissioned by P. E. Pashkov, a rich nobleman of the household cavalry and a descendant of Peter the Great's valet. The interior of the house was quite badly damaged during the 1812 fire but Osip Ivanovich Bove restored it using a gift of money from the King of Prussia who was grateful for Russia's assistance in the defeat of Napoleon. Bove altered the column and mouldings slightly; the round belvedere on the roof was also changed and some of the more decorative features removed.

The Pashkov House embodies the idea of a gracious 'palace-estate', a large town house rivalling the royal palaces in the nearby Kremlin. Its position is the foundation of its grandeur. High on a hillside, it boldly faces the Borovitsky Gate of the Kremlin, and the great palaces and cathedrals within. It also enjoys a sweeping position across the Moskva River and even today, when Moscow is becoming crushed by ubiquitous tall buildings, the Pashkov House can be seen from many unexpected vantage points. The gardens in front originally descended almost to the Neglinnaya River, which formerly flowed along the Kremlin wall, and were laid out with ponds. The street side with its imposing façade was not meant to be the main entrance: this lay at the back off Ulitsa Marksa and Engelsa where tall iron gates and a driveway along an alley of trees made for an impressive introduction to the house.

The building is in two parts, the central cube of three stories of typically Palladian

40 The Pashkov House, now the Old Building of the Lenin Library. Built by V. I. Bazhenov, 1784–6.

form with two-storey wings on either side united by single-storey galleries to the central block. The rusticated ground floor lit by tall round-arched windows forms the base for a giant order of composite pilasters which define the main body of the building. The centre is emphasized by a projecting portico of four composite columns. The flat roof is topped by the charming belvedere and enlivened by the balustrade and line of vases that are arranged along the edge of the roof. Where the fifth and sixth columns might have been placed on either side of the central four are statues, further embellishments of this highly decorated building. The house develops from the large volume of the basement, to the cube of the central core, and then to the quaintness of the belvedere. The height of the central mass contrasts with the wings on either side.

The classical profile of this building associates well with its medieval neighbours within the Kremlin, which it matches in height. Indeed, even though it now lacks the original statues that adorned the belvedere, the house's silhouette is one of its most important features, and conveys something of the rich variety of form of the Naryshkin churches of a century earlier. Its details, particularly the mouldings on Ulitsa Frunze, are very fine.

5 THE CITY MATURES

A quiet revolution was taking place in Moscow. With the abolition by Peter III of obligatory state service many of the nobility and gentry began to drift back to Moscow, the home of their forebears. In spite of its losses from the plague the city began expanding rapidly to absorb this influx of persons of influence and grew from 139,000 in 1730 to 180,000 in 1785 (St Petersburg's population was by this time about equal with Moscow's). Catherine was aware of Moscow's attractions. She wrote in her notes:

St Petersburg was completely empty. Most of the well-off people lived there out of necessity but by no means at their own wish, and when the court returned from Moscow, almost all the courtiers, in order to remain in Moscow, took leave, some for a year, some for six months, some for a month or a few weeks. Officials – the Senators and others – did exactly the same; if leave was denied then there were various pretexts, both imagined and genuine, illness of the husbands, fathers, wives, brothers, mothers, sisters or children, lawsuits, or other pressing matters.

The Empress became suspicious of the new intellectual pretensions of Moscow although she had supported the new university. By the middle of the 1770s Moscow was becoming a centre of unrest among the more conservative of the gentry who came more and more to regard St Petersburg as a focus of unwelcome foreign influence. Moscow was looked on as more genuinely Russian and in the young university renewal of interest in the Russian language, in teaching in Russian, and in the philosophy of the critic N. I. Novikov led to a great spiritual revival. Commercially, Moscow had never lost its primacy. St Petersburg, a long way to the north, did not enjoy the central geographical position of Moscow and could never pre-empt its trade.

With a resurgence of intellectual and commercial life, conditions were very favourable for an era of new building. The city was expanding in all directions, some of the curving, crooked streets were being straightened and even paved, and whole districts of the old, tottering wooden houses were torn down to make squares or new trading establishments like the *gostiny dvor* in Kitaigorod. The concept of the boulevards was born, water-pipes were laid for the first piped water from Mytishchi, and burials after the plague of 1771 were no longer allowed beside churches but were confined to the large new cemeteries outside the city boundaries. As in St Petersburg, there was an attempt to plan the growth of the city through the agency of the Commission for the Arrangement of the Capital Cities of St Petersburg and Moscow. Founded in 1762 in St Petersburg, a branch of this commission was set up in Moscow in 1773. The boundary of the city in 1785, now the Kamerkollezhsky Val, enclosed 7,100 hectares; and there were 9,000 houses of which about 3,000 were of stone. There were more than a hundred large industries and a start was being made on problems of water pollution and the spread of disease.

State interest in town planning really arose after the defeat of the Turks and the accession of the Crimea to Russia. New cities were to be founded there, requiring all the ingenuity and resources of the available architects and builders. At the same time the Commission was involved in the future planning of the two major cities. In St Petersburg it was not difficult. Here the government and the court demanded large, formal buildings and palaces in a city so recently founded as to be devoid of ancient edifices in antique styles. The Commission kept strict control and an amazing uniformity and gravity still typifies Leningrad. Moscow, on the other hand, must have been a planner's nightmare: medieval, twisting streets, gay onion cupolas, asymmetrical houses, buildings askew. The Commission said of Moscow, 'from ancient times its building has not yet been put into any sort of order.' It never really became as solidly established in Moscow as it did in the more modern city and greater variety of design and individuality in the houses and buildings are more a feature of Moscow than of St Petersburg. Moscow was still basically a great village surrounded by small villages. The new baroque and neo-classical houses and public buildings rose large and magnificent beside the charming tangle of leaning wooden houses with their carved lintels and window frames, and the many belled churches so altogether different from the regular, clean features of the classical façades.

A plan of Moscow was ordered by the Commission and in 1775 it was completed. This detailed map included a general plan envisaging the redevelopment of the centre, of which Bazhenov's plan for the Kremlin was a part, and many engineering improvements. Gracious, tree-lined boulevards were to take the place of the crumbling walls of Belgorod. There was to be a chain of important squares built in a semi-circle along the outside of the Kremlin and Kitaigorod meeting the Moskva both to the east and the west. In this way the old radial-circular structure of the city was to be retained. The central squares and the boulevards were to be enhanced by large private houses set in commanding positions like the Pashkov House.

The Kammennyi Prikaz or Stonemasons' Department came into existence to assist in realization of the plan but its major recommendations, such as the completion of the boulevards, were not fulfilled until the nineteenth century. By 1795 the embankment between the Kremlin and the Moskva River had been built and the long old buildings of the *prikazy* or Chanceries inside the Kremlin were removed, allowing the cathedrals to be clearly seen from the south bank of the river. The only other change within the Kremlin was the tactful addition of the Senate. In Kitaigorod the offices of the Gostinny Dvor, a state trading establishment, were built by the court architect, Giacomo Quarenghi. The building, erected over the foundations of the old Market Place, takes up an entire block. Its open arcade with Corinthian columns formed a place of business for the traders. (Since the Revolution it has been used as an office block.)

The new great houses of Moscow, many of which were on a par with the royal palaces, were generally built on hills overlooking the Kremlin and the centre. The Pashkov House, the new university building by Kazakov and the Dolguruky House or Nobles' Club also by Kazakov, all face the Kremlin from slight rises in the partially cleared area of the new squares surrounding the Kremlin. Further away, just outside the boundary of Kitaigorod and set lower down on the embankment, rose the huge, cold edifice of the Foundling Home, designed in a severely classical style and built in 1764–70 by Karl Blank. This new institution, the first of its kind in Russia and the largest in Europe, was founded by Catherine to discourage infanticide and to bring up orphans and abandoned children to be educated in spheres useful to the state – traders, mechanics, tailors, cobblers, seamstresses, lacemakers, embroiderers. It was one of the largest buildings erected in Russia in the eighteenth century and even today appears remarkable for the amount of space it occupies.

As it had been at the beginning of Peter the Great's reign, so in the last quarter of the eighteenth century the focus of attention in Moscow was on the former foreigners' colony, the Nemetskaya Sloboda, or, as it became known at that time, the St Germaine suburb. Here and across the river in the area now known as Lefortvo, large palaces were built, some with huge parks that truly rivalled the facilities of the court in St Petersburg. Along Novaya Basmannaya, leading to the settlement, were the palaces and mansions of the most notable and wealthy of society. Of these great houses, the only ones to remain are the poor-houses and churches of the Kurakin estate, much rebuilt, and the splendid Demidov House with its gold rooms. Other large fine houses in the area include the Razumovsky House built by the English architect A. Menelas, with its huge park descending to the Yauza, and the house on Razgulya owned by Countess Musin-Pushkin-Bruce whose husband was the famous archivist and bibliophile Count A. M. Musin-Pushkin. The Count's large library and famous ancient manuscript, *The Lay of Igor's Campaign*, perished in this house in the 1812 fire. Although now very much altered, the Musin-Pushkin House was originally built by Kazakov.

Across the river from the foreigners' colony Lefortovo was really an integral part of it and grandiose royal palaces also began to appear here. Bazhenov was invited to submit plans for yet another elaborate palace for the Empress on the site of the old Golovin Palace which had been used by the royal house since the reign of Anna Ivanovna. Bazhenov, as usual, was dismissed, and it was finally built to Quarenghi's design in 1773–96, but Camporezi, Rinaldi and Karl Blank also took part in its execution. The commencement of the palace in 1773 indicates that it may have been built to compensate for the cessation of Bazhenov's rebuilding of the Kremlin. The resultant building on the site of Rastrelli's Annenhof Palace is impressive with its giant order of sixteen Corinthian columns and loggia and its colonnade, which is the longest in Moscow. The palace, only finished in 1796 after Catherine's death, was never used as originally intended but was immediately altered into a splendid soldiers' barracks by Catherine's unpopular son, Paul I, who had a mania for military barracks. To connect the palace with the Nemetskaya Sloboda, S. Yakovliev built the Palace Bridge (Dvortsovy Most) in 1779–81 said to be a close copy of the old Stone Bridge near the Kremlin across the Moskva. The Catherine Palace has consistently been the home of the army in both tsarist and socialist Russia and is now the Soviet Tank Academy.

Kazakov's Moscow

Perhaps the equivalent in Moscow of the classicist Quarenghi in St Petersburg was Matvei Fedorovich Kazakov (1738–1813). Kazakov's ultimate style is as different from the baroque of Ukhtomsky and Bazhenov as Quarenghi is from Rastrelli. It can be argued that he alone is responsible for the change from the predominantly medieval and disordered character of Moscow into the gracious place of order and elegant houses which were characteristic of the city at the beginning of the nineteenth century. Medieval Moscow was never totally rooted out and remains today in delightful corners and unexpected lanes, but the amber and ochre classical houses, from the smallest one-storey wooden dwellings to the magnificent columns of the Nobles' Club, are also typical and essentially derive from the influence of one architect.

The so-called 'Kazakov period' or the 'Empire' style lasted nearly one hundred years from 1770 to about 1860, long after the master architect's death in 1813. The change was immense. From the complex halls and churches of ancient Rus with their many varied roofs and cupolas, richly decorative forms and luxurious colours lavished on even the most insignificant detail, it was a big step to houses in one whole, single block, their halls and rooms forming a unified, elegant system, built according to the classical orders. Smooth columns and flat pilasters replaced the old *lopatki*. Panels of relief sculpture offset the triangular plane of the pedimented portico. Stucco exterior walls were painted amber or pistachio or ochre and sculpture became common either as statues or reliefs on the most important parts of the building. The houses bore a closer relationship to streets and squares and high, forbidding solid walls disappeared to be replaced by iron railings which left the fronts of buildings visible to the street.

The development of the new large houses had been going on throughout the century but the fashion for travel in the court of Catherine was unprecedented and once abroad the rich Russian gentry were strongly influenced by the new architecture with its origin in the widespread revival of interest in Roman antiquity. There is a particular Russian quality to the otherwise international style of neo-classicism found in Moscow; and this quality is displayed in the combination of traditional and classical forms. From the 1770s onwards not only were large houses erected in the new style but a multitude of small houses were built for Moscow's emerging middle classes – government clerks, minor merchants, successful traders – which combined the complex, traditional carved window- and door-frames – the *nalichniki* – with the symmetrical façades of classical buildings. No longer of one room, and now painted on the outside in pastel colours with white details, they boasted separate quarters for the kitchen and for sleeping, and both a principal and a tradesman's entrance. This basic type with some modifications continued to be built after the 1812 fire and still holds sway over some districts of Moscow.

The neo-classical mansions were usually built inside an existing estate. Whether in town or in country it was necessary to provide gardens and grounds around the buildings. As a general rule, the façade was divided horizontally into three parts and vertically into three bays, making a total of nine equal parts. The centre was emphasized by a giant Corinthian or Ionic order. The portico would have six, eight, ten or twelve columns with five, seven, nine, or eleven window openings to correspond with the columns. The large, decorated central opening usually contained the door. This system, which reflected the interior organization of the house, made the building a unified whole, often further united by a low cupola over the central part. The ground floor provided the vestibule and service rooms, the first floor held the most important reception rooms, the second floor had the families' living and bedrooms. In the town the building either had its main section along the street with its windows perpendicular to it, or it was moved back and the side-lodges fronted the street, serving as a frame for the building. Sometimes the principal entrance was not via the elaborate façade but, as in the Pashkov House, through the courtyard at the rear.

Although the houses were perfectly symmetrical, the general plan of the estate was not. Besides the out-buildings, there was usually a large church occupying an important site, often from an earlier period with a pyramid silhouette and therefore clashing with the architectural style of the house. It was this which gave to the mansions a particular Russian character quite different from those in western Europe.

Kazakov's background differs from that of Bazhenov and other Russian architects in that he did not study in St Petersburg at the Academy of Fine Arts nor did he ever travel abroad. His entire life was centred on Moscow, and even his trips to St Petersburg were very few. The main influence on his style was the school established around Prince Ukhtomsky which he joined at the age of thirteen, the son of a poor church clerk. He studied there for nine years under a kind of apprenticeship system which involved activities as diverse as copying the classics and washing the floors. In 1760 he had attained the title of *praporshchik arkitektury*, a type of graduation certificate. For seven years he worked as Bazhenov's assistant and the influence of Bazhenov on his earlier work is quite apparent in buildings like the pseudo-Gothic Petrovsky Zamok, and the pavilions on the Khodynka fields erected in 1774 for the elaborate celebrations of the Kuchuk-Kainardji Peace at the ending of the Turkish war. He and Bazhenov must have enjoyed themselves playing with the Gothic style, adding minarets and kiosks, to match the light-hearted atmosphere of the Peace. The Khodynka pavilions have not survived. The Petrovsky Zamok not far from the Fields was built in 1775–82 and continued the manner of the pavilions. If one looks closely one can see incised decorations between the surrounds, the bulging pitcher shape of the porch pillars and other details derived from old Russian forms. Catherine had ordered the palace to be built as a place in which she could rest and change before entering Moscow after travelling from St Petersburg.

Kazakov's first important work was not in Moscow but in Tver (Klin) where a particularly destructive fire had laid the city bare in 1763. Kazakov helped design a new central square (or rather circus) and large new houses on the embankment, many of which have survived. Catherine was so pleased she called Tver 'my beautiful little toy'. For his work the architect was elevated to the rank of 'Captain' in the order of ranks of the nobility set up by Peter the Great. On his return to Moscow he helped Karl Blank with the huge, severe building of the Foundling Home.

Kazakov was also invited to serve on the Commission for the Rebuilding of the Kremlin Palaces headed by Bazhenov. He thus partook in Bazhenov's plan for restructuring the Kremlin, receiving the princely sum of 400 rubles a year for this work. In 1795, when Paul I began his short reign, Kazakov made even more comprehensive plans for rebuilding the Kremlin but Paul was not interested.

By the 1770s Kazakov was thoroughly established as an important Moscow architect. From 1776 to 1787, although nominally under Karl Blank, he worked on the construction of his greatest work, the building of the Senate in the Kremlin. With its fine proportions and brilliant resolution of an uncomfortable site this

41 The Senate in the Kremlin, by M. Kazakov, 1776–87. Now used by the Council of Ministers of the USSR.

building remains the most important eighteenth-century building in the Kremlin. Contemporaries described it as the 'masterly composition of taste and elegance'. Its form, in the shape of a triangle to fit in with the restrictions of the site, is strictly classical, a striking contrast with the light-heartedness of the Petrovsky Zamok built only two years earlier. Does it illustrate an abrupt change in Catherine's taste, or is it simply that Kazakov was allowed to have his own way? At any rate Catherine was charmed by the completed building with its fine, tall, circular hall. The Senate building was meant to provide the offices and a meeting place for the Moscow section of the Senate, the advisory body established by Peter the Great. Its site was bounded by the corner of the Kremlin walls and the formerly numerous buildings of the Chudov Monastery and the Arsenal. Only one building had to be removed for the Senate, the palace of Prince Trubetskoi. The complex shape of the new building includes three inner courtyards, each triangular, the central one containing the great hall embellished by a colonnade of Tuscan columns and bearing the great cupola. This is the compositional centre of a long-bodied building which flows from the Senate Square between rhythmically placed bays with tall, shining windows. The severity of the façade is softened by the grand main entrance into the inner courtyards. From Red Square the cupola over the hall appears to be in the middle of the Kremlin wall between Spassky Gate and the Corner Arsenal Tower, almost behind the mausoleum. The Senate is now called the Council of Ministers building and contains their offices.

The great hall, now called Sverdlov Hall, is round and over 25 metres high. Corinthian columns decorate it, over which rises the inner shell of the cupola nearly as high again as the hall. Between the columns are eighteen sculptured bas-reliefs of famous poets of the eighteenth century, the only adornment to the severity of the design. The hall, originally the meeting place of the Senate, was also used for meetings of the nobility and after the Revolution was for a time a club for Kremlin cadets. It is now used only for the bestowing of the most honoured awards, such as the Lenin prizes, and for meetings of the plenums of the Communist Party of the Soviet Union.

At the same time that Kazakov was occupied with the Senate building he designed and built the lovely, cylindrical Church of Filip the Metropolitan (1777–88), which still stands in Moscow. It has a fine classical façade. The two-storey circular church is joined to an earlier entrance-way on the west but on the north and south sides Doric porticos form the entrances. The two-storey altar extends outwards in a manner resembling that of the porticos. It was the private church of the Metropolitan, Plafon, who lived nearby, which explains its small size. Its exterior is reserved in contrast to the rich columns of the interior.

In 1783 Kazakov was given the task of designing the new city of Yekaterinoslav, Potemkin's great project, but few of his ideas were executed. He was now very busy in Moscow and for the next thirty years his touch was felt in every quarter. The Dolgoruky House (1784), later the famous Nobles' Club, with its magnificent, glittering Hall of Columns, belongs to this period. At the same time as he was involved in work for the Dolgorukys, Kazakov built a splendid house for the military commander of Moscow, Z. G. Chernyshev, on the Tverskaya (now Gorky Street). When Chernyshev became Governor of Moscow, his house was purchased by the state and became the official residence of the governors until the Revolution. The house still stands and provides offices for Mossoviet but it was so excruciatingly altered in 1945 when it was given two additional floors and an incongruous Soviet arch that it is impossible now to visualize the original building.

Kazakov is also the architect of the old block of Moscow University and its chapel, just north of the Kremlin, both of which are still used by the University. Along with many other private commissions Kazakov was given the task of building the Golitsyn Hospital in 1796–1801, near the old Kaluga Road in southern Moscow overlooking the high banks of the river. A. M. Golitsyn was the Russian Ambassador in Vienna and, as was fashionable then, desired to satisfy his philanthropic yearnings by building a hospital on his large estate. The architect had absolute freedom of design and the result is magnificent, probably his best work after the Senate. Its lay-out recalls the fashion of the town estate with the main entrance facing the street.

42 Moscow University, by M. Kazakov, 1786–93. Rebuilt after the 1812 fire by Gilliardi.

Wings extend from the main courtyard to the street. There is a fine stone staircase climbing from either side to the foyer of the main entrance. The entire scheme is unified by a large cupola over the hospital church. Behind was a lovely park descending sharply to the water. The rooms of the hospital were designed with the latest ideas of medicine in view. It is still in use as the Second City Hospital.

The indefatigable Kazakov built many more fine palaces and mansions including those at Kon'kove, Bulatnikova, Tsaritsyno, the Sloboda Palace for the Emperor Paul, the Gubin House and the Demidov House. He lived to see the great fire of 1812 destroy or damage much of his finest work and he died in 1813 after having been evacuated from Moscow highly distressed by these events. But some thirty-three of his buildings survive still, in or near Moscow, an achievement no other eighteenth-century Russian architect can boast.

Other talented architects were also busy at work in Moscow, where only forty years before there had been only one architect. Ivan Yegotov designed the Military Hospital near the Catherine Palace in Lefortovo in 1798–1802 and it still functions as such. R. R. Kazakov (no relation to Matvei Fyodorovich) built the lovely Batashov House, now used as a hospital, on International Street, its position high on a hill typical of large Moscow houses of this period, which were usually placed in commanding positions. He also is responsible for the odd features of St Martin the Confessor (1782–93) on Kommunisticheskaya Ulitsa near Taganka Square, a self-conscious imitation of Wren's St Paul's in London. It stands today deserted and unhappy, incongruous in a street of decaying plaster and leaning wooden dwellings, and permanently darkened by the profusion of trees. N. N. Legran, the most senior architect of the Commission of Building in Moscow, designed the impressive Kriegskommissariat on the south side of the Moskva in 1778–80, now used as a military training school. A canal was dug behind the Kommissariat, so putting it on a long island and removing the threat of frequent flooding.

One of the loveliest buildings of this era, that still graces Moscow, is the Strannoprimnyi Dom or Sheremetiev Hospital, now the Skliforovsky Institute (1794–1807). It was designed by E. S. Nazarov, who was a serf-architect owned by the Sheremetievs. This family encouraged the peasants of talent on their vast holdings, and ultimately gave Nazarov his freedom. They were one of the richest and most powerful Moscow families at this time, with antecedents going back to the time of Ivan the Terrible. N. N. Sheremetiev had many houses in Moscow and grand country estates at Kuskovo and Ostankino. He was a great patron of the arts and built an ingenious theatre at Ostankino where the best singers and actors of the day, many of them his own serfs, staged entertainments. He married the famous singer P. I. Kovaleva-Zhemchugova. When Zhemchugova died in 1803 Sheremetiev decided to dedicate the new hospital to her memory. Like the other philanthropists of his day Sheremetiev wanted to build a hospital for the public. Nazarov designed a long, low, semi-circular building, with a church in the centre roofed by a cupola; the left wing was laid out for the poor-house (ground floor for men, first floor for women), the right wing for the hospital. Services were in the basement. Two out-buildings in the courtyard were to provide apartments for the administration. After his wife's death Sheremetiev asked Quarenghi for his ideas for the hospital. Quarenghi changed little but what he did transformed the building with great simplicity. He added a

43 Strannoprimnyi Dom, the Sheremetiev Hospital, by E. Nazarov and D. Quarenghi, 1794–1807. Now the Skliforovsky Institute.

projecting semi-circular colonnade based on the entrance portico, providing the building with its focal point of interest and proving once again that the ageing architect had not lost his touch.

At the close of the eighteenth century Moscow had recovered well from the harrowing experience of losing its primacy to St Petersburg. The desertion of the city by the nobility and court at the beginning of the century, the emptying of its busy commercial quarters and cessation of its building activity, had, by the end of the century, been more than offset by the gradual return of the gentry who had been able to leave St Petersburg when the obligation to serve the state, and therefore to reside in the capital, had been removed in 1762. The rebirth of the city was nearly complete by the end of the century. Large new mansions with sizable gardens, miniature or town estates too numerous to mention in detail, were built in many parts of Moscow: for instance, the English Club on what is now Gorky Street, the Gubin House on the Petrovka, the Dolgoruky House (later the Nobles' Club) on Okhotny Ryad (Prospekt Marksa), the Gagarin House at the Petrovka Gate (the Boulevard), the Talyzin House and the Sheremetiev House on the Vozdvizhenka (Prospekt Kalinina), the Yushkov House on Myasniktskaya (Ulitsa Kirova), and the huge palatial residence of the Razumovsky House. Many of these palatial houses had large parks and rivalled the royal palaces. In addition to their own houses it was becoming fashionable for the nobility to own large country estates and second town houses in St Petersburg. At no other time were such huge private houses built in Moscow; it was the so-called era of 'monumental' architecture. The fine residences

of the wealthy, the round classical churches so secular in appearance, the royal palaces and pillars and pediments, and the new palatial hospitals and public buildings, overwhelmed Moscow, dominating its features from every aspect. When he stood on the Sparrow Hills Napoleon exclaimed in admiration and surprise at seeing, instead of the strange oriental buildings he had been expecting, the familiar, gracious, clean lines of a Europeanized eighteenth-century city.

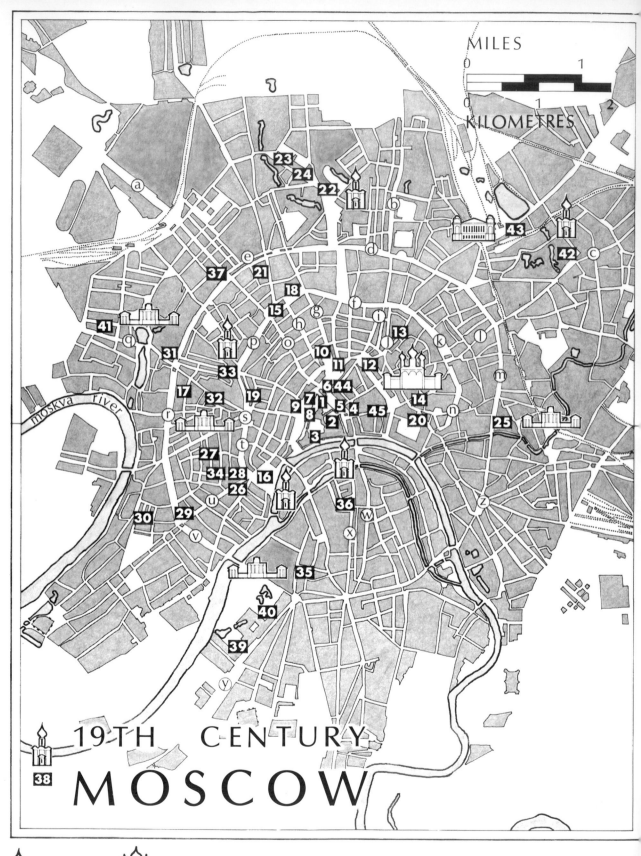

MILES

KILOMETRES

19TH CENTURY
MOSCOW

moskva river

Cathedral/
Church/
Chapel

Convent/
Monastery

Palace/
Estate/
Mansion/House

Apartment/
Hotel

Railwa
station

4 The Aftermath of Napoleon and the Rise of Eclesticism

At the beginning of the nineteenth century in Moscow, as elsewhere in Russia, a mood of optimism prevailed after the forcible removal of the cruel Tsar Paul in 1801 and the commencement of the reign of his tall, idealistic son Alexander who seemed physically and morally a complete contrast to his father. Alexander had been brought up in a liberal tradition under the tutelage of his grandmother Catherine II, and soon took measures to counter the most despotic aspects of Paul's reign. Among his first acts were the abrogation of the security police, a declaration of a general amnesty, liberalization of trade, removal of the prohibition on travel abroad, the granting of permission for the importation of foreign publications, and a start on reform of the penal system. With such an auspicious beginning, some sections of Russian society hoped for deeper constitutional and social reforms but Alexander proved to be vacillating in his attitude to these questions and towards the end of his reign increasingly took refuge in mysticism while repressive measures, including censorship and the secret police, were reintroduced. Over the years Alexander fell more and more under the influence of the extremely reactionary Arakcheev, his chief minister, who with the Tsar's approval set up the famous 'military' colonies of civilians all over Russia. Nevertheless, at the beginning of the new century, with the Peace of Tilsit in 1807 to remove the imminent threat of Napoleon's ambitions, the mood in Moscow might be epitomized by the gaiety of Natasha in *War and Peace* on her name-day when the future appeared cloudless.

Buildings

1 Nikolskaya Gate, 1801   2 Veskresensky Convent, 1823   3 Kremlin Great Palace, 1838–49   4 GUM (Upper trading Rows), 1888   5 Statue of Minin and Pozharsky, 1818   6 History Museum, 1878–83   7 The restored University and Chapel, 1817–19 and 1835   8 Alexandrov Gardens, 1821–23   9 The Manège, 1817   10 The Bolshoi Theatre, 1824, rebuilt in 1851   11 Maly Theatre, 1821–40   12 Polytechnic Museum, 1875–77   13 No. 19 Myasnitskaya (Kirova), the tea house, 1896   14 Ivanovsky Convent   15 Strastnoi Convent, 1849–55 (no longer standing)   16 Cathedral of Christ the Redeemer, 1838–80   17 Gagarin House, 1815   18 Catherine Hospital, 1812   19 Lunin House, 1818   20 Opekunsky Soviet, 1823–6   21 Medvedeva Ulitsa (Street)   22 Catherine Institute (now Soviet Army Building), 1802–5   23 Alexandrovsky (now Tuberculosis) Institute, 1809–11   24 Mariinskaya (now Dostoevsky) Hospital, 1803–5   25 Naidyonov Estate, 1829–31   26 Lopukhin House, 1822   27 Sivtsev Vrazhek Pereulok   28 Khrushchev House (now Pushkin Museum), 1814   29 Proviantsky Sklady, 1832–35   30 Dolgy Pereulok (now Burdenko Ulitsa)   31 Vdovy Dom (Widow's House), 1809–11   32 Konnozavodstvo (now Gorky Museum), 1820   33 Bolshoe Vesneseniye (Ascension) Church, 1820s   34 Gagarinsky (now Ryleeva Pereulok)   35 Igumnov House, 1896   36 Vsekh Skorbyashchikh (All Sorrows) Church, 1832–3   37 Triumphal Gate, 1827–34, moved to southwest Moscow in 1968   38 Cathedral Monument to 1812 by Vitberg, never completed   39 Golitsyn Hospital, 1796–1801   40 First City Hospital, 1828–33   41 P. I. Shchukin House   42 Bogoyavlenie v Yelokhove Cathedral, 1837–45   43 Kazan Station, 1912–26   44 City Duma (now Lenin Museum), 1890–92. Just to the southeast is the old Synod Printing House, 1814   45 Romanov House, restored in 1859

Streets

a Petrogradskoe Shosse (now Leningrad Shosse)   b I. Meshchanskaya (now Prospekt Mira)   c Vladimira Shosse (now Entusiastov Shosse)   d Sukharevskaya   e Triumfalnaya   f Rozhdestvensky   g Dmitrovka (now Pushkinskaya)   h Petrovka   i Lubyanka (now Dzerzhinskovo)   j Myasnitskaya (now Kirova)   k Chistoprudny   l Pokrovka (now Chernyshevskovo)   m Zemlyanoi Val (now Chkalova)   n Yauzsky   o Tverskaya (Gorky)   p Tverskoi   q Voskresenskoe Shosse (now Khoroshevskoe Shosse)   r Novinsky Boulevard (now Chaikovskaya)   s Arbat Square   t Prechistensky (now Gogolevsky)   u Prechistenska (now Kropotkinskaya)   v Zubovsky Boulevard   w Pyatnitskaya   x Ordynka   y Kaluzhskoe Shosse (now Leninsky Prospekt)   z Tagansky Square

The city itself still radiated the sense of order and harmony imposed upon it by the genius of Kazakov and his disciples. On seeing Moscow for the first time on 15 September, 1812, before the fire broke out, a French officer wrote: 'On entering Moscow I was seized with astonishment and delight. Although I had expected to see a wooden city, as many had said, I found, on the contrary, almost all the houses to be of brick and in the most elegant and modern style. The homes of private persons are like palaces and everything was rich and wonderful.' Napoleon's officer was wrong in thinking there were few buildings of wood but the city must have been quite a sight with its fine neo-classical façades relieved by the spires and onion-shaped cupolas of the churches of the seventeenth and earlier centuries.

Except for the Kremlin, Moscow did not have such a clearly defined central area as it was to do later when the series of main squares around the Kremlin was built. Although they did not rise higher than other, less important buildings in the vicinity, the great public buildings – the theatres, hospitals, educational institutions, charitable institutions – were larger and finely decorated and gave the city the focal points it so badly needed. Nevertheless, there was no square to set off the Petrov Theatre on the site of the future Bolshoi, and the dirty and meandering Neglinnaya River still ran free along the Kitaigorod wall then northwards past the theatre in line with what is today Neglinnaya Boulevard. Red Square boasted no open spaces but was crowded with small buildings jostling each other right up to the Kremlin walls. Not all new buildings were in the classical style moreover. Karl Rossi, then the leading St Petersburg architect, early in the century designed the spire of the Nikolsky Gate and the Cathedral of the Veznesensky Convent in the Kremlin (see p. 173) in pseudo-Gothic style. The Synod Printing House built in 1814 was designed in a similar manner.

The Kazakov contribution was continued by the Italian architect Giovanni Gilliardi, who settled in Russia and built the Catherine Institute, a school for daughters of the hereditary nobility (now the Central House of the Soviet Army), in 1803–5 and the Alexandrovsky Institute in 1809–11, a school for children of merchants and petty officials. Both buildings are severely classical. Similar in style is the nearby Mariinsky (now Dostoevsky) Hospital by A. Mikhailov 1802–5. Significantly these buildings are found outside the central part of Moscow, as the authorities were loath to disturb the central area.

The beginning of the nineteenth century marked the onset of a period of rapid industrial growth and of great developments in Russian literature. In the first decade of the century three of Russia's greatest writers came on the scene – Krylov, Griboyedov and the young Pushkin. In 1803 the historian Karamzin was granted the title of Official Historian and in 1816 published the *History of the Russian State* which was greatly to influence Pushkin.

Technical innovations were causing important changes in building, one of which was the discovery of how to use iron. In 1804–8 the first iron bridge was laid in

44 The Synod Printing House, built by A. Bakarev and I. Mironovsky, 1814.

45 A curved balcony on Khokhlovsky Pereulok dating from the early nineteenth century.

St Petersburg across the Moika. It was quicker to build than the old method of stone arches, and was lighter as well as being strong and durable. In 1808 the architect Voronikhin was the first to use a metal frame, for the huge cupola of Kazan Cathedral. It had a span of 17.1 metres. The metal factories began to proliferate as this new use of iron became more common.

In Moscow the new generation of architects was still very much under the influence of the academic classical tradition of Kazakov. They were trained in the school he helped establish, with the peculiar name of the Kremlin Expedition. In 1802 a committee was formed to assist in the administration of the city, the Committee for the Direction of City Services (Komitet dlya Upravleniya Gorodskikh Povinnostei), and under its auspices a careful plan of contemporary Moscow dated 1806–8 was drawn up under the direction of F. K. Sokolov. Over five hundred of the most important religious, state and private buildings were carefully detailed on this plan, which was to be an invaluable aid to the reconstruction that was made necessary by the sacking in 1812.

I THE FIRE

The foreign policy of Alexander I up to 1812 and after was conditioned by diplomatic manoeuvrings to obtain security against Napoleon either by going into league with him or by joining alliances against him. The disastrous Austrian campaign in 1805 where the Russian army of some 90,000 men was entirely routed at Austerlitz finally led to the Franco-Russian alliance, the Peace of Tilsit, in 1807. The two emperors subsequently argued over Napoleon's interference in Polish affairs and eventually the expansionist policy of the French resulted in the invasion of Russia in June 1812 by the Grande Armée. Russia had just signed a peace treaty concluding the six-year war with Turkey and was able to turn its entire attention to the French menace but as the Grande Armée totalled 655,000 troops (including reinforcements) and the Russian army could muster only 220,000 men, the Russian authorities had little option but to order retreat to a more defensible part of the country. The Russian attitude was summed up by Rostopchin, the Governor of Moscow, who remarked to the Tsar: 'The Emperor of Russia will always be formidable in Moscow, terrible in Kazan, and invincible in Tobolsk.'

46 Number 16 Ulitsa Volodarskovo. A typical comfortable home of the early nineteenth century, illustrative of Moscow as it appeared to Napoleon.

It is interesting that all Russia's foreign invaders in the last 700 years have regarded the capture of Moscow, the geographical and commercial centre, as the decisive goal in their occupation of Russia and that the rise of St Petersburg did not change this strategy. Charles XII also concentrated on capturing Moscow and Hitler came very close to it, but only Napoleon was to succeed in actually entering the city. Yet he soon learned that far from meaning victory the taking of Moscow was to prove his undoing. After Smolensk fell to the French in August a general disorderly flood of the population began to pour from the city, although it was not decided until 13 September by the aged General Kutuzov at Fili that Moscow would not be defended. Yet already in August Governor Rostopchin began evacuating government departments and troops. In the Foundling Home all the older children were evacuated to Kazan but, oddly, the very young toddlers and babies remained. The Kremlin treasures, including coronation valuables and important church plate, were sent to Nizhny-Novgorod and Vologda, which also received the most important valuables of the rich Moscow monasteries. However, there was not time to remove everything.

After the inconclusive but bloody battle of Borodino on 7 September the evacuation of Moscow greatly intensified. One witness of the flight, N. S. Glinka, reported from Ryazan: 'As far as the eye could see the entire Moscow road was covered with lines of carriages and people on foot fleeing from the unhappy capital. They jostled and overtook one another, and hurried, driven by fear, in carriages, cabriolets, *Drozhkys* and carts. Everyone carried what he could. All faces were dusty and tear-stained.' To add to the miseries of the crowd, thousands of desperately wounded men from the battle of Borodino limped and crawled through the streets. Although the exact number is impossible to assess, this mass exodus reduced the population of the city from 200,000 to something below 10,000.

On 13 September the rearguard of the Russian army passed through the city and on the afternoon of 14 September Napoleon viewed Moscow for the first time from the splendid vantage point of the Sparrow Hills (now Lenin Hills). For Napoleon it was the culminating point in the Russian campaign, it was his greatest triumph, greater than those of Milan or Venice or Alexandria or any of his other many conquests. Here was the connecting link between Europe and Asia, and the Tsar was about to sue for peace. But Napoleon's triumph was short-lived.

He waited impatiently on the Sparrow Hills for a deputation from the city to receive him, to acknowledge his triumphal entry into the city. However, no deputation arrived. The Russian population had vanished and of those that remained a considerable number were foreigners who expected mercy from Napoleon. By the time the French withdrew from Moscow only about 3,000 of the 10,000 inhabitants that had probably been in the city on Napoleon's arrival remained. The rest either had fled, been captured by the French, left voluntarily with them, or were killed while pursuing partisan activities. Although he could not get over the emptiness of the city, the 'terrible desert', Napoleon was nevertheless impressed by Moscow. On 16 September he wrote to his new empress, 'The city is as big as Paris. There are 1,600 church towers here and over a thousand beautiful palaces; the city is provided with everything.'

Before the first night of the French occupation was over the great fire of Moscow had begun. It seems to have started in Kitaigorod, in the rows of small trading stalls. French reports agree on this and there is a message to the Moscow Council from the Police Superintendant, Voronenko, who remained in the city, to the effect that he had been ordered by Count Rostopchin to fire the rows of stalls selling wine and the customs house. He reported that he did so on 14 September, working until ten

47 A contemporary impression of the Fire of Moscow and Napoleon's Army.

o'clock in the evening. Other fires may have originated from the French themselves, particularly the looters. At any rate by the following morning a strong wind had fanned the flames and the fire had spread to engulf half the city. Eventually the fire affected the entire city and burned fiercely for four days, not finally dying out until the sixth day. Moscow, accustomed to frequent fires, had never experienced one so terrible. By 16 September the Arbat area, from where Pierre in *War and Peace* watched in horror, was all aflame and the Vdovy Dom (Widows' Home) not far away on the Ring Road was alight with 700 severely wounded Russian soldiers inside, unable to escape. On the other side of the still largely wooden city the fashionable Nemetskaya Sloboda was also a wall of flame. The Kremlin, as yet untouched, was literally surrounded by a sea of flames. Napoleon, who had moved to the Kremlin on 14 September began to feel the heat of the fire and by 16 September, when the winds rose to a fury fanning the fire in a north-easterly direction, the Kremlin itself was threatened. Napoleon felt obliged to move for three days to the Petrovsky Palace on the northern outskirts of Moscow. Count Segur described the departure of Napoleon and his staff from the Kremlin in the early hours of 16 September as a battle through 'an ocean of flames'.

On the same day the fire crossed the Moskva River and all of Zamoskvareche was burnt. The entire central area as far as the Ring Road was in flames although the fire sometimes capriciously ignored some streets such as the Ukrainian area south of the Maroseika (Bogdan Khmelnitsky). The Yauza River too was crossed and eastern Moscow was alight. For the French it was an appalling experience. Looting went on indiscriminately in spite of Napoleon's strictures. It must have seemed to the soldiers absurd to allow the fire to consume everything. Stendhal was in the quarter-master section on Napoleon's staff and wrote that even the smoke hanging in the air was 'copper-coloured'. Boats on the river and even green trees were consumed by the terrible conflagration. About 3 a.m. on the night of 17–18 September the wind dropped and rain began to fall but the fire still burned and was not completely out until 20 September. Napoleon then issued a heart-felt bulletin, 'Moscow, one of the most beautiful and wealthy cities of the world, exists no more.'

The damage seemed incalculable. At least three quarters of the buildings were in ashes. Of the 9,158 private houses, 6,532 suffered extensive fire damage; less than one third survived. The unhappy Kazakov, then on his deathbead, was according to his son, deeply shocked: 'having beautified the capital city with wonderful buildings, he could not imagine without a shudder that his life's work was being turned into ashes and disappearing in the smoke of the fire.' The great libraries, both private and public, had gone up in smoke with many irreplaceable historical documents. A famous copy of the *Lay of Prince Igor's Campaign* in Musin-Pushkin's library was destroyed, so that controversy still rages over the authenticity of the most ancient example of Russia's literature. Miraculously most of the Kremlin survived intact although some of the towers and palaces were damaged. Indeed, the Kremlin was to suffer far more from the mines maliciously laid by the French on their departure.

After the fire, discipline among Napoleon's troops seems to have entirely disintegrated and looting became even more common, particularly of the churches and monasteries. Napoleon himself did not hold back from pilfering what he could from the Kremlin. On one of the pillars in the Uspensky Cathedral the French wrote scornfully that they had taken 325 poods (about 11,600 pounds) of silver and 18 poods (about 648 pounds) of gold. Even the huge gold cross at the top of Ivan Veliky was hauled down to please Napoleon who had thought of placing it over the Invalides in Paris.

Meanwhile, Napoleon made three overtures to Alexander suggesting peace terms, including one through Major-General Tutolmin, the head of the Foundling Home and practically the only one who had nobly remained to protect his youngest wards. But the Russians remained obstinately silent as they waited for the French to succumb to the impossibility of living in the ruined city throughout the winter. On 13 October, unusually early even for Moscow, the first snow fell, a portent of the extremely hard winter in store for the French.

The fire had made the deserted city even less hospitable than it was at the arrival of the French and left Napoleon without adequate winter quarters or sufficient food for his troops. Finally Kutuzov's victory over Murat's advance guard at Tarutino on 18 October convinced the emperor of the impossibility of remaining over winter. The long line of French soldiers began dispiritedly leaving the capital. The Emperor and his suite followed on the morning of 19 October. Before leaving, however, he bitterly ordered that the Kremlin and other parts of Moscow be blown up in retaliation for Alexander's obduracy in refusing to reply to his three messages. The mines were duly laid, mostly by Russian labourers, and on 19 October the wine stalls in Kitaigorod where the fire was said to have originated were blown up. On the same day the Simonov monastery on the eastern outskirts of Moscow which had not suffered in the fire was deliberately burned. On 21 October explosions began in the Kremlin. The Arsenal was hit, part of the Kremlin wall was blown up, the Nikolskaya Gate and Beklemishev Tower were damaged and fires broke out in the Faceted Palace and some of the cathedrals. But not all the mines exploded, perhaps partly because some were defused by rain. Other explosions occurred on 22 October and early on the following morning when the last of the French army left.

Napoleon had spent in all only thirty-three days in Moscow. Finally forced out he suffered a humiliating and harrowing retreat across the thousand miles of cold and snowbound Russian land. Even before reaching Smolensk the French army was starving. Stendhal wrote in a letter to a friend that one of his keenest pleasures after taking eighteen days to reach Smolensk was in finding a few potatoes and some damp army bread to eat. Harried by partisans, weak from hunger and wounds, only 25,000 of the original vast army of over half a million finally crossed the Niemen on 14 December.

Shortly after the last French troops left on the morning of 23 October the Russians marched back into the city. An appalling sight met their eyes. Rubble, wreckage and filth greeted them. There were thousands of bodies lying in the streets. The ancient capital had become a ruin. One eyewitness wrote, 'There is almost no Moscow left.'

2 RECONSTRUCTION

However, the dismay of the returning populace over the ruin of their beautiful city was largely offset by the exhilaration and pride at the defeat of the apparently invincible Napoleon. There was an awakening of national self-consciousness, a pride in being Russian, that had not existed before. Some historians argue that 1812 marks the turning point in Russian history, the watershed between historical and modern times. To oversimplify, without 1812 there would have been no Decembrist rebellion and without the Decembrists there would not have been the spark that ignited the later revolutionary movements. The experience of 1812 also led to an increased awareness of Russian history and Russia's destiny which profoundly affected writers like Pushkin.

Be that as it may, the destruction wrought on Moscow by the fire, compounded by the looting and the explosions, led to the unfolding of a new city. A few months after the fire, in early 1813, the Commission for the Construction of the City of Moscow was formed and continued in existence until 1842. Imbued with patriotic ideals and with the strong support of the court, the architects, many of them old pupils of Kazakov, formed a plan of reconstruction and strictly regulated its implementation, even down to the smallest details like the colour of the roofs. The architects on the Commission were familiar with the ideas of planning a city as a whole from the experience of the building of St Petersburg and, more recently, from Catherine the Great's interest in and patronage of town planning, and were well equipped to begin their work. Their task was twofold: to rebuild as quickly as possible the burnt-out residential quarters with attractive and comfortable homes; and to achieve the rebirth of Moscow as the 'second capital' with a strong centre distinguished by groups of squares and public buildings.

The Commission architects had behind them the plan of 1775, the first conscious attempt to view Moscow as a single entity and to plan for its growth and transportation needs. The scheme had provided for new central squares, the freeing of space in the broken circle around the Kremlin and Kitaigorod, for new squares at important junctions along the soon-to-be-dismantled Belgorod walls, the planting of trees in the spaces vacated by the walls, and for the building of a canal on the Moskva River. These projects had not been realized in the eighteenth century even with the formation of a special section of the original planning commission in 1790–97. No state money was allocated for the purchase of land for the new squares and the public were hostile to the prospect of massive uprooting in the central areas of the city.

Thus, by the end of the century very little had been done to change the essentially village atmosphere of Moscow and to accommodate the rapidly growing population. The misfortune of the fire was to provide the opportunity to effect most of the 1775 plan.

The Tsar himself, who was ultimately responsible for leaving the city undefended, took a personal interest in its rehabilitation. He chose William Hastie, the engineer-architect of Tsarskoe Selo, to draw up a comprehensive plan for the reconstruction of Moscow. Hastie, an obscure Scottish engineer, came to Russia in the 1780s. By 1808 he was employed by Count Rumyantsev and was responsible for some of the earliest iron bridges in St Petersburg, including the one over the Moika on the Nevsky Prospekt. His experience seems not to have included Moscow however. The best feature of Hastie's plan for the new Moscow was that it did not concentrate exclusively on the centre but included the wooden workers' suburbs that were burgeoning around the city. The weakest part of his plan was that it would have swept away the historical centre by creating long, straight, broad streets and huge squares which would have dwarfed the relatively low buildings planned for them. It would have made Moscow into a pale imitation of St Petersburg and would have entirely altered the more comfortable scale of the older city. The grounds on which the plan faltered, however, were not so much aesthetic as financial.

In September 1813 Alexander approved the Hastie plan and sent it back to the Moscow Commission for its agreement. The Commission quickly prepared a strong attack on account of the cost which it estimated at 19·5 million rubles and returned it in October to the Tsar. Meanwhile the Moscow architects were busy preparing their own scheme of repairs and rebuilding based on the natural relief and form of the city ignored by the geometrical Hastie. The new plan was firmly built on the proposals of the 1775 plan. Whereas Hastie had suggested forty-seven new squares, the Commission recommended only half that number, mainly confined to the circle around the Kremlin and Kitaigorod and at the former Belgorod wall-junctions. The proposals included the enlargement and clearing of Red Square as far as St Basil's, the enlarging of Petrov Square (later Theatre or Sverdlov Square), a large square on the eastern side of Kitaigorod extending from the Nikolskye Gate to the Varvarka (Ulitsa Razina) to be known as New Square, and a boulevard from the Varvarka to the river to be known as Kitaisky Proezd. Other new squares were to be at the Arbat, Krasnye Vorota (Lomonovsky Square) and the Taganka, and many existing squares were to be straightened. Markets were re-established at four places: Polyanskaya, Smolenskaya, Kudrinskaya and Nemetskaya Squares. It was decided to improve the area bordering the Zemlyany Val and the old Belgorod wall, to build hotels at the main junctions of the new boulevards as had been approved by Paul in 1798, and to establish houses of masonry along Zemlyany Val and on some central interconnecting streets. Both in the area formerly occupied by the Belgorod wall and the old Zemlyany Val, boulevards with trees planted in the centre of the road were to be built. The outer customs barrier, the Kamerkollezhsky Val, was to be strengthened. It was estimated that the whole plan would cost 4·8 million rubles – a quarter of the cost of the Hastie plan. Basically, the Kremlin would continue to form the centre and dominate the city; the radial-circular systems were to be unchanged; trees and greenery would spring up in place of the old fortifications; and the natural topography and history of Moscow would be retained.

The plan was ready in 1814 and the Commission's chief architect, O. I. Bove, took it to St Petersburg for the Tsar's approval. But Alexander was busy pursuing Napoleon on the road to Paris and permission for the plan was not obtained until his return in December 1815. The Commission in the meantime could only engage on restorative work in the Kremlin and Red Square and on preparing a detailed map of Moscow. However, they were very busy giving advice, helping to provide materials, and finding labour for the reconstruction of private houses which had begun immediately Moscow was reoccupied. Finally the Tsar officially approved the plan in nearly every aspect and work began at last on the general features of reconstruction. However, the construction of the large public buildings, the new boulevards, the general improvement of intersecting streets and new squares was not complete for more than a decade. As the cost was borne by the tsar, the money was not always immediately available and the work could not proceed too rapidly.

The rebuilding of private homes was a different matter, however. The homeless Muscovites returned to their city in late 1812 to ruin and desolation and had to make immediate preparations for shelter for the winter in cellars, old food stores, or anywhere that had walls and a roof. The Commission's main problems were to obtain the necessary building materials quickly and to provide labour for private rebuilding. They established brick-works, firms for obtaining building stone and for the preparation of mortar. The problem of labour supply was partly solved by the requisitioning of two battalions to assist in the building jobs. The Commission also provided interest-free loans to private persons for the rebuilding of their homes. For this they were given a fund of 5 million rubles (the loss from the fire was estimated at 270 million rubles). The loans had to be repaid within five years. In some cases the Commission purchased the house outright from the owner, repaired it and sold it again. In 1816 the Commission received 3·8 million rubles for this purpose.

Private houses were rebuilt rapidly and within five years the city had virtually replaced its residential areas. As in the past the most common building material was wood and progress in replacing masonry buildings was much slower. By 1816, when the Commission was ready to begin on the larger jobs, construction of small dwellings declined as much of the necessary rebuilding was accomplished. Between the beginning of 1813 and the end of 1815, in all 4,814 houses and outbuildings were rebuilt and 2,187 repaired. Although most of the reconstruction was in wood, the relative smallness of the number of stone houses in old Moscow meant that by 1816 72 per cent of stone houses were repaired and rebuilt while only 54 per cent of

48 Pechatny Dvor. An old seventeenth-century printing house cleverly rebuilt in 1879 after it had been largely destroyed in the 1812 fire.

wooden houses had been similarly rebuilt. The *ryady*, or rows of trading stalls within Kitaigorod where the fire had originated, were replaced very quickly. Although most were of masonry, by 1815 over 5,000 had been repaired and rebuilt.

In spite of the rapid pace of rebuilding, the ravages of the fire were evident to visitors' eyes for many years to come. In 1819 more than 300 private houses were still not rebuilt, had no fence around the ruins, and the roads in front were often in chaos. Some houses remained in ruins until the 1870s, such as the Gurev house in a prominent position on the Tverskaya, and the Vsevolozhsky house at number 7 Prechistenka (Kropotkinskaya).

The Commission occupied a commanding position throughout this rebuilding programme. Although the director was M. D. Tsitsianov, the head of the planning department, S. S. Kesarino, played the major role in formulating the plan eventually accepted by the Tsar. One of the principal characters in the Commission was Osip Ivanovich Bove, an Italian by origin who lived all his life in Russia, and who was in charge of all the architectural sub-sections. Before the fire he had been employed in the Kremlin Expedition and had imbibed the Kazakov tradition. His position meant that by 1814 he was responsible for the plans and supervision of the rebuilding of all state buildings. In addition he had a special responsibility for the façades of all buildings in Moscow, which meant that he could oversee the plans for virtually all private homes. He actually was responsible for building about 500 buildings himself.

In the summer of 1816 Alexander visited Moscow and noted the progress of reconstruction. One of his objections was to the 'coarse colours' of the new houses and suggested that in future they be painted in soft, pastel colours such as pale grey, flesh-colour, straw and pale green and that the masonry decorations be contrasted in white. This led to the commission's drawing up strict rules governing not only the colours of the houses, both private and public, but regulations concerning the façades, the size of the houses, their position vis-à-vis the street, etc. The use of green, red, cherry, dark grey and pale blue colours was expressly forbidden. Roofs were to be painted grey, green or red.

Strict directives on the main architectural features were laid down. Houses were usually of one or two stories, rarely of three and hardly ever of four. Outbuildings were always of one storey. The size of the house and number of stories was decided partly by the importance of its owners and partly by its position in the street. The Commission seems to have been anxious to achieve a city unified in both form and volume. Façades of the houses had to be chosen from a study published between 1809 and 1812, *Collection of Façades Appropriate for Private Dwellings in Towns of the Russian Empire*. As a rule private houses were divided into two groups: those with separately expressed centres where the pediments and porticos predominated, and those with flat façades where the centre was all simplicity and harmony and did not stand out from the rest of the house. Although the Commission's rules were strict, there was individuality in the way each house was built and the freshness and intrinsic harmony of this era is still a delight in some corners of Moscow like the Arbat. In the change from medieval fortress to nineteenth-century city not only were the old walls and fortifications removed but the rebuilt houses were placed squarely on the line of the streets, their gardens to the rear greatly reduced in size from those of the previous century. The Commission even laid down the measurements of windows and doors and other architectural details such as the horizontal lines that dominate the lower floors, and the loggias, and the simple mezzanines with their pediments in the central part of the façade. Occasionally stone swags, wreaths or medallions were added. Inspectors were employed to ensure that the houses were built as the regulations demanded. Whole streets and squares were built in this way. Although few survive, there are still examples in the Arbat area, such as Gagarinsky Pereulok (Ryleeva Ulitsa) and Sivtsev Vrazhek Pereulok, and in other parts of Moscow, for instance Dolgy Pereulok (Burdenko Ulitsa) and Staropimenovsky Pereulok (Medvedeva Ulitsa).

Much work had to be done in straightening the crooked little lanes and streets of the old city. However, they were not straightened arbitrarily. The principle was that they were to be straightened where it would not interfere with important masonry buildings, taking into consideration the transportation needs of the city, local relief and intersecting or alternative lanes. Streets were straightened and widened with as little expense to the state as possible so the easiest possible course was taken resulting in the attractive circular and winding streets that still prevail in some central districts of Moscow.

Public rebuilding

The first part of Moscow to be tackled after the fire was Red Square. It was very different from the Red Square of today, even after the rebuilding. New stone trading stalls had been put up in the form of a U in 1786 along the Kremlin walls opposite the place where GUM stands today. The U nearly met the corresponding U of stalls from the opposite side at their open ends, turning Red Square into a confined, enclosed courtyard. In 1813 Bove set to work estimating the damage from the fire. As it had started in the stalls, it was extensive, and Bove drew up plans for a differently organized square. He opened the square by removing the recent stalls along the Kremlin walls and rebuilding the old stalls on the east side of the square, the so-called upper, middle and lower rows descending to the Moskva River. The new building boasted a wide Doric portico and a powerful pediment and squarely faced the Senate cupola peeping over the Kremlin wall. With the removal of other buildings crowding the square the wonderful forms of St Basil's were no longer hidden. The Commission decreed that only single-storey buildings were to be allowed in the southern part of the square. However, the hill from St Basil's to the river was still crowded with buildings.

The restoration of Red Square was completed with the unveiling in 1818 of the first piece of sculpture to grace Moscow, the statue of Minin and Pozharsky, heroes of the uprising against the Polish invasion in 1612, just two hundred years before the rout of Napoleon. It originally stood in the centre of the square opposite the Senate. Executed by I. Martos it was the first monument to be financed by public subscription. The sculpture, in the classical tradition, is an attempt to depict Russia in heroic battle. Situated halfway between Bove's new trading stalls with their strong portico and shallow dome, the statue provided a vertical accent in the same way as the Nikolsky and Spassky Towers opposite did for the Kremlin.

The next square to be tackled by the Commission was Petrov, later Theatre Square (now Sverdlov Square). In 1816 with the help of Gilliardi and others, Bove laid out the square, for so long a project in the minds of the eighteenth-century planners. It was to be rectangular. Two long two-storey wings terminating in three-storey blocks

---

49 The Maly Theatre. This is the only original building left of the replanned Theatre Square after the 1812 fire.

were planned. At the head of the square, facing the Kremlin, was to be the new theatre. The burnt out Petrov Theatre was replaced in 1824 by the Bolshoi (or 'Large') Theatre designed by Andrei Mikhailov, a St Petersburg architect, in collaboration with Bove. This theatre burnt down in 1850 and was rebuilt by Kavos in 1851 since when it has not been significantly altered. The later theatre is not so fine as the 1824 building since it was changed internally by the addition of rich, elaborate decoration in the heavy neo-baroque manner of the middle of the century. The oppressive red velvet and gold mouldings date from this time. In the Mikhailov-Bove building Ionic columns were used, the walls were plain except for the rusticated ground floor, and the central part of the building with its hipped roof displayed a niche in which a statue of Apollo and his horses sat. Now Apollo rides free and the simplicity of the exterior wall has been lost. In 1826 a fountain was placed in front of the Bolshoi in line with its axis to the Kremlin. This was later enhanced by a charming sculpture of playing cherubs by Vitali. (In 1961 a sculpture of Karl Marx was placed in front of the fountain.) The Maly (or 'Small') Theatre is the only original building to have survived from Bove's plan of Petrov Square.

The general scheme continued providing a threshold approach to the Kremlin and Kitaigorod on Red Square, Theatre Square and the spaces later to be created by forcing the Neglinnaya River underground. The Pashkov House, the University and the Nobles' Club were already in existence and orientated towards the Kremlin in a majestic arc. Their repair and restoration, especially that of the badly damaged University building, was put in hand.

The task of restoring the damaged University building was given to Domenico Gilliardi, son of Giovanni, the Italian architect who designed the Marinsky Hospital. He retained Kazakov's basic U-shaped plan as favoured by the late eighteenth century, but altered the exterior significantly. Gilliardi exchanged the light Ionic portico of the Kazakov building for heavier Doric columns, raised the height of the building 6 metres by adding an attic and completed it by a broad cupola, crushing the pediment. In the central portico, where the pilasters of Kazakov dividing the wall into vertical sections had been removed, he also placed bas-reliefs depicting the achievements of Russian education. In effect he altered the University by making it a more monumental public building situated in a commanding position. In 1835 Y. D. Tyurin added the attractive rotunda of the University chapel, St Theresa, with its fine wrought-iron railings. It is now used as the University club. The University library built up with the aid of the wealthy Demidov family was lost in the fire but by 1835 it has been replenished and contained 30,000 volumes. In the same year the University had over 500 students and five faculties including the physical, mathematical and medical sciences, and twenty-eight professors.

In 1821–23 Bove planned and executed the lovely Alexandrov Gardens by the Kremlin wall in the now empty bed of the Neglinnaya, which had been placed in the underground pipes while Gilliardi was rebuilding the University. The first public garden in Moscow with its fine iron gate by E. Pascal still enhances what is now Revolution Square. (A second set of gates opposite Herzen Street was removed in 1935.)

Alexander also left his imprint on this part of Moscow. Deciding to visit the city in the autumn of 1817, the Tsar proposed in the spring of that year that an exercise house or *manège* should be built in which a whole troop of infantry could manoeuvre. By June A. A. Betancourt, in charge of communications and public buildings in St Petersburg, submitted a plan which was approved. General L. L. Carbonnier undertook its execution, choosing the site opposite the Kremlin on the west side near the University. Alexander requested that the building be completed by 1 October 1817. The interior space was to measure 166 metres by 45 metres without the support of any sort of pillar. To support the roof, long wooden struts were placed across the width of the building but these proved too weak and in 1824 the roof had to be completely rebuilt. After frantic activity the building was officially opened in the presence of the Tsar on 30 November 1817 only one month later than the Tsar had ordered. However, the exterior was not properly finished and in 1824–5 Bove, now the city architect, had the building plastered and mouldings made. In spite of representations by the Governor of Moscow he refused to add any sort of decoration or sculpture to the large pediments to the west and east, partly because he believed the University should dominate the square.

The completion of the *manège*, the rebuilding of the University and the laying out of the Alexandrov Gardens imprinted on this part of Moscow the late Russian Empire classical style not to be found elsewhere in the city.

The conclusion of the magnificent achievement of rebuilding the burnt-out city was marked by the erection of the Triumphal Gate (1827–34) designed by Bove. The gate was to commemorate the 1812 'Fatherland' war and was to act as a ceremonial entry into Moscow from the St Petersburg road. It stood on the Leningradsky Prospekt until it was dismantled in the 1930s and was a great arch of brick, stone and iron. Columns cut into the body of the structure bear bas-reliefs surmounted by iron sculptures at the arch depicting Glory facing St Peter. The sculptures were made from drawings by Bove and were executed by Timofeyev and Vitali. The gate was re-erected in 1968 on the main road to Kiev in connection with the setting up of the Kutuzov museum, along the axis by which Napoleon had first approached Moscow and then departed from it.

3 MOSCOW REBUILT: THE CULMINATION OF THE CLASSICAL ERA

Bove, like Kazakov, seems to have been endowed with great energy. Besides being responsible on the Commission for virtually all the rebuilt houses and buildings, new squares and street improvements, he designed and built many private houses. One, the Gagarin House on Novinsky Boulevard (now Chaikovsky Street) was considered his best work, similar to the early Bolshoi, but sadly it was one of the few buildings in Moscow to disappear during the short German bombardment of the Second World War.

Bove also repaired and redesigned another house belonging to the Gagarin family, originally designed by Kazakov in the late eighteenth century, on the Boulevard where it meets the Petrovka. He rebuilt it as the Catherine Hospital. It had been used for some years as the English Club and had been badly damaged in the fire (Stendhal speaks of having been billeted there until the fire came too close). Of particular note is a splendid Ionic dodecastyle portico over the central wing which is unique in Moscow.

Bove was the architect too of the First City Hospital built between 1828 and 1833 on Bolshaya Kaluzhskaya Ulitsa (Leninsky Prospekt). This part of the city was still dacha country in the early nineteenth century although Kazakov had also built the Golitsyn Hospital there. Bove's hospital is one of his best works; hidden behind the trees of a broad front garden, the long body of the building, its Ionic octastyle portico and typically fine moulding of the frieze give it a gracious and peaceful character.

Bove also completed the lovely church originally designed by Bazhenov, the Vsekh Skorbyashchikh (All Sorrowing) on the Ordynka in 1833. This functioning church, with rounded lines and light interior, is utterly different from the traditional dark and cloistered Russian churches of earlier times that still predominated in Moscow.

Domenico Gilliardi, the restorer of the University, and Afanasii Gregorievich Grigoriev were two other principal architects of this late classical era. One of Gilliardi's more important buildings was the Opekunsky Soviet, the loan bank responsible for financing the Foundling Home. It was built in 1823–26 on the

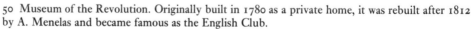

50 Museum of the Revolution. Originally built in 1780 as a private home, it was rebuilt after 1812 by A. Menelas and became famous as the English Club.

Solyanka next to the Foundling Home and was designed to blend cleverly with the latter's long, austere lines. (It is now used by the Academy of Medical Sciences.) The central façade with its light columns, pediment and wide decorative cupola succeeds in lightening the more severe lines of the Home. In addition to charging interest for loans the Opekunsky Soviet held a monopoly on the sale and manufacture of playing cards, received 10 per cent of the receipts from plays, concerts and public baths, and the income from taxes on navigation in the Moskva River and from the sale of ice for the cold cellars. This money was needed to support the 20,000 children in care at the Foundling Home or fostered out in the countryside. No children were turned away. They were received at all hours of the day or night, vaccinated, fed, washed and given a bed. Indigent parents who wanted to bring up their own children at home were granted a small sum for their board and the opportunity to have them educated at the Home later on. They were taught languages, history, geography, physics and maths, and the girls also received instruction in music, dancing and needlework. The boys could enter military or civil service and the girls could become midwives, governesses or housekeepers.

Attractive large houses called *osobnyak*, smaller than the mansions of a half century earlier, were springing up around the newly laid out circular main roads, the former Zemlyany Val (now the Garden Ring Road) and the inner ring of handsomely laid-out boulevards. Gilliardi built some of these like the Lunin House, number 12 on Nikitsky (now Suvorov) Boulevard, and the impressive Usachevykh (later Naidyonov) Estate, of 1829–31, on the Garden Ring Road. The latter is now used as a sanatorium called Vysokie Gory or High Hills. Overlooking the Yauza River from a height, the house faced the Garden Ring Road and behind it a lovely park with pavilions was laid out descending to the banks of the river. Although confined by the strict regulations of the Commission, Gilliardi managed to create an estate and house of great individuality. Unusually, the front and rear entrances both received equally elaborate attention. The main part of the house fronting the Garden Ring Road bore the customary portico put behind, at the entrance to the garden, Gilliardi placed a magnificent staircase leading from the first floor. A vase-lined walk culminated in a doorway flanked by massive Doric columns distyle in antis (two circular pillars between two square piers) within a niche with a richly decorated architrave and a tympanum over. The complicated effect of light and shade caused by the arched niche and entranceway breaks up the bareness of the stark walls with their wreath medallions. The main garden situated behind the house is bounded by outbuildings, and beyond them a green park descends to the river. Gilliardi seems to have excelled in laying out parks and pavilions. Among the latter was a semi-circular Tea House at the Naidyonov Estate with rich but finely sculptured ornamentation.

The *proviantskie sklady* or official store-houses cannot be ignored at the boulevard end of Metrostroevskaya (formerly Ostozhenka) Street on Krymsky Square. This humble building, built in the 1830s by F. M. Shestakov from a design by V. P.

Stasov, epitomizes the late classical style. It has a simple and powerful form, each of the three buildings that constitute the whole is modestly sized, and the usual columns are absent. But this plainness is wonderfully relieved by fine architraves to the doors, surmounted by large lunettes, by stone wreaths and by a Doric frieze. Across from the *sklady* at number 49 is a modest, wooden, late classical house of the gentry, a typical example of the sort of building that dominated Moscow after the fire.

Although Moscow completely adopted the late classical or Russian Empire style, it continued to retain its own character and kept its identity quite separate from that of St Petersburg. In St Petersburg in the early part of the century almost the entire centre was rebuilt, chiefly by Karl Rossi. The new state buildings were carefully harmonized with entire complexes of streets and squares. Although a certain harmony was achieved, in Moscow the strict unity of form and style that so severely created the St Petersburg personality was missing. Great houses still stood beside less pretentious ones, and gardens were still placed behind the houses. Moscow's buildings and houses remained less monumental than St Petersburg's more important government buildings and despite efforts to regulate it after the fire, its architecture remained colourful and diverse. This impression was heightened by the survival of the distinctive old stone churches, which were carefully restored after the fire and still form the chief feature on the skyline.

In both cities sculpture came to play an increasingly important role in squares and prominent buildings. In Moscow sculpture provided the focal point for new squares like Red Square and Theatre Square.

The great central markets had been rebuilt and were again bustling with commerce. In a city of over 300,000 inhabitants where there were few shops, the markets were of central importance. The main market was on Red Square, the great hall of the upper trading rows rebuilt by Bove between the Nikolskoye (25th October Street) and the Ilinka (Kuibyshev Street). Here there were stalls or 'rows' of fruiterers, tobacconists, knife-grinders, saddlers, boot-makers, bell-founders, cloth-makers, coachman's tailors, cup-makers, bast shoemakers, ironmongers, trunk-makers, thread-mercers, furriers, lace-makers, silversmiths and chandlers. In the middle or new trading rows between the Ilinka and the Varvarka (Ulitsa Razina) one could buy wooden vessels, leather, needles, drugs, looking-glasses, wine and brandy, locks, fruit, wax, crystal, silk, honey and fish. The lower trading rows between the Varvarka and the river sold seed, bags, fish, honey, leather, hides, meat, oil and fishmeal.

The Marquis de Custine, a French aristocrat and intrepid traveller, paid a visit to Russia in 1839. His journals contain a fascinating account of the perils of travelling to that country in the reign of Nicholas I. In fact some of his comments might not seem out-of-date to a modern traveller to the Soviet Union. Having been advised by the Tsar to visit Moscow, he gives an ecstatic description of the city as it is seen from a distance, then a more realistic account as it came more clearly into focus:

A multitude of bell-towers shone above the dust of the road and the mass of the city disappeared under this swirling cloud. . . . The low houses still remained hidden in the undulations of the earth, while the airy spires of the churches, the bizarre shapes of the towers, of the palaces and the old convents already attracted my eyes like a fleet at anchor of which one can make out only the masts soaring into the sky. . . . But I have not yet told you what is most singular in the appearance of the Russian churches – their mysterious domes are, so to speak, armoured, so elaborate is the work on their covering. One would say it is like damascened armour, and one is left speechless with astonishment in seeing this multitude of roofs shining in the sun – tooled, scaly, enamelled, bespangled, zebra-striped, streaked by bands and paints of diverse colours, but always very lively and very brilliant. . . . Picture for yourself rich tapestries spread from top to bottom the length of the most outstanding edifices of a city whose masses of architecture stand out against the water-green background of the solitary countryside.

As the Marquis drew closer, however, his tone changed:

'But at three quarters of a league from the entrance to the city the prestige vanishes . . . the disenchantment constantly increases, to such an extent that on entering Moscow one ends by no longer believing what one has perceived from a distance . . . it is a vast commercial city, hilly, dusty, badly paved, poorly constructed. . . .

51 The fashionable Tverskoi Boulevard from a nineteenth-century lithograph.

Nevertheless, he concludes:

It is the most picturesque of all the cities of the Empire, and the Empire continues to recognize it as the capital in spite of the almost supernatural efforts of the Tsar Peter and his successors. . . .

In spite of the apparent reinforcement of autocracy in Alexander's reign, the effect of the Napoleonic wars was to create a situation in which thoughts of reform and liberal ideas became widespread, particularly among the young officers. De Custine aptly remarked: 'One word of truth hurled into Russia is like a spark landing in a keg of gunpowder.' The guards officers in Alexander's army were the sons of the eighteenth-century rationalists. They differed in that their travels across Europe and their lengthy sojourn in Paris had given them experience of more enlightened societies at first hand. These wealthy and aristocratic officers noticed that even Poland and Finland had their own constitutions, that nowhere was autocracy so unremittingly entrenched as in Russia. On their return they formed secret societies, debating clubs where the subject was the reform of the state. The St Petersburg club was led by representatives of the most respected noble families – Prince Sergei Trubetskoi, Colonel Pestel, the brothers Muravyov. In 1822 it became known as the Northern Society when Pestel moved to the Ukraine to set up the Southern Society. Although there were differences on such issues as whether to form a republic or a constitutional monarchy, the groups eventually agreed to assassinate the Tsar in May 1826 when he was to attend a troop review in the south. But the Tsar died on 1 December 1825. His death precipitated a constitutional crisis as the heir, Constantine, had renounced his claim to the throne. Hurriedly the society set about trying to organize a *coup*. They decided to mount their opposition the day the soldiers were to take their oath of allegiance to Nicholas, the Tsar's younger brother and next in line after Constantine, but the plot was defeated by treachery and a collapse in the rebels' morale. When the moment came, some of the officers on Senate Square in St Petersburg neglected to give the order to charge. For six hours insurgent and loyal troops faced each other until finally Nicholas had cannon turned on the mutineers. Five people were sentenced to death and over a hundred exiled to Siberia. All mention of the plot was kept out of the newspapers; however, not only was it not forgotten, but it later served to inspire the Nihilists, Populists, Anarchists, and, finally, the Marxists. For the immediate future, though, the Decembrists' rebellion ushered in a reign of even harsher state control and unremitting autocracy.

4 THE DECLINE OF CLASSICAL ARCHITECTURE AND RISE OF ECLECTICISM

Even before the Commission for the Rebuilding of Moscow ceased its activities in 1842 the purity of the classical style had been eroded. Bove, who died in 1832, just missed witnessing how the Greek Revival began to be corrupted by the indiscriminate addition of other styles. Gradually a more colourful mixture of styles came to be preferred to the cold academic discipline of the classicist. One of the first examples of the change was in the work of Yevgraf Dmitrievich Tyurin (1792–1870). As the designer of the Cathedral Bogoyavlenie v Yelokhove (1837–45) – the Epiphany Cathedral, now the main cathedral in Moscow – he was persuaded by church officials to add five cupolas instead of the single classical dome he favoured. This produced a confusion of styles between the upper and lower parts of the church. The age of eclecticism had arrived. Even a classicist such as Tyurin could not withstand the onslaught and as a consequence the aesthetic quality of his work and that of his fellow architects declined precipitately.

The debasement of the classical style coincided with increased repression in the latter part of Nicholas I's reign, and the imposition of strict censorship especially in relation to the arts. He was a harsh ruler. Although capital punishment had been abolished in Elizabeth's time, official knouting and whipping still led to many deaths. One of Nicholas's cruellest acts was the mock execution of Dostoevsky and his collaborators in 1849. He established the notorious Third Department responsible for internal affairs which was to provide the model for the Okhrana, the Cheka, MGB and KGB, the secret police of the twentieth century. When the interests of such an insensitive, autocratic man focused on architecture, the results were not happy. The Tsar himself took a personal hand in fostering the rise of the spurious 'Russo-Byzantine' manner. Architects were thus officially encouraged to mix disonant styles regardless of the incongruities.

Mikhail Dorimedontovich Bykovsky (1801–85) was one of the leading architects who began to combine opposing styles voluntarily. He invented an original pseudo-gothic and an unusual form of the Renaissance mode. In 1831 he rebuilt an estate at Marfino near Moscow in a pseudo-gothic style, the house resembling a romantic castle. In Moscow he was responsible for the rose-coloured bell-tower and walls of the Strastnoi (Passion) Convent (1849–55), a dry, uninspired application of Renaissance architecture. The still extant Ivanovsky Convent in Khokhlovsky Pereulok between Bogdan Khmelnitsky and the Solyanka is also by Bykovsky and illustrates perhaps more than the Strastnoi Convent the heaviness and lack of proportion that characterize his work.

Architectural standards declined rapidly, as is shown by the restoration of the Bolshoi Theatre by A. K. Kavos in 1856. The result, the building that is still with us today, is poorer than the original Bolshoi executed only twenty-five years earlier both externally and in the heavily gilded and over-luxurious interior.

The turbulent history of the building of the special monument to honour the war of 1812 demonstrates the move away from classical forms and the resounding victory of eclecticism. As early as December 1812, Alexander, then in Vilnius, issued a special manifesto announcing his intention to build a memorial church in Moscow; a

52 The Romanov Palace after its restoration by F. F. Richter in 1859.

few months later a competition for the best design was held. In 1815 Alexander personally selected the winning entry, a design by a young artist of Swedish origin, Alexander Laurentievich Vitberg. Vitberg had a mystical view of Christianity and this was what he hoped to express in the huge church. Of the three enormous tiers, the lowest part was to be a rectangular basilica in the shape of a coffin below ground containing monuments and inscriptions in memory of those who died in 1812 with a portal of great Egyptian columns; the second to be above ground in the form of a gigantic Greek cross with statutes of Old Testament personalities and the history of the evangelists and apostles; and the third to rise from the centre of the cross in the form of a mighty cylinder, the church of the spirit, of peace and eternity, at its summit a colossal cupola. The Tsar was by this time also interested in mysticism and for this reason may have found Vitberg's design appealing. At first Vitberg thought the best location for the monument would be in the Kremlin but he finally decided that the Sparrow Hills (Lenin Hills) would be more appropriate.

On 12 October 1817 a grand earth-turning ceremony was staged in the Sparrow Hills reminiscent of the elaborate inauguration of the similarly ill-fated Bazhenov Kremlin palace in 1775 that was also never completed. The Vitberg church was an extremely complicated building made more difficult by the fact that Vitberg, an artist with no previous architectural experience whatsoever, continually altered the plans and supplied unsatisfactory measurements. Quarrels with the Building Commission, the vast expense of the building (he had been granted 24,000 rubles to do the job), and unfortunate misappropriations added other complications. After

Alexander's death in 1826, the whole matter of the monument was reviewed. In 1827 the Senate ordered all work to cease and Vitberg was brought to trial for misappropriations and bad management. In 1835 he was exiled to Vyatka for ten years where the sympathetic Herzen, also in exile, found him living in extreme poverty and shared quarters with him for two years. Herzen argued in his memoirs that Vitberg had suffered a great injustice, that his vision had been immense and that political changes had caused his downfall.

With the abandonment of the Vitberg plan, the idea of a national monument to celebrate the defeat of Napoleon fell into abeyance. However, it was not forgotten and Nicholas I managed to find an architect who was able to reflect his own views precisely. This was Konstantin Andreevich Ton (1794–1881), who by the 1830s had firmly rejected classical architecture and was intent on reintroducing traditional Russian forms.

In the Simonov Monastery he built a huge bell-tower eighty-five metres high in imitation of Ivan Veliky (1835–39, no longer extant). It was admired in official quarters where the formula 'autocracy, orthodoxy, nationality' had become the motto of the reign. Ton's architecture seemed to the Tsar to be the concrete form of these ideas and he became the executor of the architectural style of Nicholas I. He ignored all the logic of previous architectural experience by borrowing indiscriminately from every period of Russian architecture and superimposed on buildings that bore the classical cube the styles and façades of the seventeenth,

53 The Simonov Monastery on the outskirts of Moscow as it appeared in 1829.

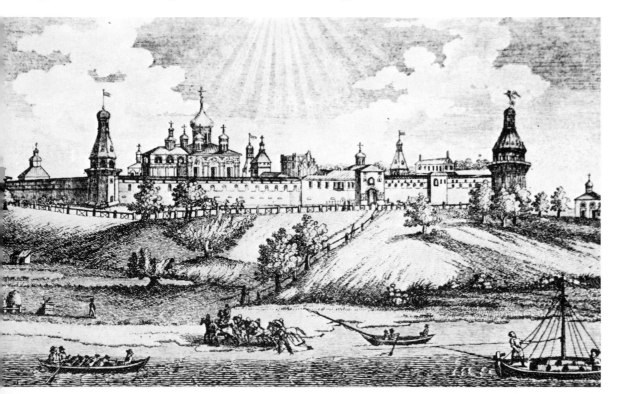

sixteenth and fifteenth centuries, in complete disregard of the practical use for which the styles had originally evolved. One of Ton's first official commissions was the designing of a set number of churches in the pseudo-Russian manner which royal decree determined were to be the model for all new churches in Russia.

But the outstanding example of the basic confusion of Ton's work was the monument to the 1812 victory. It was his largest creation, an overpowering edifice eventually called the Cathedral of Christ the Redeemer. This huge church was essentially a cube bearing an enormous cupola on four massive piers with bell-towers at each corner. The many buildings of the Alekseevsky Monastery to the west of the Kremlin were entirely removed so as to clear a site of four hectares to make space for the monument. So much material and labour was required that it took forty-three years to build and had to be financed by public subscription. Although capable of holding 10,000 people it was built in a style that had been used in the past for the small intimate medieval churches. When it was finally finished in 1880 the huge church appeared lugubrious and depressingly heavy, vastly dwarfing buildings for some distance around, its scale entirely out of place. Viewed with the Kremlin in the background, it was a grotesque overstatement against the graceful group of churches and cathedrals within the Kremlin walls. The cathedral was blown up in 1934.

Nicholas was more at ease in Moscow than St Petersburg and decided to build a modern palace in the long empty Kremlin. As court architect Ton received the commission for the Kremlin Great Palace, the spiritual successor to the abandoned Bazhenov palace.

The palace was built in 1838–49 adjacent to the traditional site where Russian tsars and grand princes had placed their residences since the fourteenth century. The huge new palace included between its two wings the long body of the old Terem palace of the seventeenth century and contained within its courtyard the oldest church in the Kremlin, the Spas na Boru or Saviour in the Pine Forest (removed in the early 1930s). Nicholas destroyed one charming building in the realization of the project: the lovely Rastrelli palace known as the Winter Palace, built for the Empress Elizabeth in 1758. It had been badly damaged during the Napoleonic invasion but had then been carefully restored.

The new palace was replete with bastardized forms of ancient Russian and Byzantine styles. The late classical style is evident in the large, single foundation-block but borrowings from the seventeenth century are found in the impression of graduated tiers (there is really only one upper floor), in the high pitched roof, the arcaded front of the lower floor, and the decorative window architraves. The lower floor contained Nicholas's personal apartments – sitting rooms, bedrooms, study, etc. – and the upper floor contained the reception halls named after the grand orders of the Russian Empire: Georgievsky, Yekaterinsky, Vladimirsky, Alexandrovsky and Andreevsky. The Georgievsky or St George's Hall was the largest and was used as the principal reception room. V. V. Stasov, the archeologist and critic and son of

54 View westwards from the Kremlin with the huge edifice of the Cathedral of Christ the Redeemer (1838–1880) in the background.

the architect, wrote contemptuously about the palace: 'The new palace in the Kremlin is also a multi-million-ruble loss, precisely in the same manner as the Cathedral of Christ the Redeemer. It displays a great amount of richness, a mechanical repetition of aspects of folk-lore on the outside, and no evidence of a sincere feeling for Russian national architecture, no evidence of real talent.'

Russia was not alone in moving away from classicism. In Europe the great debate between the rival merits of classical architecture and Gothic was raging. The difference was that in Moscow the classical era had received an unexpected boost near the end of its sway with the almost complete rebuilding of the city after the fire. Once this had been achieved, there was an about-turn to more grotesque forms. In Europe and especially in England the adoption of neo-Gothic forms was carefully considered, whether Perpendicular or Early English, thirteenth-century or fourteenth-century. The architects there had deeper archeological studies behind them and a greater knowledge of the use to which these forms had originally been put than their Russian counterparts. The latter struggled with the then unknown and completely unresearched country of traditional Russian architecture where no distinction was made between the fifteenth-century and utterly different seventeenth-century styles. When a movement was made away from neo-Gothic to an adoption of Renaissance and baroque forms in Europe it was done with knowledge and confidence. In Russia at this time the styles were more crudely mixed and the results less successful.

5 INDUSTRIAL GROWTH AND LACK OF DIRECTION IN ARCHITECTURE

The second half of the nineteenth century was ushered in by the accession in 1855 of Alexander II and the optimism aroused by his efforts to reform the more despotic aspects of government. His most important change was to free the serfs in 1861, but he also sponsored reform of local government, autonomy of the universities, reform of military service and trial by jury. On the same day that he signed the decree setting up a representative assembly, 1 March 1881, the People's Will, the anarchist group, finally succeeded in assassinating him. The decree establishing the assembly was never implemented, and his other reforms with the exception of emancipation of the serfs regrettably fell into abeyance. The hopes generated by his reign were quickly stamped out by the rule of Alexander III.

In the course of the nineteenth century, particularly in the latter half, a profound industrial revolution took place in Russia. Although production of heavy industry increased at a steady pace, the expansion of light industries, particularly cotton textiles and sugar-refining, was phenomenal. Agriculture did not in general share in the boom and in some areas virtually stagnated causing peasant unrest everywhere. In the cities increased demand for labour led to the rapid expansion of their population and by 1862 the population of St Petersburg exceeded that of Moscow for the first time. In the country as a whole between 1804 and 1860 the number of those involved in hired labour increased 8·6 times. Between the end of the eighteenth century and 1862 the population of Moscow had increased by 115 per cent to reach nearly 400,000. But between 1862 and 1897, when the value of industrial production increased by over 300 per cent, the population of Moscow more than doubled and by the end of the century exceeded one million. By that time the economy had begun to diversify and the textile and sugar factories no longer held the pre-eminent position. This tremendous expansion led to a corresponding rush of building activity that exceeded even the exceptional construction period in Moscow after the 1812 fire.

With the increasing industrialization of Moscow came the railways. The first line was the route to St Petersburg which was arbitrarily designed by Nicholas I with the help of a ruler and which even incorporated the three kinks where his fingers extended on the map. The journey to St Petersburg was cut to 18 hours, compared with 48 in Peter the Great's time. The first railway station, now the Leningrad Station, was designed by Ton in a restrained mixture of styles. Other railways quickly followed, speeding up the communications network with other cities and changing the nature of Moscow by making possible the growth of suburbs at some distance from the centre.

In 1900 a circular railway was built around Moscow. Kitaigorod, once the market of Moscow, became the centre of financial, banking and trading institutions and the suburbs were transformed from the villages they resembled into factory blocks and worker's quarters.

During the reign of Alexander 11 censorship and harassment of the arts eased, literature and music blossomed and the art of painting slowly began to emerge from the doldrums. Architecture on the other hand was still confused and directionless and remained so throughout the rest of the century.

In contrast to the single-minded discipline of the past, particularly in the classical period, several trends now pervaded architecture simultaneously. Many new kinds of buildings were required owing to the constant demands of the new industries, of the rapidly growing population, and of Alexander's social reforms. They were built in the prevailing international style, a sort of pseudo-Renaissance, their façades bearing no relation to the use to which the building was put. Examples include the central bank on Neglinnaya, and the Sandunovsky baths. Railway stations, offices,

55 Veznesensky (Ascension) Convent in the Kremlin. Neogothic features added 1817. (See page 146.)

large factories, hotels, special educational institutions and, for the first time, blocks of flats were needed and were put up in numbers, their façades masking the innovatory interiors. A spinal corridor lit from skylights or through several passageways was introduced for schools, banks, offices and shops. New apartment houses were built hurriedly to cater for the rapid influx of the population into the cities, the more exclusive of them lavish and ornate, resembling the old mansions of the previous century. Because of the use of iron new buildings could be erected without many heavy supports, windows could be larger and walls could be thinner, but it was some time before architects took advantage of these possibilities. Although the internal core of the building was heavily masked by the external attempt to resemble the palaces of the past, by the end of the century reinforced concrete came gradually into use, as it did in Europe and America. Along with these social and technical changes introduced slowly throughout the second half of the century the economics of a building became more important than its architectural merit. Because of this development the important buildings of the past, the palaces, churches and large estates, suffered a decline. The large houses of even fifty years ago were no longer so convenient and were giving way to the smaller, more comfortable *osobnyak* as people, no longer so wealthy, kept fewer servants. The large palaces came to be used for museums and institutions like the Rumyantsev Museum housed in the Pashkov House and the Duma in St Petersburg which held its meetings in the old Tauride Palace. The old architectural concepts and even the language formerly used to describe buildings were inadequate for the new architectural types.

The anarchy and capriciousness prevailing in architecture in these years is clearly shown in the following examples of two houses belonging to rich and eccentric merchants. On Ulitsa Kalinina, number 16 once belonged to A. A. Morozov, a member of one of the principal merchant families in Moscow. Built in 1894 to give the appearance of a sixteenth-century castle he saw and admired during a visit to Spain, it looks most incongruous on the streets of Moscow. However, like other buildings of this era the exterior belies the interior. The resemblance to a fortified castle extends only to the view from the street and the interior is organized in the usual manner of a large house of this time. (It is now used as the headquarters of the Friendship Societies with Foreign Countries.) Number 19 Ulitsa Kirova is in the same genre. Once the headquarters of the tea business of S. V. Perlov, the entire façade was rebuilt in 1896 in the Chinese style when the young Chinese Regent was expected in Moscow for the coronation of Nicholas II. However, the Regent disappointed Mr Perlov greatly by choosing to reside with his chief competitor, also called Perlov, on Meshchanskaya Street.

The great achievements in town planning that had taken place in Moscow in the first half of the century were not irretrievably lost in the welter of new building. Central control had entirely given way in the face of the wishes of private owners and firms, influenced by the fashion for eclecticism in western Europe. Even the largest

56 Battlement of the Morozov House, built in 1894 by V. Mazyrin in the style of a Spanish castle. Now used as the headquarters of the Friendship Societies with Foreign Countries.

buildings were not subject to building or planning controls and because the vogue was for originality differences were encouraged. Many buildings belonging to the classical period were pulled down or rebuilt in the new spirit of diversity and Moscow lost that sense of unity that had been so important a part of the city in the eighteenth and early nineteenth centuries.

The development of the pseudo-Russian style begun by Ton and Bykovsky continued unabated during the second half of the nineteenth century. Ancient motifs were imposed on the three- or four-storey regular cube-shaped buildings inherited from the classical era. Their derivation and meaning was completely lost in the arbitrary way they were placed about the surface and in the way in which they were translated into stone or brick when originally they had developed in wood. The Polytechnic Museum is one of the earliest of these large buildings. Built between 1875 and 1877 by I. Monigetti and N. Shokhin in response to a new awareness of the

57 GUM, formerly the Upper and Middle Trading Rows, now the State Universal Store. Built by A. Pomerantsov, 1888.

need for museums and finally finished in 1905–7, Russo-Byzantine forms are easily apparent on the façade. The building itself seems to be more like a palace than a museum. Another pseudo-Russian example was the building of the Upper and Middle Trading Rows, now known as GUM, designed by A. Pomerantsev in 1888 to replace the Bove building housing the old trading rows. The exterior decoration is a mechanical copy of the forms on the churches and palaces of Rostov Veliky and Borisoglebsk. However, if the exterior decoration is contrived the interior is admirably organized. The three main corridors well lit from the skylights above serve as avenues off which a multitude of small stalls are situated on two floors, or rather the ground floor and a mezzanine, for the central space is left clear for the light

to enter from the roof and shine on the fountains at the bottom. GUM was one of the first buildings in Moscow to incorporate the use of steel and glass in the roofing. The History Museum designed by V. O. Sherwood and Semyonov between 1878 and 1883 at the end of Red Square – like the former City Duma, now the Lenin Museum, around the corner – illustrates even more dramatically the basic contradictions of the Polytechnic Museum and GUM. The interior is rationally laid out and great attention is paid to lighting from the large windows but again the exterior is too detailed, too replete with towers and octagons. It appears as an unsuccessful adaptation of medieval Russian motifs, perhaps in an attempt by the architects to reflect the glory of St Basil's opposite.

58 Lenin Museum, built in 1890–92 as the City Duma by D. Chichagov borrowing indiscriminately from medieval Russian styles.

The adaptation of the pseudo-Russian style went even further than these somewhat absurd buildings which might not have been out of place in Victorian England in spite of their Russian characteristics. The Igumnov House at number 43 Bolshaya Yakimanka (Ulitsa Dmitrova), now the building of the French Embassy, demonstrates the increasingly fantastic element in the reign of the pseudo-Russian style. Designed by N. Pozdeyev and built in 1896, it is heavy and asymmetrical, with differing roof sizes and odd porches, complete with hanging arches and every kind of florid decoration. An amalgam of every seventeenth-century palace, it is so grotesque as to be almost charming. P. I. Shchukin's house on Malaya Gruzinskaya, used by the owner as a museum for his collection of Russian artifacts, resembles the Igumnov House in the fantasy of its execution (it is now the residence of the German ambassador).

59 The Igumnov House, now the French Embassy, built by N. I. Pozdeyev, 1896.

The architects of the new railway stations that were springing up around Moscow also shared in the enthusiasm for ancient Russian architecture. The results of their work still endow the grey streets of Moscow with an aura of whimsy a bit like Disneyland. Aleksei Viktorovich Shchusev, a most versatile architect who was to figure prominently in the Soviet period, was the designer of the Kazan Station, one of three on Komsomol'skaya Square. Although built in 1912–26, it is a typical late manifestation of the pseudo-Russian style. The strange and colourful features of the station are like the giant tower of a wedding cake encrusted with replicas of familiar forms: arches, *nalichniki*, a clock-tower, pitched roofs, and even a model of the Siumbeki Tower in Kazan. Again, although its function, as with GUM and the History Museum, is so well hidden behind the extravagant façade, it is well served by the rational lay-out of a large railway station.

6 MOSCOW AT THE END OF THE NINETEENTH CENTURY

The salient features of life in Moscow just before the turmoils that were to overwhelm the citizens of the twentieth century still depended upon the layers of society clearly defined by the old hierarchy of ranks. They loosely comprised the nobility, the gentry, the merchants who belonged to one of two guilds and were predominantly Old Believers, and the most numerous group of all, the workers, for whom the only legal associations were sick-benefit funds. Moscow was still a city dominated by its churches. Although the Muscovites were not a particularly pious people, religious services and religious holidays, of which there were nearly a hundred a year, were an essential part of life. Indeed, for the workers toiling for $11\frac{1}{2}$ hours a day (10 on Saturday) the numerous holidays were a welcome relief. The many workshops scattered around the industrial suburbs were dismal affairs, dirty, damp and very dark; as yet the climate and heating problems precluded more generous use of glass. There had been some progress in labour legislation: children under twelve could not be employed, women could not work at night, in factories of more than 100 workers employers had to provide medical services. But the miserable conditions of the workers was scandalous. Although conditions of industrial workers the world over at the turn of the century were far from ideal, in Moscow they were made that much more pitiful by the terrible housing which workers and their families were forced to accept. Many worked, slept and ate in the workshops themselves – foul-smelling and dirty tanneries, mills, small dye-works or woollen-factories. Others were allocated bunks in dormitories put up by employers near the factories. No rent was charged but these civilian barracks quickly became overcrowded, specially when the worker, usually a peasant, brought his family from the country to join him. Here there was no private life or modesty; in fact, in some cases the bunks were used on a shift system. Industrial workers were carefully controlled and had to carry internal passports and employment documents. However, one custom still united all Muscovites. Regardless of rank the entire population partook in the ritual weekly excursion, usually on Saturday night, to the steam baths, an established Russian custom for many centuries. The more well-to-do rented private rooms and the ordinary people used the large communal bath. Little birch twigs bundled together were bought at the door and people beat themselves to cleanse the innermost pores. In spite of the universal prevalence of bathrooms nowadays Moscow citizens still cherish their weekly steam bath.

The famous markets of Moscow still handled most of the retail trade. Trubnaya Square on Sundays was filled with the noise of the central pet market, where it was the custom to purchase caged birds in order to set them free. The birds, tamed by their owner, simply flew back to their cages where they were kept until the next unsuspecting citizen appeared. Equally well-known was the Khitrov Market in eastern Moscow where the Boulevard meets the Yauza. It was famous as a dangerous den of thieves and murderers and Gorky drew extensively upon it in his play *The Lower Depths*. Drunkenness in Moscow was a major problem, although, as in earlier centuries, the state held the monopoly on the sale and manufacture of vodka. Then as now, many policemen constantly patrolled the streets, and a careful check was kept on the comings and goings of guests at inns and hotels.

Thus at the start of the twentieth century, the city faced many social and planning problems that would eventually have to be tackled.

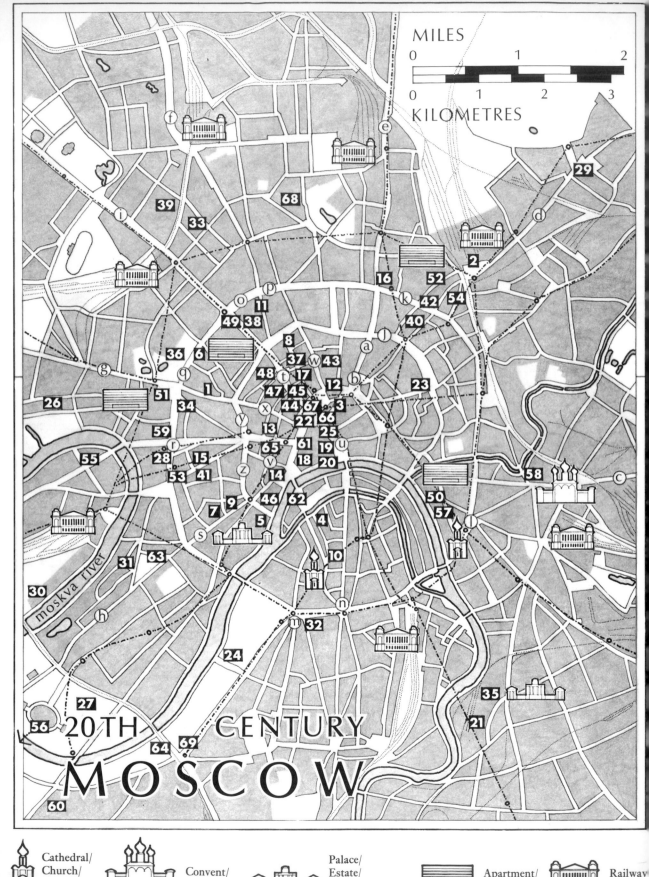

MILES

0 1 2

0 1 2 3

KILOMETRES

20TH CENTURY

MOSCOW

Cathedral/
Church/
Chapel

Convent/
Monastery

Palace/
Estate/
Mansion/House

Apartment/
Hotel

Railway
station

moskva river

5 The Tumult of the Twentieth Century

I THE SEARCH FOR A NEW ARCHITECTURE

The unsatisfactory nature of architecture at the end of the nineteenth century caused some of the younger Russian architects to turn to the pioneer work of such European leaders in modern design as William Morris, van der Velde, Charles Mackintosh, J. M. Olbrich, and Otto Wagner. Articles in journals like *Mir Iskusstva* (World of Art) had made their work known in Russia and Olbrich and Mackintosh had even participated in exhibitions of design in Moscow and St Petersburg. As in western Europe the debate concerned the rapid expansion of the machine and its aesthetic qualities, and the honest, imaginative and constructive use of materials like iron, steel, glass and reinforced concrete. Although it was shown that the traditional materials of brick, stone, coloured tiles and wood could be used inventively, particularly by Russian Art Nouveau designers, use of steel, glass and concrete was widespread as they allowed design almost unlimited expression. Walls could be thinner, windows could widen, freed from the traditional vertical form, until they

Buildings
1 The Ryabushinsky House, 1900–02 2 Yaroslav Station, 1903–4 3 Metropole Hotel, 1899–1903 4 Tretyakov Gallery, 1906 5 Pertsov Apartment House, 1905–7 6 Apartment House by Gelfreikh, 1906–8 7 Apartment House by Kekushev, 1900 8 Moscow Arts Theatre, 1902 9 No. 10 Ostrovsky Pereulok 10 Church of the Community of Sts Martha and Mary, 1912 11 Publishing House 'Utro Rossi', 1900 12 TsUM, formerly Moor and Merrylees Department Store, 1909 13 Univermag Voentorg, formerly Moscow Officers' Trading Society, 1912–14 14 Pushkin Museum, 1898–1912 15 Vtorov House, 1900 16 Sukharev Tower, 17th/18th century, demolished 1928 17 Golitsyn Palace, 17th century, demolished 1928 18 Spas na Boru Church, 14th century, demolished 1932 19 Chudov Monastery, demolished 1932 20 Voznesensky Convent, demolished 1932 21 Cathedral of the Simonov Monastery, 15th century, demolished 1934 22 Kazan Cathedral, 17th century, demolished 1930s 23 Assumption Church of the Pokrovka, 17th century, demolished 1930s 24 Site of the Agricultural Exhibition, 1923 25 Lenin Mausoleum, 1929–30 26 Sokol village, 1923 27 Usachevsky village, 1924 28 Dom Narkomfin, 1928–9 29 Rusakov Worker's Club, 1927 30 Frunze Worker's Club, 1927 31 Kauchuk Worker's Club, 1927 32 Burevestnik Worker's Club, 1929 33 Zuyev Club, 1925–9 34 The Society for Political Prisoners (now Cinema Actors House), 1931–34 35 Palace of Culture of the Likhachev Automobile Workers, 1930–7 36 Planetarium, 1928 37 Lenin Institute for Marxism–Leninism, 1927 38 Izvestiya Building, 1927 39 Pravda Building, 1929–34 40 Centrosoyuz, 1929–36 41 Melnikov's House, 1927 42 Ministry of Agriculture Building, 1928 43 Central Bank (now Gosbank), 1927–9 44 Building on the Mokhovaya, 1934 45 Central Telegraph Office, 1925–7 46 Palace of Soviets, begun 1937 but never completed 47 No. 6 Gorky Street 48 Mossoviet, rebuilt 1939–45 49 Chaikovsky Concert Hall, 1940 50 Kotelnicheskoe Naberezhnaya, 1949–53 51 Tower Block Apartments, Vosstaniya Square 52 Leningrad Hotel, 1954 53 Ministry of Foreign Trade, 1953 54 Ministry of Communications, 1953 55 Ukraine Hotel, 1957 56 University, 1949–53 57 Church Nikita shto za Yauzy, restored 1958–60 58 Spassky Sobor at Andronikov Monastery, restored 1938–60 59 Comecon Building, 1967 60 Pioneers Palace, 1961–2 61 Palace of Congresses (in the Kremlin), 1960–1 62 Government Building, 1928–31 63 Frunze Military Academy, 1936 64 All-Union Council of Trade Unions, 1934 65 Lenin Library, 1937 66 Council of Ministers Building, 1932–5 67 Moskva Hotel, 1935 68 Red Army Theatre, 1940 69 Kaluga Gate Apartments, 1940

Streets
a Dzershinskovo b Dzerzhinsky Square c Entusiastov Shosse d Rusakovskaya e Prospekt Mira f Dmitrovskoe Shosse g Khoroshevskoe Shosse h Pirogovskaya i Leningradskoe Shosse j Sretensky k Spasskaya l Tagansky Square m Oktobrsky Square n Dobrynin Square o Triumfalnaya p Karetnaya q Kudrinskaya r Chaikovskaya s Kropotkinskaya t Gorky u Red Square v Frunze w Petrovka x Gertsena y Suvurovsky z Gogolevsky

formed horizontal ribbons or could encompass an entire wall, and concrete, especially when reinforced with steel, could simplify the problem of supports for roofing. These developments led logically to the next stage: an almost unlimited freedom in handling volume and space, rejection of decorative façades, and a desire to express the organic unity of the building from the inside outwards, its spines and bones no longer hidden under a crust of baubles but 'well formed and comely in the nude' as Louis Sullivan put it. The difference between eclecticism and modern design was not only in the use or absence of decoration but in the basic attitude to function, in the new freedom of volume, the new understanding of plasticity.

Parallel with the influence on architecture of new materials and machines were the fundamental social and political upheavals of the period 1900 to 1917. The disaster of the Russo-Japanese war, Bloody Sunday, the 1905 revolution, the brief achievement of some measure of representative government, the rapidly growing political consciousness of the people, the blood-bath of the First World War, the February and October revolutions, were all factors influencing the search for new expressions in architecture.

The period before the Revolution in Russia encompasses the short flirtation with the seductive, serpentine charm of Art Nouveau; a progression to clearer and simpler lines; an exciting reappearance of traditional Russian forms captured in a dynamic and sometimes outstandingly beautiful way; and a return to familiar neo-classical features by 1910 as the heavy hand of the autocracy regained supreme control of the country.

The historical development of the modern movement in Russia can perhaps be said to have begun at Abramtsevo near Moscow in the 1860s where the great art patron Savva Mamontov, a sort of Russian William Morris, gathered around him the leading artists, architects, actors, singers and theatrical directors of the day and allowed them to work comfortably and unencumbered, voluntarily uniting their skills to produce theatrical performances and works of art. Among his guests were the painters Ilya Repin, Vasily Surkov, Vasily Polenov, Mikhail Vrubel, the Vasnetsov brothers, the singer Fyodor Shalyapin, the director Konstantin Stanislavsky. Mamontov's colony was dominated by a group interested in Russian medieval forms, the Wanderers, and was the birthplace of developments in art that flowered at the beginning of the century: Art Nouveau, primitivism, futurism, rayonnism (as in Larionov's works), cubism, suprematism (pure, geometrical, abstract art as in the work of Malevich), and finally, constructivism. It also led to the publication of a flurry of journals, such as *Mir Iskusstva* (World of Art), *Zolotoe Runo* (Golden Fleece), *Apollon*, and *Starye Gody* (Past Years), which did much to disseminate the views of the artists of Russia and Europe. This had a decisive impact on the development of architecture where artist and architect began to work closely together, indeed in some cases were one and the same person. Perhaps the first building in this genre is the little church at Abramtsevo built in 1881-2 by the artists

Apolinarius Vasnetsov and Vasily Polenov in the combined spirit of Novgorod-Pskov and Vladimir-Suzdal architecture.

Another landmark in the search for a new architecture was K. A. Korovin's pavilion of the Far North at the 1896 All Russian Industrial Exhibition of the Arts in Nizhny Novgorod. The pale grey, unadorned building looking like a huge lump of ice was an attempt to express in emotional terms the icy waste of the north. It was an innovatory idea for Russian architecture and a very advanced building for its time.

In Moscow the arrival of modern architecture is represented by buildings as dissimilar as the Ryabushinsky House and the Yaroslav Station both by F. O. Shekhtel, the Metropole Hotel by W. Walcot, Vasnetsov's Tretyakov Gallery and Milyutin's Pertsov House. However different in appearance, all these buildings betray a common approach: the free treatment of space and volume unhindered by the rigid rules of the past, an attempt to achieve original façades, and, above all, respect for the function of building. In other words, the aim was a strong architecture in which simplicity and clarity predominate, even in the superficially extravagant Art Nouveau buildings.

Both Vasnetsov and Korovin were artists rather than architects. At that time it was very rare to find collaboration between architects on the one hand and artists and sculptors on the other but jointly they succeeded in producing the most interesting buildings of this period in Moscow. Exteriors were enlivened by fine sculpture, by majolica, by the use of coloured tiles, and integrated with the building in a way that had not been possible in the separate treatment of façades in the late nineteenth century. Paintings and mosaics were moved from the interior to the exterior and were not just placed on any free space that happened to provide symmetry but with care so that they became an integral part of the building, as with the compositions along the upper part of the Metropole Hotel. These exterior decorations were either positioned in contrast to the clear form of the building or blended into it in an abstract design. Interiors, on the other hand, could be either stark and bare like the lobby and auditorium of the Moscow Arts Threatre, or saturated with the stylized, irrational décor of the Ryabushinsky House.

The most vigorous exponent of modern architecture in Moscow and the leading architect of his age was Fyodor (Franz) Osipovich Shekhtel (1859–1926). An artist by training, his earliest work, for the festivities of the coronation of Nicholas II, was in the embellished pseudo-Russian 'Ropet' style, but by 1900 he had advanced not only to the forms of the neo-Russian revival but also to the international manner of Art Nouveau. He worked under the patronage of the rich factory owner S. P. Ryabushinsky. In the Ryabushinsky mansion (1900–02), a large private house which would not have been out of place in Vienna or Brussels at this time, Shekhtel juxtaposed the strong lines, flat roofs and asymmetrical form with the undulating curves and sinuous branch-like forms of the window-frames, the doorways, and the wide mosaic frieze in which brown and cream-coloured orchids blend with the grey-green of the walls. An overhanging cornice emphasizing the frieze betrays the concrete and metal construction. Large windows stare out provocatively from the almost bare walls and the design of the window-frames is matched by wrought-iron railings in rhythmic running spirals. Inside the ornamentation seems to have run wild, plant motifs climb and bend in the furniture, in the splendid staircase and in the paintings. The Ryabushinsky House, where Gorky lived for a time after his return from America, is both grand and a little mad, showing the extravagant and irrational side of the modern movement.

There are other examples of Art Nouveau in Moscow. Some of them are also closely linked with the neo-Russian style, such as the Yaroslav Station, a fantasy of northern architecture. Art Nouveau is also evident in the design of the Metropole Hotel built by an Englishman, William Walcot, between 1899 and 1903, although here there is a certain echo from the nineteenth century in the use of small gothic towers on the corners. The hotel bears a huge coloured ceramic panel, the 'Princess of Dreams', from designs by M. A. Vrubel, the foremost Art Nouveau painter in Moscow. Walcot was also the architect of 10 Ostrovsky Pereulok built for the Moscow Housebuilding Society. The construction of the house is clearly outlined by strong cornices, metal brackets, and hard vertical lines between the large double and triple lights of strongly accented windows. The spiral motif is repeated in the iron railings, around the door, on the balcony and porch. The design above the door and windows in majolica is an abstract of greeny brown toned against the grey of the plaster.

Although Art Nouveau was essentially a dead end in that further development of such extravagant decoration in blind opposition to the technical improvements that were the hallmark of the new architecture was impossible, it signalled the movement away from eclecticism. Essentially, architects were striving for expression and dynamism in the architectural mass, plasticity of volume, refinement of decorative elements, and clarity of construction. Inevitably they would move towards a strict, almost ascetic architectural form.

The neo-Russian style
The neo-Russian style that emerged early in the twentieth century arose from the renewal of interest in ancient Russian architectural forms which had begun about 1840 and continued during the second half of the nineteenth century. It differed from the nineteenth-century revival in that it was greatly influenced by the use of modern materials and modern design. Artists were the first to grasp hold of the opportunity to turn away from the academic emphasis of the art schools by making use of the information revealed by the studies of medieval Russian forms. In her pioneering work *The Great Experiment: Russian Art 1863–1922* Camilla Grey notes that it was to Moscow that these artists were drawn: 'For Moscow became the centre of this nationalist movement which lies at the base of the modern movement in

Russian art. The repudiation of international neo-classicism which had dominated the Russian artistic field since the end of the eighteenth century, and the ensuing rediscovery of the national artistic heritage, was the starting point of a modern school of painting in Russia.' Moscow architects were also attracted by the possibilities of using traditional styles to design contemporary buildings with a new, but historically familiar look. The modern interpreters of the old Russian styles did not choose fragments from the design of the old buildings and blindly force them onto alien structures but abstracted the forms and motifs from the totality of medieval architecture and gave these strong emphasis. The results were often fantastic, not always successful, but usually colourful, clearly understood, and more acceptable as works of art than those of the earlier pseudo-Russian architects. The builders did not turn for inspiration to the heavily encrusted forms of the Yaroslav churches of the seventeenth century but to the simpler, more monumental forms of Novgorod and Pskov, the sharply etched pyramid shape of the Voznesenskaya (Ascension) Church at Kolomenskoe, and the splendid wooden architecture of the north where one or many ascending cupolas are superimposed on the cube.

The leading architect of the modern movement, F. O. Shekhtel, was equally attracted to the forms of the neo-Russian revival. In 1901 he designed the Russian pavilion at the Glasgow exhibition of architecture in the spirit of wooden architecture of the north using as his model the splendid Church of the Transfiguration at the Kizhi *pogost* with its twenty-two cupolas ascending to the summit in a pyramid. The pavilion did not imitate the church but recalled it by association using the colour, dynamism, placement of volumes, and the sharpness of the overall form. Shekhtel went on to design the Yaroslav Station which was even more of an abstraction than the Glasgow pavilion. It evokes the north wonderfully, with its tall pitched roofs and its decorations from Kostroma and Yaroslav. From the outside it is utterly unlike a railway station yet inside it is plainly functional with a large waiting-room and easy access to the platforms.

A. V. Shchusev, later to become the leading architect of the Soviet period and the designer of Lenin's mausoleum, had a prolific youth first as a restorer and then as a builder of churches in the neo-Russian manner. The outstanding example of Shchusev's earlier work still extant in Moscow is the lovely church built in 1908–12 at 38 Bolshaya Ordynka for the former Community of Martha and Mary, a sisterhood founded in 1905 by the Grand Duchess Elizabeth. It is now used as a workshop for the restoration of icons for the R.S.F.S.R. Modelled on the simple, early churches of Novgorod and Pskov and also on the former Spas na Boru (Saviour in the Wood) in the Kremlin, it has completely captured the spirit of artless elegance that distinguished those early churches. Nesterov painted the frescoes inside.

The former home of the eminent art collector P. Tretyakov at number 10 Lavrushinsky Pereulok, rebuilt in 1906 as the Tretyakov Gallery with a unique collection of Russian art, was a natural choice for the traditional Russian style. It has

61 Church of the Community of Sts Maria and Martha, by A. V. Shchusev, 1912. A detail of the wall.

60 *Opposite* Church of the Community of Sts Maria and Martha, by A. V. Shchusev, 1912.

a beautiful façade designed by Viktor Vasnetsov; the bare walls relieved only by the frieze and gable of the upper wall and by the projecting porch with its steep roofs recall the porches of the seventeenth century. These devices mask the basic functionalism of the building, which is seen in its wide galleries lit successfully from roof lights.

Although many buildings were erected in the neo-Russian style, there is one other that more obviously combined aspects of both the modern movement and ancient Russia. The Pertsov Apartment House at number 1 Soimonovsky Prospekt across from the Moskva Swimming Pool was built as a block of flats in 1905–07. S. V. Milyutin designed a huge frieze which accommodates the interruptions of windows

62 Tretyakov Gallery, the gallery of Russian art, by V. Vasnetsov, 1906.

and roofs in the upper floors in an intricate design sometimes forming the sharp triangle of the central gable, sometimes filling in odd corners or composing a frame around a window. It was intended to forestall any impression of a repetitive, multi-storey building and to provide an atmosphere of the *byliny* (epic songs) of Russian fairy stories. The tall sharp gables and the deliberate lack of symmetry give an unusual character to the house.

The modern movement
The neo-Russian style eventually blended with the modern movement to such an extent that it became indistinguishable. The elaborate ornamentation of Art Nouveau had an even shorter life and the new architecture gradually became more austere as the centre of interest focused on the use of windows and the rhythmic composition of the exterior. This is particularly true of several commercial buildings erected at this time by the talented Shekhtel, such as the publishing house Utro Rossii built in 1900 at number 3 Skvortsova-Stepanova Ulitsa. Rational and clear and dominated by large windows, its best feature is the meeting of the curved exterior wall and the recessed entrance. It is one of the most modern-looking buildings in Moscow prior to the Revolution.

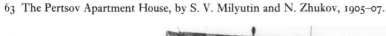

63 The Pertsov Apartment House, by S. V. Milyutin and N. Zhukov, 1905–07.

The Moscow Arts Theatre was redesigned in 1902 in the spirit of the intense artistic and theatrical activity of the time. The architect, again Shekhtel, had the problem of rebuilding in the shortest possible time the old Korsh Theatre into one where, according to Stanislavsky, three-quarters of the space would be assigned to the foyer and auditorium and only one quarter set aside for the actors, stage, scenery and so on. The simple design of the interior was almost totally without decoration to ensure that, as Stanislavsky remarked, the audience would not be distracted from what was going on on stage. Shekhtel strengthened the stage with metal supports and devised mechanical lifts and rails for the easy movement of the scenery. There was not time to alter the classical façade but Shekhtel changed the symmetry of the building by moving the entrance from the centre to the right wing. An Art Nouveau wooden doorway was designed by A. S. Golubkina depicting a woman's head looking down on the theatre goers, her hair undulating along the lintel. The Arts Theatre is still unique among theatres in Moscow for its deceptively simple décor. (A new Arts Theatre on Tverskoi Boulevard was completed in 1972.)

There are many other buildings in Moscow with modern characteristics, such as the department store, Moor and Merrylees, by R. I. Klein on the Petrovka (now the Central Universal Store – TSUM) and the House of the Moscow Officers' Trading Society, now Univermag Voentorg, on Prospekt Kalinina 2, built in 1912–14 by S. R. Zalessky. Blocks of luxury flats were also built at this time whose interior design caters particularly well to the needs of the tenants.

Neo-classicism

By 1910 the incipient modern architecture was eclipsed by the revival of that recurring favourite, neo-classicism. Neo-Russian forms continued to appear sporadically but in a more traditional, less inspired way than when the style had been connected with the modern movement. That neo-classicism should have reappeared and halted the development of modern architecture just when it was beginning to be generally accepted is surprising and can only be explained in the context of the social and political events that were taking place at that time. The purity of form and basic functionalism of modern design was most appreciated after the revolution of 1905, during the brief reign of representative government in the form of the DUMA. This was a brief lull before the autocracy once again assumed all power and stifled the political aspirations of the people, particularly those of the workers in the new, burgeoning industries. When hopes for reform failed to crystallize and the heavy hand of unrepresentative government fell once again, a reaction was also set in train in architecture. In this field, unlike painting, there is little room for individual experiment and what is not officially approved or tolerated usually cannot survive.

There are some carefully constructed buildings in the neo-classical style in Moscow from the years just before the Revolution, such as the Pushkin Museum by R. I. Klein (p. 205) or the Vtorov House on Spasopeskovsky Square, now the

64 The Vtorov House, now the residence of the American Ambassador, by V. Mart and V. Adamovich, 1900. The return of neo–classicism.

US ambassador's residence. However, there are many turgid, tiresome examples. The leading architects were I. Fomin, who had turned abruptly from some daring early experiments in modern design, V. Shchuko and I. Zholtovsky, all three of whom were to become major figures in the late twenties and thirties when Soviet architecture took an about-turn from the functional, constructivist architecture of the twenties to more traditional and monumental forms. There is even a small house by the ubiquitous Shekhtel in the classical style on Bolshaya Sadovaya which he built as his own home in 1900. Perhaps the attraction of classicism was the return to established, carefully laid-down rules, to symmetry, to known proportions, and an escape from the almost limitless possibilities released by modern techniques and design. The careful copying of classical forms was also part of the general reaction against the eclecticism of the late nineteenth century. But the flirtation with neo-classicism did not succeed in stemming the tide of modern design, for after 1917 a flood of new ideas, the successors to the experience gained in the first years of the century, were expressed on drawing-boards and some of the designs were actually built in the honeymoon of the Revolution.

2 THE REVOLUTION

In retrospect, considering the disasters of war and the extent of social unrest, a major upheaval was inevitable in Russia. Even in 1913 disillusionment with the royal family was apparent in the coldness with which the masses viewed the elaborate celebrations and display of pomp for the tercentenary of the Romanov dynasty. The war of 1914 found an army incredibly poorly equipped and badly led, in many cases without footwear or proper weapons, or equipped with bullets that would not fit the rifles. In the first ten months of the war the Russian army suffered 3·8 million casualties and by the end of 1916 general disillusion caused mutinies and the collapse of the front. Mismanaged and futile, the war inevitably led to a total loss of confidence in the government. At last discontent turned against the Tsar. On 12 March 1917 (new style) a Provisional Government was formed by the reactivated DUMA. Three days later the Tsar abdicated. For the next eight months the Provisional Government floundered on trying to deal with ever-mounting problems but prevented from doing so by the lack of strong central control. The Petrograd Soviet of Workers' and Soldiers' Deputies gradually assumed a governing role parallel to and in co-operation with the Provisional Government.

In April Lenin arrived at the Finland Station in Petrograd. Pressure from Lenin and the continuing support given to the Allies in the war began to arouse popular discontent against the Provisional Government. In Petrograd on 7 November the almost bloodless Bolshevik coup took place practically unnoticed by the mass of the population – even the theatres did not close. In Moscow, however, it was otherwise. Fierce fighting went on from 7 to 14 November between the White troops loyal to the Provisional Government and the Red Guard insurgent troops. On hearing the news of the *coup* in their headquarters in what is now the Mossoviet building on Ulitsa Tverskaya (Gorky Street) the Bolsheviks ordered the Red Guards to seize strategic buildings. The Moscow Duma thereupon hurriedly formed a Committee of Public Security and, with the help of the local garrison, occupied the important buildings circling the Kremlin, forcing the besieged Red Guards out of the Kremlin the next day. However, the Bolsheviks began to receive reinforcements via the railways which they controlled; troops were even rushed in from Petrograd. The fighting became concentrated on the important positions occupied by White troops: the Passion Monastery on Pushkin Square, the Metropole Hotel, the military barracks in Lefortovo, Kaluga Square, Krasnaya Presnya, and the Kremlin itself; and by 14 November the Red Guards were victorious. The Metropole Hotel, the Beklemishev Tower, Nikolsky Gate and Uspensky Cathedral in the Kremlin and many other buildings all suffered extensive damage. Considerable loss of life was also sustained; the Red Guards buried 250 dead at the end of the week of fighting.

In Petrograd Maxim Gorky's newspaper *Novaya Zhizn* (New Life) reported on 15 November that severe fighting was taking place in and around the Kremlin. On 16 November *Novaya Zhizn* published an emotional resignation letter by Anatoly Vasilievich Lunacharsky, the new Commissar for Enlightenment, who had heard rumours that St Basil's and the Assumption Cathedral were destroyed in the Moscow battle. 'I cannot bear it. My cup is full. I am powerless to stop this

65 Damage to the Uspensky Cathedral in the Kremlin sustained during the 1917 Revolution.

awfulness. It is impossible to work under the pressure of thoughts which are driving me mad.' But Lunacharsky withdrew the resignation almost immediately and explained in the pages of Gorky's paper that the Sovnarkom (Council of People's Commissars) had pressed him to remain. Later the rumour about St Basil's was found to have been false and the damage in Moscow, although considerable, was much less than had been feared. Trotsky excused Lunacharsky at the Sovnarkom meeting of 16 November explaining that he was not a 'militant politician' and had been very upset at the news.

Although the beginning of Bolshevik rule was so deceptively easy the problems facing the new leaders were formidable. The first two decrees of the Bolshevik Government – withdrawal from the war with Germany and redistribution of land – were an attempt to deal with the two most urgent issues, war weariness and the insatiable land-hunger of the peasants. The solutions created other, equally serious, problems. The subsequent treaty of Brest-Litovsk with Germany can only be described as an utter defeat for the Russians. They were forced back within frontiers that reduced the western area of the country almost to the size of the Grand Duchy of Moscow in the fifteenth century. The Germans thereby gained the most arable land and the most important mining districts. The redistribution of land which had in any case been going on spontaneously for a year was an attempt to win over the peasants to the Bolshevik cause but the breaking up of the large estates into 25 million tiny plots was to result in a sharp drop in agricultural productivity.

Other problems no less important faced the Sovnarkom. Fearful of a German victory after the collapse of the Russian front the Allies decided upon a policy of intervention which, although badly organized and mismanaged, did at times succeed in controlling large areas of Russia. At the same time the forces of counter-revolution began to draw together after the first shock of the take-over in Petrograd and Moscow. In the south and west, in the north and in the east, Deniken and Wrangel, Yudenich and Kolchak raised formidable armies. In January 1920 the Allies withdrew their troops but the civil war continued sporadically and it was not until 1922 that the Red Army was able to enter Vladivostock. During this period, known as 'war communism', government was conducted under a series of measures designed to meet the exigencies of the moment. Nationalization and grain-requisitioning were resorted to only as emergencies. In 1920–21 a terrible drought on the lower Volga produced famine and caused the death of five million people. What with the war against Germany, the civil war, the famine and outbreaks of diseases like typhoid and cholera, the population declined by about 28 million between 1914 and 1921.

The troubles were further complicated by the 1921 Kronstadt Revolt against Bolshevik power, which marked the lowest point in the fortunes of the new government. Lenin decided that palliative measures had to be introduced to save the Revolution and in 1921 introduced the idea of the New Economic Policy. Under the NEP the government would allow the revival of some measure of a market economy, with incentives for peasant production, and would tolerate trade being controlled largely by private traders. State control was established only over the 'commanding heights' of the economy. This situation remained in force until 1928 and it was precisely during this period of cautious freedom that there was an extraordinary blossoming of modern architecture. But first an event of great importance to Moscow took place, the transfer of the capital from the banks of the Neva back to its old habitat. The 'purple clad dowager' got back her inheritance.

Moscow in 1918

Early in 1918, in its exposed position on the northern flank of Russia Petrograd was being pressed by the anti-Bolshevik forces of Yudenich from Finland and by advancing German troops. Knowing full well that the Bolsheviks did not yet control much more than the two major cities, the Sovnarkom decided it would be expedient to transfer the capital to Moscow, a more central position, easier to hold and from which it would be easier to govern. On 11 March, therefore, Lenin arrived at the Northern Station (now Leningradsky) in Moscow and Moscow again became the first capital, the position she had surrendered to St Petersburg for just over two hundred years.

Lenin was given a suite of two rooms at the National Hotel. It was early spring, the thaw had set in and rivulets of melting snow were running everywhere making the streets wet and dirty with slush. Nevertheless, the day after his arrival Lenin took a walk around the Kremlin and decided that the offices of the government should be there. The decision to place the offices of a new government which had taken power by revolutionary means in the ancient buildings of the Kremlin, traditionally the seat of power of medieval Russia, meant that events had come full circle. The move from Petrograd, once St Petersburg, the 'Window to the West' created by Peter the Great, to the traditionalist, conservative city of Moscow, still associated with the dark intrigues of Byzantine traditions, was perhaps a foretaste of the darkness and secrecy, the cunning and unpredictable rule of the Stalinist future. The immediate consequence of the move was that the Kremlin and all its treasures were closed to the public, the monasteries and great cathedrals stopped functioning as religious institutions and the red banner of the Revolution was raised over the buildings. Power had indeed returned to Moscow.

In early 1918 Moscow was a large city still dominated by wooden buildings, although the proportion had fallen to just over half of the total. The population had grown to about 1·7 million and the overcrowding and appalling housing conditions of the poor and industrial workers had become a scandal. One of the earliest decrees of the Soviet government was the forcible sharing of housing among the entire population of the cities. House-owners were restricted to one or two rooms, the rest were allocated to the people who had suffered the worst sort of housing in damp, unlit cellars and unheated shacks. A million and a half people were resettled in this way. During the next few years over one million people emigrated, mainly from the upper classes, and Moscow's population declined by hundreds of thousands during the famine and fuel shortages in 1919 and 1920, as people fled to the relative safety of the country. As a result of this sudden process of depopulation, the crisis in housing was postponed for the time being. During the NEP wealth increased and the flow of the population reversed, so the cities, particularly Moscow, again became overcrowded and the problem of new housing could no longer be postponed.

Early successes in protecting ancient monuments

Despotic and autocratic as the new leaders undoubtedly were from the beginning, they had no intention or interest in destroying or annihilating the products of bourgeois culture, whether in art, architecture, music or the theatre. Contrary to what was generally believed at the time, damage to buildings in Petrograd during and immediately after the Revolution was minimal, amounting to some broken glass and the pilfering of the Tsar's wine cellar in the Winter Palace. In Moscow where there was shell damage the cost was higher, but apart from the activities of some anarchist groups there were few cases of indiscriminate looting. Although amongst the Kremlin's countless valuables were the crown jewels, which had been brought there for safe keeping during the war, not a casket was opened before 1922 when a special commission analysed its worth and transferred its contents to the Almazny Fond (Diamond Fund) where some of the jewels are now on public view. The countryside fared differently. Here the peasants often took matters into their own hands, burning and looting the manor houses.

The solicitude with which the historical monuments and other valuables were treated after the Revolution is partly explained by the actions of a group of dedicated art historians, archaeologists, architects and museum keepers who had been striving for decades to achieve some sort of state control over the protection of ancient buildings. Before the Revolution they had been severely frustrated by the lack of progress in eliciting government action to protect buildings of historical value. By 1910 the Society for the Defence and Preservation in Russia of Monuments of Art and Ancient Times had been founded, the first volumes of the comprehensive *History of Russian Art* by Igor Emmanuelovich Grabar were appearing and the journal *Starye Gody* (Past Years) was attracting widespread interest in the heritage of Russian architecture. It was hoped the government would take a more vigorous role in the protection of historically valuable buildings but the war interfered. The Provisional Government, in its turn, also had little time for ancient monuments but Gorky took it upon himself to lead a crusade for their preservation in his publication *Novaya Zhizn* and campaigned for a ban on the selling of valuables abroad.

Thus by 1917 there was a strong body of interested, influential persons who would have welcomed any government of whatever persuasion which assisted them in their goal of providing finance and help in the protection of old buildings. In Lunacharsky they found a sympathetic ear and in Lenin a genuine interest if not in actively preserving old buildings at least in preventing unnecessary demolition. Although Lunacharsky was a lightweight politician, not one of the inner council (his resignation in the early days of the Revolution was always treated scornfully), he had Lenin's trust and embarked on his new job with the greatest enthusiasm and energy.

In Moscow the leading role in the remarkable achievements made in the preservation of architectural monuments in the first ten years of Soviet power was played by Igor Emmanuelovich Grabar. Immediately after the Revolution he helped to persuade the employees of the main museums in Moscow to accept the new government and co-operate with it. Early in 1918 Grabar agreed to organize the Collegium for Museum Affairs under Narkompros, the People's Commissariat for Enlightenment, particularly that section dealing with conservation of works of art and architecture. (Lunacharsky in return promised Grabar that some Petrograd workers who had moved into part of his large flat would be evicted.) Grabar's prestige meant that the most respected figures involved in restoration were encouraged to work for the new Collegium. At first the Collegium covered general questions of art and invited artists like Tatlin and Konenkov to its meetings, but it found that the continual debate detracted from the problems of building conservation. Accordingly, in May 1918 it changed its title to Department on Museums and Preservation of Ancient and Artistic Monuments and was given more specific tasks.

The new government had been quick to issue decrees to prevent wholesale looting and destruction of property. As early as the day after the Revolution, on 8 November 1917, Lenin called on the peasant land committees immediately to 'confiscate all the landlord's property, putting it to the strictest account and complete order, protecting in the strictest way the former landlord's property which henceforth has become the property of all the people and which, therefore, these very people must protect'. Early in 1918 the Government issued a declaration that clearly reflected its genuine concern for the heritage of the past:

Citizens, the old masters have gone, leaving behind a vast heritage. Now it belongs to all the people.

Citizens, take care of this inheritance, take care of the paintings, statues, buildings – it is the embodiment of your spiritual strength and that of your forefathers. Art is something wonderful, that talented people were able to achieve even under the yoke of despotism, that bears witness to the beauty and strength of the human soul. Citizens, do not even touch one stone, protect the monuments, the old buildings, articles, documents – all this is your history, your pride. Remember, all this is the soil from which will grow your new, people's art.

Executive Committee of the Council
of Workers' and Soldiers' Deputies.

In this way began the most productive period of restoration ever undertaken in Moscow in conditions that would have daunted less dedicated enthusiasts. Anarchists were still terrorizing the streets, and public transport, distribution of food, factory production were all functioning at less than one third of their pre-war level. Even Lenin was not immune from the prevailing chaos – in 1918 in uprisings in Moscow and Yaroslav led by the Social Revolutionaries an attempt was made on his life. The protectors of ancient buildings were further dismayed by the consequence of the fuel crisis in the winter of 1919–20 when any building of wood, no matter what its age or value, was in danger of being dismantled to stoke the fires in the blue cold of the winter.

Their achievements, therefore, were all the more outstanding. In the first eight years after the Revolution 10,000 buildings of special interest were brought under state protection and 3,000 of these were actually restored and repaired. The system of authorization was deceptively simple in those early years. Any suggestion of plans for the demolition or rebuilding of a historically important building had to have the sanction of Narkompros and Lunacharsky. Even in the uncertainties of the civil war in 1919 and 1920 expeditions were organized to the upper and middle Volga region, the upper reaches of the Moskva and the Oka and even to the northern Dvina and the White Sea. These areas had been practically untouched by earlier archaeologists and art historians and provided a great wealth of material and led to the cataloguing of many formerly unknown buildings.

The restorers' honeymoon began to draw to an end in about 1924 when responsibility for the fate of the monuments, until then under central control, was gradually transferred to the care of local authorities, into the hands of people with no experience in the care of old buildings and no genuine interest in providing expensive maintenance. In 1927 some of the central organs empowered with a veto over the tearing down of old buildings were dissolved. At the same time there was a move towards the rebuilding of the major cities, particularly Moscow, and interest declined in preserving its ancient edifices. Grabar fought a losing battle in the pages of *Stroitelstvo Moskvy* (Moscow Building) trying to educate the readers in the history of the development of the city, in the historical origin of threatened edifices like the Sukharev Tower and the Kitaigorod Walls. Shchusev, too, tried to defend the preservation of the central core of the city, arguing that this did not mean turning Moscow into a 'museum city'. In the end they failed, and even the unique Golitsyn Palace was pulled down after much research and effort had gone into the possibilities of its restoration. The Sukharev Tower, moreover, crumbled into dust only a few weeks after it had been carefully repaired. In 1930 Grabar resigned from the restoration department, ostensibly to devote himself to painting but he must have felt powerless in the face of the increasing tendency of the government to discard the old buildings of the past lightly. Lunacharsky left Narkompros in 1929 after the defeat of his educational policy and in 1930 the restoration section was closed.

---

66 Poster of 1918 imploring citizens to protect monuments.

Now began the blackest period in the history of preservation of ancient buildings in Moscow. Destruction of important buildings went on voraciously in the period 1928–34 and continued intermittently up to the Second World War. There is no space to list all the buildings that disappeared in this period but besides the Golitsyn Palace and the Sukharev Tower, a few of the more important were:

In the Kremlin: the Church of Spas na Boru (Saviour in the Wood), built in 1330, the Chudov (Miracle) Monastery and the Voznesensky (Ascension) Convent, and the Nikolaevsky Palace (1775–6).
Most of the buildings of the Simonov Monastery, some of which dated from the fifteenth century.
Kazan Cathedral on Red Square built in 1636 in honour of the liberation of Russia from the Polish interventionists.
The Assumption Church on the Pokrovka built in 1696–99, an outstanding example of Moscow baroque.

Thus the character of Moscow, where not even the Kremlin was inviolate, altered almost beyond recognition.

The Revolution and architecture

Although architects played no part whatsoever in the first flurry of the Revolution, except for those involved in restoration work, they could not but be influenced by the fact that many avant-garde artists aligned themselves with the government. These artists thought they recognized in the revolution a parallel with their own new, experimental art. Encouraged by the benevolence of Lunacharsky in allocating teaching commissions and studies, they believed that Bolshevism was more responsive to modern painting than the old regime. Chagall and Malevich taught in Vitebsk, Punin worked in Petrograd and many left-wing artists in Moscow joined Narkompros and worked under the auspices of the Department of Fine Arts (Otdel Izobrazitalnykh Iskusstv or IZO). Tatlin himself, the leading constructivist, headed the Moscow branch and constructivism, as represented by Tatlin and Malevich, gradually came to have a decisive influence on the new generation of architects.

In April 1918 the Lenin Plan of Monumental Propaganda was announced. Under this imaginative idea the streets of Moscow and Petrograd were to be decorated with fifty statues of admired revolutionaries, philosophers and progressive personalities of the past (even including Florence Nightingale), buildings were to be gaily painted with appropriate revolutionary themes, and a plaque in honour of the first Revolution was to decorate the Kremlin wall. The Plan was not a great success. The sculptors had only six months to complete the busts before the first anniversary of the Revolution and the cheapest materials were used, such as gypsum and wood, which meant that however well they were made they could not have a long life in the open in a Russian climate. In the event, only a dozen were ever built and of these many were poorly received by the traditional-minded politicians and the even more conservative populace. The art departments of Narkompros which chose the sculptures were blissfully unaware of this problem and were shocked when the cubist bust of Sophia Perovskaya by O. Grizelli in Petrograd was sharply criticized by the local authority there. In Moscow the bust of Bakunin by B. O. Korolev was also in a 'non-realist' style, and although hotly defended by IZO it was not unveiled but remained on its plinth at the boulevard end of Ulitsa Kirova covered with boards until the bad winter of 1920 when the wood was stolen for firewood. The press attacked the revealed bust and it was soon taken down (it is now on view in the Museum of Architecture). In contrast with the revolutionary lines of the street sculpture, a traditional, partially finished obelisk in honour of the constitution was ceremoniously unveiled on Soviet Square by Lenin on 7 November 1918. In July 1919 the sculpture by Andreyev astride the obelisk was completed and unveiled; it depicted a classical lady representing the liberation of man. Here there was no experimentation, no economy of form or exciting lines, but a mildly prosaic figure that could have been at home at any time in the previous century.

In spite of the abolition of private property and the possibilities this created for planning and building, architects were not so free as artists in their ability to experiment. After the Revolution they had grouped themselves in the various ateliers of the former established architects like A. V. Shchusev or I. Fomin, or were eagerly working with sculptors and artists in the newly established Free Art School, later the Vkhutemas (Higher Artistic-Technical Workshop, renamed Vkhutein in 1926). The Moscow Vkhutemas was set up in the former School of Painting, Sculpture and Architecture at number 2 Ulitsa Kirova, the old Yushkov house designed by Bazhenov in the eighteenth century. Here they were given studios, were invited to teach and conduct limited experiments, and were given every opportunity to collaborate with the left-wing artists. A few architects established before the Revolution emigrated but on the whole those with the most secure reputations remained and took an active part in architectural activity. Some, like Shchusev, tried to adapt themselves to the new ideas; others, like Zholtovsky, rarely strayed from their classical past. Although partially eclipsed by their more brilliant colleagues in the twenties, they were never entirely pushed into the background and were more than ready to emerge when they received the call for traditional architecture in the thirties. The most innovatory of the modern architects at the turn of the century, F. O. Shekthel, was nearly seventy in 1917 and was no longer the active force he had been. Nevertheless he continued to act as chairman of the rather conservative Moscow Architectural Society until 1922.

The early years of the revolution saw a synthesis between architecture and the fine arts that lay in the early work of artists like Malevich and his 'Arkhitektonica', El Lissitsky and his 'Prouns', Mayakovsky, Aleksander Vesnin, Gabo and Tatlin. Vesnin, the architect, designed stage scenery; Lissitsky, the artist, frequently turned to architecture; Gabo, the sculptor, was attracted to large constructions; and Tatlin, the supreme sculptor, in 1919 designed the Monument to the Third International, or the Tatlin Tower, the romantic symbol of the Revolution. The tower embodies a conscious desire to invalidate all previous architectural experience, be it Gothic, Renaissance or eclectic, and to start anew, to examine fundamentally the basic tenets of building and design. As the Revolution meant absolute change, so must architecture too respond to these entirely new conditions with radical solutions. Within the iron mesh of the spiral tower three glass chambers, the offices of the Third International, were to be perpetually revolving: the lower one in the shape of a cube was to turn on its axis once a year and was intended for general meetings; the middle, a pyramid in shape, was to revolve once a month and was to be used for meetings of assemblies and executive bodies; and the uppermost, for information purposes, in the shape of a cylinder, was to revolve once a day. A model of the tower was built out of bits of old tin and other scrap material and shown in the streets of Petrograd but the construction of the tower itself was never a real possibility, for the technical resources were too few. It remained a brilliant paper project, a source of inspiration for subsequent architects. Tatlin's group in 1920 had been the first to use the term 'constructivism' in relation to architecture and in 1923 *Lef* magazine, the left journal of the arts, published a thoughtful interpretation: 'Constructivism is the organization of the given material on the principles of tectonics, structure and construction, the form becoming defined in the process of creation by the utilitarian aim of the object.'

3 THE FIRST DECADE

The early twenties

Those attracted to the new architectural faculty of the Vkhutemas included the young Konstantin Melnikov, Professor N. Ladovsky, the Vesnin brothers, the Golosov brothers, and Moishe Ginzburg, the future constructivist philosopher. The Vkhutemas also included faculties of industrial design and art. During the early twenties the 'psycho-technical', the mechanical, the geometrical, colour and form – all aspects of architecture were examined and experimented with as far as was possible within the confines of the studios. Forms were given emotional content: the spiral, as in Tatlin's Tower, was symbolic of the Revolution, the cube an expression of tranquillity, the square a form with no movement.

Slowly as the country overcame the terrible problems of civil war, famine and pestilence, and as the NEP began to work its way through the economy, a new building programme became possible and several design competitions were held. This was still the romantic era, the period of absolute rejection of all pre-1917 experience, the search not only as elsewhere for a new architecture but one powerful enough to express the essence of the Revolution. Such was the idea behind the decision of the government to build a huge Palace of Labour between the lower part of Gorky Street, Sverdlov Square and Okhotny Ryad, the first example of the Soviet predilection for huge buildings. The main auditorium was to be large enough to seat 8,000, a second, smaller one was to seat 2,500 and the building was to contain offices, a meteorological observatory, a radio station, a social science museum, a library and a restaurant for 6,000. This, the first major building in the new communist state, was to be a memorial to the Revolution as Sergei Kirov clearly explained in a speech to the First Congress of the Soviets on 30 December 1922:

I believe that . . . this building should be a symbol of the growing might and triumph of communism, not only among ourselves but also over there, in the west. . . . And on that new, magnificent, splendid and revolutionary earth, we, the workers, born in miserable hovels, will leave those hovels in comradely ranks to enter our enchanted palaces to the strains of the great 'Internationale'. . . . [We] are capable of embellishing this wretched earth with monuments such as our enemies could never imagine, even in their dreams.

The architectural committee selected in 1923 to judge the entries included among its members some familiar faces, for example, Shchusev, R. I. Klein (the architect of the Pushkin Museum), and the aged Shekhtel. First prize was awarded to N. Trotsky for a peculiar building with a scalloped effect which remained true to some classical canons. However, the entry which received third prize excited the most comment. This was the design by the Vesnin Brothers, Alexander and Leonid. Complete absence of decoration allowed the forms of the building to express their

67 Pushkin Museum (formerly Alexander III Museum), by R. Klein, 1912. (See page 192.)

own power. The auditorium was circular and was juxtaposed against the square of the main body of the building, and the whole superimposed by the wire mesh of a radio tower. This project is widely accepted as the first design in the constructivist genre. However, the Palace of Labour was never to be built. Although ten million rubles had been allocated for the monument, there was disagreement over the results of the competition and a second one was organized. Eventually, as more urgent problems occupied the building section of Mossoviet, it was quietly dropped.

The young Soviet state was anxious to show off its economic achievements and in the autumn of 1922 *Pravda* announced that an Agricultural Exhibition would be built in the area between the Krymsky Bridge and the Golitsyn Hospital along the embankment now occupied by Gorky Park. As well as Shekhtel, the organizing committee included the ubiquitous Shchusev and other *ancien régime* academicians like Klein, Chernyshev and Rylsky. Shchusev was to be chief architect but Zholtovsky was to have control over a number of pavilions and the restaurant. N. Kolly, the young architect of the modern group who was later to work closely with Le Corbusier on the Centrosoyuz building, was appointed to work with Zholtovsky and his influence is discernible in the completed pavilions. The most interesting of the pavilions in the modern style was the Makhorka tobacco pavilion by Konstantin Melnikov. The exhibition was a mixture of modern and eclectic, one of the few occasions in which the modern and more traditional architects collaborated successfully.

Architectural organizations

There was as yet no pressure from the government to join officially sponsored unions and the architects began to group themselves in like-minded organizations. Before 1923 the only architectural society in Moscow was the Moscow Architectural Association, MAO, a pre-revolutionary local society founded in 1867 which had a large membership exceeding those of all the other societies. Immediately after the Revolution the society co-operated with the architectural section of Narkompros and offered the government advice on repair and restoration. Although it had not actively supported the Revolution MAO had not actively opposed it either, but had offered its co-operation in the early days. Many commissions were given to its rather conservative members, even in the middle and late twenties, usually considered the most active period of the modern architects.

In 1923 some of the architects most interested in experiment and the search for new structures formed the Association of New Architects, ASNOVA. Their credo included the total rejection of the past, the fullest use of modern techniques and materials, and the synthesis of art and architecture. They believed that architectural form is the object of scientific research, that it is 'rational'. For this reason the ASNOVA group are often called 'rationalists'. The group was formed by Professors Ladovsky and Dokhuchayev of the Vkhutemas. Included in the membership were Lissitsky,

S. Mochalov, V. Balikhin and Konstantin Stepanovich Melkinov as well as engineers like Artur Ferdinandovich Loleit who was an expert on reinforced concrete. By 1926 they had thirty-five members and were associated with the new psycho-analytical method of teaching introduced by Ladovsky. Although much of the work of ASNOVA's members remained on the drawing boards, Melnikov's many workers' clubs and a few other buildings provide examples of the group's work. In the second half of the twenties they moved away from the analytical method and the emotional appreciation of architectural form to a more functional approach. An example of the Association's imaginative approach was Lissitsky's designs for 'horizontal' skyscrapers, or the Cloudprop project, an outcome of the 'Prouns', or studies of the transitional stage between painting and architecture. One of the chief occupations of ASNOVA was to engage in a spirited polemic with the constructivists and their organization, OSA, although with the advantage of retrospect the similarities between the two groups appear greater than their differences.

The Association of Contemporary Architects, OSA, had its origins in the activities of constructivists like Tatlin and Gabo. OSA members believed, to put it simply, in refuting the old architecture and rationalizing the labour of building. The theory was first expressed in tangible form in the Vesnin brothers' design for the Palace of Labour in 1923. The Association was formed in 1925 by the Vesnin brothers, Barsch, Gan, Burov and Moishe Ginzburg whose book *Style and Epoch* published in 1924 explained the philosophy of the new movement. Officially, the Association was described in the petition to Mossoviet as 'an association of architect-innovators working on problems of new contemporary architecture of the great industrial centres'. Unlike ASNOVA, OSA published its own journal, *Contemporary Architecture*, and engaged in correspondence with most of the leading modern architects abroad. It organized the first exhibition of modern architecture after the Revolution with the help of Narkompros in 1927. OSA criticisms of ASNOVA were based on the issue of utilitarianism, of 'transformation of the way of life', of striving for the new socialist type of building, of finding concrete solutions instead of pursuing the abstract ideas they believed typified ASNOVA. With a larger membership than ASNOVA, OSA also had a branch in Leningrad and most of the best buildings of the 1920s with the exception of those by Melnikov, were built to the designs of architects associated with OSA.

One of OSA's leading members was Ivan Ilyich Leonidov, a young graduate of Vkhutemas and one of the most visionary of the post-revolutionary generation of architects. He was an exponent of the 'socialist transformation of the way of life' and contributed much to new ideas in town-planning, such as the separation of residential areas from industrial areas, the use of low-level housing interspersed with towers, and imaginary use of the most advanced construction methods. He submitted many plans – for the Lenin Library, the Central Union Building, the House of Industry etc. – but unhappily the only project ever realized was a complex of park terraces with steps in a sanatorium at Kislovodsk in 1937–8.

68 The temporary wooden mausoleum for Lenin's body erected by A. V. Shchusev in 1924.

The new architecture gathers momentum

In 1924 Lenin died after a protracted illness. His widow, Natalya Krupskaya, urged his followers not to create memorials in his name: 'Do not let your sorrow for Ilyich find expression in outward veneration of his personality. Do not raise monuments to him, or palaces to his name, do not organize pompous ceremonies in his memory.' Her wishes were totally ignored. In a short space of time Petrograd became Leningrad and Lenin Libraries, Lenin Institutes and Lenin Streets began to proliferate in every city in the union – so much so that five Lenin Streets in Moscow had to be renamed recently to avoid confusion. But the most important step in transforming Lenin worship into a new religion was in Moscow where Stalin went against the wishes of some of the Politburo in erecting a mausoleum to enshrine the man and turn his body into a symbol of the state. With the mausoleum of Tamerlane in mind Shchusev built in two and a half days the first wooden edifice to shelter the body. Konstantin Melnikov designed the sarcophagus. Five months later the original building was replaced by a stronger one, also of wood, intended to serve as a tribunal as well as a mausoleum. Although in form it resembled a Greek temple, its modest size did not disturb the arrangement of Red Square where it was placed. In 1929 Shchusev replaced the wooden mausoleum with a permanent building of red granite, again in pared-down classical style. The mausoleum was put just in front of the Kremlin Wall which had come to be used as a burial place of honour for leading revolutionaries as early as 1918.

Meanwhile the NEP was tempting people back into the cities and Moscow again began to feel the pinch of overcrowding. The houses of the former well-to-do had already been redistributed and there was no alternative but to build anew. At that time there was a great vogue for garden cities and a real attempt was made to design workers' houses either individually or in pairs on the model of the English garden cities. One of the leading exponents was N. V. Markovnikov who in 1923 designed one of the first housing estates for workers in Moscow, the Sokol village in Krasnopresnye Rayon. He produced a group of cottages with gardens and even picket fences of which a few still remain, making an English-looking incongruity among the sea of blocks of flats. However, the government soon decided for reasons of economy and space that garden cities were feasible only as groups of dachas in the countryside. Instead, the architects began to concentrate on planning blocks of flats for industrial workers. One such development in 1924 is the Usachevsky village by A. Meshkov on the street of that name near the Novodevichy Convent, a complex of small apartments each not larger than three rooms. It was carefully placed on a north-south axis so that all the flats could benefit from the sun; it was built with wide, green courtyards and generous, well-lit staircases; nursery schools, baths, shops and similar amenities were all part of the plan. In comparison with the miserable barracks for workers provided in pre-revolutionary Moscow this was a major step forward, one of the first examples of planned quality housing for the less well-off. Other such 'villages' were created in Moscow on Dubovka Street, Mytnaya Street and Khavsko-Shabolovskaya Street. But gradually problems became evident with these small two- and three-room flats. The overcrowding now endemic in Moscow meant that a flat built for one family of three rooms plus kitchen and bathroom quickly deteriorated into a flat for three families all sharing the inadequate kitchen and washing facilities.

The architects of OSA and Narkompros recognized the problem and solutions were sought in which the housing concerns were to act as 'catalysts in the transformation of the way of life', as Ginzburg described it. In 1925 two competitions were organized for communal housing, both of which were to include communal dining-rooms where 40 per cent of the inhabitants were to eat. Every floor was to have a cubicle containing gas-rings for making tea and feeding children. Because all the units would be small the communal house would eliminate the problem created by more people than intended crowding into one flat. It would also be more economical in that there would be no duplications of expensive kitchen facilities. Finally, it would pave the way to socialism by providing the opportunity for a collective life together. A few communal houses were actually built in Moscow like the one on Khavskaya Street in 1927–8, but they tended to deteriorate into cheap hostels and were not popular.

At the same time the OSA architects were trying to find ways of using new building materials mass-produced in standardized sections. One of the most interesting buildings in this genre was by Moishe Ginzburg. Ginzburg the theoretician of OSA, also designed the F type one-family living unit on two floors. It contained a single living area plus a bathroom and small kitchen which could be removed when communal catering was introduced. With Ignaty Fransovich Milinis, Ginzburg built the Dom Narkomfin (House for the People's Commissariat of Finance) in 1928–9 just off Chaikovsky Street. A number of F type units were included in the block. Long horizontal lines of glass containing the corridors along the exterior and the flat roof gives it a strong modern look. At first it stood on open pillars or *piloti* like a Le Corbusier building, but later the open spaces were filled in. Ginzburg himself had one of the flats on the top floor where the editorial policies of OSA were often discussed.

Gradually, the fantasies of the modern architects about communal housing reached such a pitch that Melnikov could envisage a garden city where orchestras in huge dormitories would drown the snoring and induce sleep and Kuzmin could contemplate the complete elimination of family life, and regimentation of the day strictly according to the clock. When the Soviet authorities turned against modern architecture at the end of the twenties they picked on ideas such as these to ridicule the whole movement. Ironically, although forgotten for forty years, the last decade has seen a move to reintroduce a modified form of communal housing in the new blocks of flats in recent suburban developments, as at Novyi Cheremushky.

By the middle of the twenties Soviet architecture was beginning to assume a definite shape and with the Paris Exposition of Decorative Arts in 1925 it reached the outside world to make an impact on the most avant-garde architecture of the time. The selection of Melnikov's plan for the Soviet pavilion was a brilliant choice. Winner of the Grand Prix, it proved to be one of the most exciting designs of the Paris exhibition. It was simple in its use of wood and glass but revolutionary in its form, in the way interior and exterior space were interconnected. It was one of the few national pavilions to use modern architecture and its functionalism and interior design with photomontage by Rodchenko and notes by Mayakovsky made it a true collaboration of all the arts.

After the success of the Paris Exposition modern architecture became completely acceptable in the Soviet Union. During the latter half of the decade there were many opportunities for the modernist architects in the pressing need for buildings to fulfil new functions like the hydro-electric enterprises, the information and communication media, and – an entirely new concept – the workers' clubs.

Workers' clubs were envisaged as a necessary part of the social revolution. They were to be 'effective centres of mass propaganda and development of the creative talents of the working class', according to a party resolution. But more than that they were intended to replace the role of the Church, to stimulate the education of the workers, so many of whom were illiterate, and to provide them with a focal point for comradeship and social well-being. At first they were haphazard affairs set up in any suitable premises like the requisitioned Tarasov house on the Spiridonovka. Eventually, as the clubs were intended to be used as libraries, reading-rooms, dining-rooms with kitchens, auditoriums, museums, theatres, rooms for meetings and information centres, the stately homes were found to be inadequate and it became clear that purpose-built buildings would be more suitable. The huge Palace of Labour was just such a club intended to serve the whole of Moscow, a huge centre of culture and education. But the demise of the idea of the Palace of Labour resulted in the happier and more realistic idea of smaller clubs serving particular localities or industries. By 1925, with more means at their disposal, a few enterprising architects were commissioned to design clubs for particular enterprises.

For the ideologically minded architect here was a chance to put into practice some of the ideals of the Revolution. Konstantin Melnikov proved to be the most energetic and one of the most imaginative designers of clubs. In the short period between 1925 and 1930 he built six clubs, four of which were in Moscow. All four, the Rusakov Club, the Frunze Club, the Kauchuk Club, all of 1927, and the Burevestnik Club of 1929, are still functioning although their original close connection to a particular enterprise has been eroded and they are in more general use as 'houses of culture' and cinemas rather than clubs. The Rusakov Club is the most interesting of the four with three great cantilevered sections each holding an assembly hall protruding from the first floor. Here Melnikov made use of reinforced concrete to support the sections

69 The Rusakov Club for Transport Workers on the Stromynka. By K. S. Melnikov, 1927.

but in general he relied on the versatility of cheaper materials like wood, glass, bricks and plaster and so did not have the problem of relatively inexperienced Russian builders working with unfamiliar new materials. The clubs were also not expensive to build; even the Rusakov Club cost only 600,000 rubles. Melnikov's clubs were not only functional and very different from each other (compare the rounded form of the Kauchuk Club with the Rusakov) but flexible in that the halls could be enlarged or made into a number of smaller rooms by the use of moving partitions, an idea first expressed in the Vesnin brothers' design for the Palace of Labour.

The Zuyev Club on Lesnaya Street by I. Golosov, built in 1925–29, now a house of culture but still used essentially as a club, was also an original and totally modern building. It consciously resembles factory architecture with different levels of roofing, large sections of glass and a glass cylinder which encloses the staircase held by square frames on the lower and upper levels. When built, the assembly hall with seating for 950 made it the largest of the Moscow clubs.

By 1928 the theory behind the clubs was beginning to alter. It was felt that there was too much emphasis on the theatre side of the clubs and that the usual proscenium stage was outdated. Some architects wanted to expand the activities of the club extravagantly to include winter gardens for botany, zoology rooms, playgrounds and more facilities for sport, films, planetarium showings, laboratories for specialized research and even tracks for car racing. Meanwhile the first Five Year Plan of 1928–33 was being implemented. Its emphasis on expanding heavy industry as rapidly as possible meant that in future clubs would be built within the context of the large new housing and industrial estates that were planned all over the country (fifty new cities were envisaged) making clubs for individual enterprises redundant.

In Moscow two more clubs were still to be built, both by the leaders of the constructivists, the Vesnin brothers. The Club for the Society of Political Prisoners, now the House of Cinema Actors (the society was abolished in the thirties), on Ulitsa Vorovskovo, was built in 1931–34. From the outside it is deliberately asymmetrical with varying roof levels and volumes united by the broad steps in front of a large entrance. However, this impression belies the unity of the interior groups of rooms and the warmth of the main hall where the walls are finished in rosewood panels. The last club of this period, the Palace of Culture of the Likhachev Automobile Works, was also built by the Vesnins between 1930 and 1937 in the grounds of the partially demolished Simonov Monastery. A three-storey building, it is the largest and most lavish of the clubs. The architects have made prominent use of marble, and produced an auditorium seating 1,200, together with a large library, lecture hall for 400, children's rooms, gymnastic rooms, a winter garden and fountain and many other rooms besides. Almost palatial in the use of space and marble columns, it lacks something of the more functional approach of the earlier clubs. It is best viewed from the River Moskva where it sits astride a high cliff silhouetted against the sharp towers of the remains of the Simonov Monastery next-door.

70 Club for the Society of Political Prisoners (now the House of Cinema Actors), by the three Vesnin brothers, 1931–34.

Public buildings

In addition to clubs and housing projects, large new public buildings for the different sort of world that the Revolution had ushered in were built during the twenties. Lenin's plan of electrification formulated in 1920 meant that many hydro-electric projects were contemplated. Two of them were built in Moscow to the designs of Kuznetsov and Zholtovsky, who, untypically, designed a line of beautiful grooved glass-clad columns. Other projects were also coming to fruition: new buildings for the information services such as the telegraph and the newspapers, the rebuilding and completion of railway stations such as Kazan and Kursk, economic institutions like the State Bank and offices of Exportkhleb (the wheat exporting body), the new ministries, and para-educational institutions such as the Planetarium and the Lenin Institute for the study of Marxism-Leninism.

The Lenin Institute was part of a plan to rebuild Soviet Square. In the depths of the square dominated by the classical lines of the Kazakov building opposite (Mossoviet) and the old-fashioned figure of the Liberty Obelisk the severely regular shape of the Institute built in 1927 to the design of S. Chernyshev can be seen. For all the many schemes that were proposed it is in fact the only building of those years which was of a genuinely monumental nature. The blank, almost forbidding geometrical shape of the exterior, broken in a steady rhythm by wide squares of glass, conveys an impression of deep seriousness.

Meanwhile in 1927 the great newspaper building for *Izvestiya* was being erected in Pushkin Square. Even today its shape and innovations are exciting – in fact it is probably true that for a building of this size Soviet architecture has nothing better to show. It was built by G. B. Barkhin, an untypical member of MAO and an architect of munitions factories before the Revolution. It has something in common with the Zuyev Club in the squared projections which act as a frame for the glass façade, and in its borrowings from the functionalism of industrial architecture. Here the exterior is not monotonous as in the Lenin Institute. Balconies placed on only one side and the circular windows on the editorial offices of the top floor lend interest to the façade and break up the otherwise severely regular shape. Framed by vertical piers and a horizontal string course of reinforced concrete, the exterior is again predominantly glass. It is self-contained; the printing presses are located at the rear and the editorial offices overlook the square. The original giant lettering of the upper floor has been altered and reduced to include the *Izvestiya* symbol and it is now less robust than originally.

The *Pravda* newspaper building was erected in 1929–34 on the street of the same name by P. Golosov, a member of OSA and brother of the designer of the Zuyev Club. Again a strictly modern building, its large area is divided into two parts, the seven-floor editorial building and the smaller printing works adjacent to it. The façade is marked by horizontal fenestration and the entrance portico is a solid sheet of glass. Glass bays also project from the ends of the building. The large lettering that distinguishes the Zuyev Club and the *Izvestiya* building also appears here at roof level.

Abroad, foreign architects were curious about the new buildings being erected in Soviet Russia. They noted enviously that, in spite of a lamentable backwardness in technology, the state had assumed the ownership of all land and planning, making possible the careful regulation of the growth of cities and the building of low-cost housing on a vast scale. Compared with the prevailing anarchy of private ownership in the countries of western Europe and America conditions for architecture in the USSR must have seemed very attractive. Many of the foremost foreign architects expressed their views in the pages of *Contemporary Architecture* and in 1927 many architects from abroad sent projects to the first exhibition of contemporary architecture organized by OSA. In 1928 a competition was held for an administrative building to house the offices of the Centrosoyuz (Central Union of Consumer Societies) and Le Corbusier's design won first prize.

The building took six years to erect and was not ready until 1936. Much of the time the vulnerable framework with steel reinforcing rods sticking out of concrete

71 *Pravda* building, by P. Golosov, 1929–35.

blocks was exposed to the severity of the Russian climate as the materials needed had been made scarce by the demands of the Five Year Plan. N. Kolly, one of the leading constructivists, collaborated with Le Corbusier and took charge of the work when the master was not in Moscow. Situated on the old Ulitsa Kirova, it was built to face the proposed new Kirov Prospekt on the other side of the building but has had to wait until the 1970s before its proper entrance could be exploited. It is still a breath-taking building. Originally raised on *piloti* in Le Corbusier's manner it has since been enclosed to the detriment of the structure. Nevertheless, it is still possible to admire the unbroken glass façade and the dull red solid block of tufa at the end of the wings facing the street and on the interior side of the wings. Sadly, the solid glass impression of the exterior has been marred by the use of white ruffled curtains that are most incongruous against the clean lines of the building. Soviet authorities refused to contemplate the introduction of a sophisticated ventilating system Le Corbusier had created especially for the building which would have made the curtains redundant and would have overcome the problem created by the large areas of glass of exposing the inhabitants to the vagaries of the climate. The building housed many social amenities including a modified version of a club.

Before leaving the modern architecture of the twenties one other building must be considered that does not belong to any easy category. There has been very little private house building in the Soviet Union since its inception, except for private dachas in the countryside and the homes of some of the important leaders, but an exception to this is Melnikov's own house built in 1927 in central Moscow just off the Arbat on Kirvoarbatsky Pereulok. The house is formed from two intersecting cylinders which meet at the point of a spiral staircase. The rooms are consequently wedge-shaped or have other unusual shapes. The best room is the first-floor study with its huge plate-glass window, while above it is the studio, filled with diamond-shaped apertures. The bedrooms are not separate rooms but are divided by free-standing partitions. In all there are 200 apertures in the house, making it unusually light. An under-floor heating system was installed, a novelty for its time. Many journals and the central press were hostile to the building but there were at least two favourable reviews when it was completed. Melnikov still lives in his unique home, the old man of architecture in Moscow and probably the only Soviet citizen to live in a private house of his own design.

72 The unique private house of the architect Konstantin Melnikov, built in 1927.

The old guard

The architects of the old regime managed to adapt very well, although they had been suddenly jolted in mid-career from the strong currents and predictability of neo-classicism to the unknown world of plain exteriors, asymmetrical shapes and innovatory use of materials. In 1918 when the architectural section of Mossoviet was formed it did not seem unnatural that A. V. Shchusev, already an academician, and I. V. Zholtovsky, almost as equally highly regarded, should take charge of it. They were therefore instrumental in the direction architecture was to take in the early days. Shchusev is in many ways the most interesting character of the old regime. Aged in his early forties, he had made his reputation before the Revolution designing churches and the fabulous Kazan Railway Station. A careful imitator, Shchusev had shown that he could build in almost any style he chose. His versatility became even more marked in the twenties. Although he spent much of his time in an advisory capacity on juries and in Mossoviet, he was not hostile to the new architecture and even helped the younger, unestablished members of the profession by channelling commissions from Mossoviet. Melnikov even lived with him for a time in Serebryany Pereulok near the Arbat. Shchusev seems to have been as influenced by the avant-garde architects as they were by him and he managed to adjust quite successfully to the modern idiom. In 1928 construction began of his Ministry of Agriculture along the Sadovo-Spasskaya Ring Road. Here he used the horizontal fenestration and the steel and concrete frame of his colleagues, although not with so much verve or flair. The most remarkable aspect of the building is the rounded end on Orlikov Pereulok, a glazed circular bay, which effectively relieves the monotony of the sharp-angled building. Walking around Moscow one is struck by the many buildings modelled on the Ministry of Agriculture. Slightly repetitive, they are nevertheless a direct result of modern design as it developed in the 1920s.

73 Ministry of Agriculture (formerly the People's Commissariat of Land), by A. V. Shchusev, 1928–33.

The same flexibility is not to be found in the work of I. V. Zholtovsky. Although not unaffected by the younger generation, particularly in his design for the Moscow Power Station, Zholtovsky, an academician since 1909, was much less susceptible to change than Shchusev. Throughout his career he concentrated exclusively on clever imitation of the forms of the Renaissance, as in his Tarasov House on Aleksei Tolstoy Ulitsa (1909–10). Fifty years old in 1917, after the Revolution he worked with Shchusev in Mossoviet and was in charge of part of the Agricultural Exhibition plans in 1923. Here, as mentioned earlier, his assistant was N. Kolly, and the sparsely decorated pavilions designed by Zholtovsky betray Kolly's touch. From 1927 to 1929 Zholtovsky was in charge of the reconstruction of the central bank, now Gosbank, built originally by Bykovsky in the 1890s. The reconstruction was fundamental, leaving only the central core of the building. Zholtovsky based his design on the early period of the Renaissance in contrast to the baroque favoured by Bykovsky. But Zholtovsky was a more careful imitator than his nineteenth-century predecessor. His *pièce de resistance*, although it belongs more properly to the next decade, should be mentioned here as it was built just at the time of the change-over to the new policy and illustrates the care with which he adapted the Renaissance style. Called simply the 'building on the Mokhovaya', it stands as the first example of Soviet architecture of the thirties. Its great order divides the windows criss-crossed with the rich balustrades of the balconies and the string course. A large overhanging cornice lends it an impression of importance which is reinforced by the fact that it protrudes somewhat into the street; the total effect resembles that of Palladio's richest building, the Loggia del Capitano (1571). For some time it was used as the American Embassy but is now the offices of Intourist.

Another important building of the old guard is the Central Telegraph Office designed by the engineer Rerberg. His design did not even figure among the winners of the competition but, inexplicably, Mossoviet decided to award him the commission. The huge size of the building and its entirely modern function did not prevent Rerberg from designing a sort of office block of the late nineteenth century, the windows carefully held in by the large stone frame, the central entrance unnecessarily large, dwarfing the two wings on either side. The German architect, Bruno Taut, dismissed it as that 'horrible academic misconception of the Main Telegraph Office'.

Thus, Moscow had two parallel streams of contemporary architecture which sometimes merged into each other but more often were in strong competition. OSA and ASNOVA were very hostile to architecture such as the Central Telegraph Office and it seems that deep-seated animosities were bound to arise between the young architects and those of the old guard.

The demise of artistic freedom
By 1928 Trotsky, Zinoviev and Kameniev were ousted. Stalin had consolidated his

74 Central Telegraph Office, by I. Rerberg, 1925–27. Non-revolutionary architecture.

primary position in the party leadership and there was a return to harsher policies. The first Five Year Plan was announced in 1928 and the period of relaxation in the economy was over. Because the backwardness of small agricultural units proved to be a major barrier to the plan for industrialization, a programme of collectivization was forcibly imposed, driving millions off the land and discriminating against the better-off peasants. The labour camps, which Solzhenitsyn reminds us had existed since the Revolution, began at this time to swell their numbers. Within a short period of time the end of limited freedom in the economy was followed by restrictive measures against the few private publishers who had continued to function after the Revolution, and by a more critical attitude to experimentation and liberalism in the arts. The writers were the most obvious targets but even music was forced to come under the direct control of the Party. Although at first architecture was less directly affected, soon there was curtailment of the debate about the merits of planned cities, of communal housing, workers' clubs, and relations with foreign architects. In 1929 VOPRA, the All-Russian Association of Proletarian Architects, was formed. This society believed in the proletarian basis of socialist architecture and attempted to apply the dialectics of Marxism-Leninism to the planning of industrial estates and the future development of Moscow. They were opposed to OSA, the most vociferous of the modern architectural societies, which they accused of a utopian attitude, of elevating the use of technology to the detriment of art, and of imitating the modern architecture of the west. Although on the whole VOPRA's standard of architecture did not approach the level of OSA, a few gifted architects such as Berthold Lubetkin were associated with the society.

By 1929 some members of OSA had sensed the growing hostility of the Party to modern architecture and realized that fragmentation of the architectural societies would not help their cause. They suggested a federation of all the societies, including the small Association of Urban Architects, ARU, which had broken from ASNOVA in 1928. With the exception of VOPRA, all the societies federated to become VANO (MOVANO joined by MAO in 1930 was the Moscow section) and began to campaign for a genuine workers' architecture. They even formulated their own five year plan. Within VANO, OSA became known as SASS – Sector of Architects of Socialist Construction. But even this amalgamation was unacceptable to the Soviet Government. Following reorganization of all the arts on 23 April 1932, the Organization of the Union of Soviet Architects was formed in July from an amalgamation of all the previous societies. This forcible union of the architectural societies represents the dividing line in Soviet architecture between the first era of modern design and the abrupt return to officially sponsored eclecticism.

Ironically, just at the time in the early thirties when Soviet architecture began to look backwards, thousands of foreign engineers, technicians and architects arrived to help in the massive building projects of the first Five Year Plan. The architects were attracted by the opportunity to build for a new workers' state unfettered by private ownership and where the grandiose ideas of the planner could be easily implemented. Le Corbusier was already a frequent visitor to Moscow in connection with his Centrosoyuz building. For the German architects Russia seemed a haven from the reactionary policies of the growth of Fascism. Hannes Meyer, who had replaced Gropius as a director of the Bauhaus, was obliged to leave Germany in 1930 and the Nazis forced the closure of the Bahaus soon after. Meyer was at first happy to settle down to the life of an ordinary architect in Moscow and worked there for some years as chief consultant of GRIPOGOR, the National Institute of Urbanism, where he spent much of his time on the general plan of Moscow. Eventually he left the country for Mexico, probably because he too could not accept the imposition of state control over architecture.

The notable German town-planner Ernst May arrived in Moscow in September 1930 with twenty assistants to take charge of part of the vast new building programme. Among other things he was associated with the development of Magnitogorsk in which many of his ideas on communal housing were incorporated. He recalls, however, that there was the greatest difficulty in obtaining decisions, even over which bank of the river the city was to be built on, and that this was not decided even by the time he left. May also designed a plan for Moscow which envisaged that the city's population would grow to four million (it is now nearly double that number) and grouped twenty-four satellite towns around the centre. It was a great disappointment to him when his plan was rejected although some aspects of it were taken up again in the fifties. May stayed for three years.

It is an extraordinary thing that leading foreign architects who were highly critical of decorative architecture in their own countries, went to great lengths to make allowances for the Soviet adoption of a retrogressive style. However, a few like Bruno Taut and Andre Lurcat plainly saw the writing on the wall. Taut left abruptly in the summer of 1933, quitting the work he had undertaken precisely because of official interference. In an unpublished article he said wistfully, 'In time the present overriding tendency to express the heroism of the revolution in monuments and buildings will hopefully be overcome.' Others, however, saw it differently. Hannes Meyer felt that there were special conditions for the new 'academism' which foreigners could not appreciate, and the normally outspoken Le Corbusier refused to condemn official sponsorship of eclecticism even when his plan for the Palace of Soviets was rejected in favour of a peculiar version of neo-classicism. He said that statues, columns and entablatures were easier for Russians to appreciate because they were still at an early stage of architectural development.

The Russian architects seem to have submitted to the abrupt change in policy without the suicides or attempts to emigrate that occurred among the writers at this time and many of them found it possible to alter their styles just enough to go along with the changes. Of course, the new emphasis on neo-classicism meant that the pre-revolutionary architects of the neo-classical schools, such as Shchusev and Fomin, rose unchallenged to take over the architecture of the thirties, but many of the modern designers like Alexander Vesnin remained on the highest councils, active throughout this decade in design and administration and honoured to the end.

Others, like Melnikov, Leonidov and Ginzburg managed to keep busy teaching or painting and editing general histories or living from commissions quietly passed on to them by colleagues more in tune with the regime. Melnikov's career after the twenties epitomizes the isolation of these resolute architects. He alone was brave enough to publish in 1934 a manifesto refuting criticisms of the buildings he had designed. Two years later, with Leonidov, he was obliged to appear before the Moscow Architectural Institute and was sharply rebuked. After 1936 he spent much of his time painting and teaching in the Building Institute in Moscow but he also persistently designed pavilions for international exhibitions like the New York Exhibition in 1939 and the Seattle World Fair in 1962. After 1930 he received no architectural work in the USSR except for the interior of a department store in Saratov in 1949. During the temporary thaw in relations with the west in 1944 made expedient by the exigencies of war he was awarded an honorary degree but his rehabilitation was only momentary. He was left alone in his amazing cylindrical house and ignored until 1963 when he was again subjected to personal abuse, this time by Khrushchev. Although rehabilitated in the mid-sixties (it became respectable again to praise the work of the modern architects of forty years earlier and a carefully phrased article generally favourable to his work appeared in *Arkhitektura* SSSR in 1966) his many designs remain on the drawing board.

The debate between the modernists and the neo-classicists went on in a muted way until in 1936 all modern design was unequivocally censured as 'formalist'. An amazing fact is that none of the leading avant-garde architects were arrested in the waves of mass arrests and exile that swept through the intelligentsia, the party, all levels of government and all walks of life during the dreadful period of the late thirties. One can only assume that they were too necessary to the regime's dreams of monumental buildings to be discarded. Perhaps also, in spite of past disagreements, a strong fraternity existed between the architects of all schools that preserved them from the mania of mutual denunciation that affected so many of the intelligentsia.

The year 1937 is generally accepted as the beginning of the worst period of the purges in which ten million were reckoned to have lost their lives. It was in this atmosphere that the First Congress of the Union of Architects was held. Obligatory, fulsome eulogies of Stalin took up much of the congress. Molotov made a speech emphasizing even larger monumental buildings and stressing that the Party was sole arbiter of rules governing architecture. 'Formalism', the euphemism for modern architecture, was unanimously attacked. To this semi-political forum came a highly respected foreign guest, Frank Lloyd Wright. Appalled at what he saw in Moscow and at the trend towards ever larger and more imposing buildings, he spoke out frankly at the congress and his speech was even published in *Pravda*. Noting that architecture in the USA was once in the position of contemporary architecture in Russia he said, 'We once had a great opportunity – a "clean slate" as we say. We had to choose between crawling back into the shell of an old culture or going bravely forward to the new one we needed in order to become a strong new culture ourselves. In our new-found freedom we made the wrong choice. We chose the inferior path of the slave. . . . [We] foolishly built upon forms we took from the bargain counter of dying or decayed cultures.' Referring to skyscrapers as false architecture Wright remarked, 'I have seen a dismal reflection of that falsity in your own work palace. . . . And elsewhere among you I see your old enemy, Grandomania – I see it even in your subways.'

However, there was probably little need to remind the architects of their mistakes. Wright later wrote that architects like Shchusev, Alabyan, Vesnin and Kolly were fatalistic about the buildings being put up at that period and told him that all, even the Palace of Soviets, would be torn down in ten years' time.

Although the megalomania for large, monumental buildings had subsided in the late twenties except for occasional hiccups, it was revived on an unimagined scale with the decision in 1930 to build the Palace of Soviets. However, the Palace of Labour planned in the early twenties was never even begun; the projected Palace of Industry on Red Square which would have extended down to the Moscow River and for which the Kitaigorod walls were removed, never got beyond the stage of pouring concrete; and the Palace of Soviets, grandest of all, was not to be completed. Central Moscow was to become a litter bin of huge abandoned building sites some of which remained eyesores for thirty years.

75 The projected Palace of Soviets with the massive statue of Lenin surmounting it.

The Palace of Soviets was planned in honour of the first Five Year Plan, and a competition was opened in 1931. In all, 160 designs were sent in including many from abroad, among which was the one by Le Corbusier. The site for the Palace was to be the territory of the demolished Cathedral of the Redeemer, itself an unrepentantly ugly memorial to the 1812 victory. In this way it was intended that the Kremlin, until now the focal point of Moscow, was to be dwarfed on both sides by two huge buildings, the Palace of Industry flanking it on one side and the Palace of Soviets on the other. Fortunately neither was to get beyond foundation level. In the summer of 1933 the Commission, under Molotov, judged the projects and announced that although there was no outright winner, the design by the Russian architect Iofan was to be accepted as a working basis for the Palace and that Shchuko and Gelfreikh would work with Iofan to revise the plans. The main change suggested by the Commission concerned a statue of a representative of the liberated proletariat.

It was to be replaced by a statue of Lenin and enlarged from the mere 18 metres of the original design to 75 metres in height, the whole Palace acting as a pedestal for the statute. It was intended that building would start by 1 January 1935 but it was not until 1937 that the revised plans were accepted.

Commenting on the design for the Palace of Soviets in the pages of *Stroitelstvo Moskvy* (Moscow Building) Lunacharsky went to some lengths to justify the change of direction in architecture. Although he criticized the eclecticism of the nineteenth century, the butt of his main attack was the functional architecture of recent years, the same architecture he had so enthusiastically supported in the early days of the Revolution. 'Architecture of the bourgeoisie for the past ten years has fallen under the influence of pure engineering and proclaims that beauty lies where a building completely coincides with its purpose like a machine or modern steamship.' Of recent box-like buildings he stated unequivocally that 'the sooner they are expunged from the face of the earth and forgotten by man, the better it will be for everyone'. In their place, he suggested the finer features of Greek architecture and found a convenient quote from Marx in praise of Greek civilization. In speaking of the plans submitted to the competition Lunacharsky half-heartedly admired some aspects of Le Corbusier's project but said finally that it resembled 'a huge hangar for an immense Zeppelin'. Zholtovsky's plan was also dismissed; its fault lay in too closely adhering to the Renaissance style. He praised Iofan's plan both for not avoiding antique motifs but also for not being entirely classical, having a tower growing out of each cylindrical layer. Here was the essence of the approved style of the future – based on classical forms but at the same time not hindered by them.

The great Palace with its two huge halls to seat 20,000 and 8,000 respectively, offices, restaurants, and other amenities, was intended to accommodate meetings of the Supreme Soviet, Party congresses and the like. The site occupied 110,000 square metres and the foundations for this, the largest building in the world, had to be very deep and very strong. Thirty-two pairs of steel columns were to provide the main support and the amount of cement consumed by the foundations amounted to 16 per cent of the annual output in those years. Early in the construction work a major problem connected with water seepage arose and the base was covered with bitumen in an attempt to counteract it. A huge avenue approaching the Palace was to be built from Sverdlov Square. Only the Manege and the University would survive the onslaught of street-widening necessary to obtain the appropriate perspective for the grand edifice. The huge avenue would then swing off across the river and make its way to the Lenin Hills.

Water seepage could well have been expected in a low site so close to the river and it continued to plague the builders. However, by 1941 the huge skeleton was protruding far into the air. The war and subsequent emergency coupled with the increasingly insoluble problem of an unstable foundation not only called a halt to the massive construction but, because of the shortage of steel, eventually resulted in the dismantling of the precious metal from the frame for use in the war effort. The project was really abandoned at this stage although lip service continued to be paid to it for many years. The name of the palatial Palace of Soviets metro station built in 1935 in anticipation of the huge building was changed to the more prosaic 'Kropotkinskaya' in 1953. But the idea of a monumental Palace of Soviets lingered for some time and in 1955 a new competition was held for a palace to be located in the higher and drier Lenin Hills. This too came to nought, as the jury were unable to agree on a design. In 1960 a massive swimming pool was constructed over the foundations of the former Palace of Soviets and the old ladies of Moscow cackled and whispered that the site had been cursed when the great Cathedral was destroyed. Finally the whole question was resolved by the impatient Khrushchev with the building in sixteen months of the Palace of Congresses inside the Kremlin in a thoroughly modern style in 1960–61. Although a direct descendant of the Palace of Labour and the Palace of Soviets it is functional, modern, built on a human scale, and not conspicuously monumental in form. None of the more important buildings in the Kremlin were removed to clear the site and it does not interfere with the age-old panorama of cupolas and bell towers.

76 Palace of Congresses in the Kremlin, by A. Mndoyants, E. Stamo, P. Shteller and N. Shchepetilnikov, 1960–61.

4 ECLECTICISM IN SOVIET ARCHITECTURE

Buildings in the thirties

By 1934 a new term, 'socialist realism', had come into currency, describing what was
required by the regime in all the arts. It was first used at the Congress of the Union of
Writers in 1934 by Andrei Zhdanov. A contradictory theory, calling on the one hand
for revolutionary enthusiasm and on the other for an 'objective' view of reality, its
meaning has always been obscure, thus ensuring that those engaged in the arts do not
clearly understand how it should be interpreted and end up practising a form of self-
censorship. In 1936 Alabyan explained in *Arkhitektura* SSSR that the essence of socialist
realism was sincerity – 'like the buildings at Pompeii, like the harmony of classical
architecture, the complete answer to the questions of the time.' Auguste Perret, the
French architect, was the example most often quoted for Soviet architects in the
thirties. In 1905 he had been one of the first architects to display the concrete frame
of buildings but by the mid-twenties he relapsed into using classical features with the
most modern techniques.

77 Number 6 Gorky Street as rebuilt in the late thirties by A. G. Mordvinov.

The change to socialist realism became conspicuous in all buildings started after 1931, as it became the officially approved style. Those modernist buildings which were not completed until the mid-thirties, like Le Corbusier's Centrosoyuz, received little praise or recognition from the media. When the Vesnin brothers' Palace of Culture was finished in 1937 it was similarly cold-shouldered. However, Zholtovsky's building on the Mokhovaya completed in 1934 was received with warm applause. A few buildings straddle the styles of out-and-out modern design and the reappearance of heavy, decorated architecture. One, by B. M. Iofan, the principal architect of the Palace of Soviets, is the so-called Government Building built in 1928–31 on the south side of the Moskva River. It contains luxury government flats, one of which was inhabited by Svetlana Stalin, in a large building almost featureless except for its geometrical form, the three courtyard entrances and the glazed stairways. It contains 500 spacious flats, a club, stores, a library, a nursery school, laundry and the Udarnik Cinema. Grey and forbidding, it broods over the cheerful seventeenth-century estate of the *Dumny Dyak*. Its façade is free of decorative devices although an elaborate portico marks the entrance to the club, now the New Theatre.

The Frunze Military Academy at Novodeviche Pole designed by L. V. Rudnev, the author of the Monument to the Victims of the Revolution in Leningrad, and V. Muntz, is also not entirely of the new genre. Although without its massive stylobate the building would belong more squarely to the neo-classicist school, with this huge horizontal support it achieves a certain simple strength. On the east corner a square pedestal supported a large, splendid model of a tank which was later removed.

Another transitional piece of architecture is the buildings of the VTSOS, the All-Union Central Council of Trade Unions on Leninsky Prospekt designed by A. V. Vlasov as hostels for students of the new free school, KOMVUZ. The era of the free schools had come to an end by the time the buildings were finished and it was taken over by the union organization. Although the original design was considered too functional in 1934 and was radically revised, it is still interesting, standing as it does on piles. The exterior is marked with loggias and the buildings are placed in a zig-zag fashion instead of facing the street uncompromisingly like the majority of buildings of the thirties.

One construction by a group of architects, Kolly, Orlov and Andreyevsky under the direction of Victor Vesnin, should be included in this survey because although not built in Moscow it was one of the last and best examples of truly grand modern design. This was the great dam built over the Dnieper River, the Dneprostroi. The sweeping, clear simplicity of the curve of the enormous dam with the power station on one side and the flood-gates on the other was, as Lunacharsky put it, 'power, lightness and fitness in the architecture of an industrial building'. Unfortunately it lay in the path of the advancing German armies and was blown up by the retreating Russians in 1941. It was rebuilt after the war but not to the same design.

Other buildings of this time edged more and more towards a franker use of classical and Renaissance motifs and were designed on an increasingly larger scale. The Lenin Library, not completed until 1937, was the result of no less than three competitions held between 1927 and 1929. Finally the design by V. A. Shchuko and V. G. Gelfreikh was chosen in preference to those of more modern architects like the Vesnin brothers. The huge building is dominated by strong vertical piers only slightly softened by recessed windows and manifests the growing fascination with size. The porticos and the statues representing famous figures along the roof place it unequivocally in the architecture of the thirties for all that it was designed earlier. There was no attempt to blend the design with that of the eighteenth-century building by Bazhenov, the Pashkov House, next-door. The only factor important to the designers was its position flanking the new broad avenue that was to lead to the Palace of Soviets.

The heavy Soviet style is clearly evident in four major buildings of the thirties. The first was the Building of the Council of Ministers of the USSR (formerly the Council of Labour and Defence) on Okhotny Ryad on the site of the unbuilt Palace of Labour. Built in 1932–35 by A. Langman, it is a forbidding building with thick vertical lines to its piers, strong cornices, large square entrances and relatively insignificant windows. As yet it lacks the baubles, the prettified mouldings and towers that were to become the symbol of Stalinist architecture; nevertheless it consciously dominates the fine lines of the old Nobles' Club next-door.

Across the street is an equally impressive edifice, the Moskva Hotel built by A. V. Shchusev and his collaborators for Mossoviet and completed in 1935. This granite and concrete structure is larger than life, its portico and ground floor dwarfing the people passing on the streets below. But in spite of its serious appearance, the building harbours a perverse joke. The story goes that Stalin was shown two variants of the plan juxtaposed. Assuming them to be a single design, he approved it as it stood. No-one dared to point out the error and it was built to both designs, the left and right wings differing in almost every respect. More than any other building except perhaps the Red Army Theatre, the Moskva illustrates the effect of Stalin's personal idiosyncracies on architecture.

One of the leading members of the architects' union, Alabyan, was the architect of the Red Army Theatre building, completed in 1940. Symbolism and grandeur had gone mad here. The vast building was in the shape of a five-pointed star, the symbol of the Red Army and a shape utterly unrelated to the functions of a theatre, despite the clever use of the points of the star as staircases and dressing rooms. It was encumbered with numerous classical excrescences – Alabyan told Frank Lloyd Wright that he had put all the columns he would ever use for the rest of his life in the design of the theatre. The idea of the theatre, so utterly different from the functionalism of the constructivists a decade earlier, was so unrealistic that even Khrushchev, who as Moscow Party Secretary was closely involved with building in

78 Moskva Hotel, by A. V. Shchusev, L. I. Savelyev and O. A. Stapran, 1932–35. Compare the right wing with the left. The difference arises from Stalin's approval of two variations of the plan, not realizing that they were meant to be alternatives.

---

79 The Red Army Theatre, in the shape of a star. By A. Alabyan, 1935–40.

Moscow in the thirties felt strongly enough about it to deride the plan in 1961 pointing out that the star shape of the building could only be appreciated from the air.

Where the Kaluga Gate, formerly the eighteenth-century boundary of Moscow, opens onto the broad reaches of Leninsky Prospekt, there are two curved buildings like huge wings separated from each other by the ribbon of the seven-lane highway, a modern adaptation of the ancient Russian tradition of triumphal entry gates into the city. They were built by Fomin, Leninson and Arkin in 1940 and are a prime example of the monumental prevailing over the utilitarian. In this case, the buildings were intended as living accommodation but their position astride the highway must make them very uncomfortable for those living in the flats. Mikhail Andreyevich Il'in in his 1961 guidebook to Moscow has an interesting comment to make about the apartment houses of this period:

The desire to make every building a 'monument of the epoch', a monument of victory and triumph, resulted in a breakdown of the architecture of buildings into their volume and external 'form'. The use of original elements in the construction of every building slowed down the development not only of industrial construction but of all construction. Such a situation was especially sharply evident with apartment houses. Architecture had lost touch with the living needs of the Soviet people.

Such was the development of Russian architecture that at the Paris Exhibition of 1937 certain similarities were noticed between the Soviet and German pavilions. In general, both Soviet and German architecture of the thirties was expressed in the need for large squares for demonstrations and emphasis on heavy solid façades where the windows were only of secondary interest, in a yearning for size and monuments to the glory of the state.

The real achievement of the thirties lay not in the erection of stultified buidings but in engineering. The Moskva River which regularly flooded its banks was finally tamed in the mid-thirties by the building of a series of embankments and quays which somehow have the period stamp without being grossly ugly. Between 1936 and 1938 seventeen bridges were built or rebuilt in Moscow including seven over the Yauza River. At the same time the Moskva-Volga Canal was constructed providing the city with a reliable source of water and, for the first time, a direct water link to the Volga. Two huge statues of Lenin and Stalin stood on either side of the main sluice-gates. But the greatest engineering feat was undoubtedly the metro. Even before the revolution the planners had discussed the possibility of building an underground railway and in 1923 a plan was published which envisaged six lines. The decision to begin building was taken in 1931 and the first line was opened in May 1935. Kropotkinskaya (Palace of Soviets) station received the most attention but on the whole the metro stations are distinguished by their sheer size and spaciousness, the lavish use of expensive materials like marble, a certain element of palatial grandeur

80 Kaluga Gate, by I. I. Fomin, E. A. Leninson, and A. E. Arkin, 1940.

and a definite feeling of coldness. The lack of colour, the subdued tones, the fanatical cleanliness, and the silent, hurrying masses, make it a slightly unreal world. Contrasted with the Art Nouveau stations of Paris or the design of stations like Arnos Grove in London they appear forbidding, not on a human scale.

The reconstruction of Moscow

Town planning had preoccupied Mossoviet since 1918 when the idea of the reconstruction of Moscow first came under discussion but at that time priority was given to cleaning up the city in preparation for rebuilding at a future date. Little stalls and kiosks that cluttered the pavements were removed, the sprawling markets taken away, and factories and garbage dumps moved to outside the city.

In 1924 a new plan for Moscow by Shestakov was agreed in which most of the new building was to be concentrated in the outer, relatively empty fringes, and the centre, apart from the Palace of Labour, the Palace of Industry and the enlargement of Soviet Square, was to be untouched. The plan was criticized in *Izvestiya* and other publications for treating Moscow as a museum of ancient buildings. Gradually the Shestakov plan became discredited and by the late twenties the debate had moved to a more theoretical level. The urbanists, such as L. Sabsovich, planned new cities of communal houses. They were opposed to the de-urbanists, such as M. Okhitovich of OSA. He favoured individual houses isolated from each other by plots of land and woods dotted all over Russia and joined to places of work and schools by superhighways. For the de-urbanists there was to be no difference between town and country; Moscow was to be depopulated and turned into a great park. In May 1930 the Central Committee issued a decree against utopianism in architecture and roundly criticized the town-planners, both urbanists and de-urbanists.

In 1932 Kaganovich, the Soviet leader, who with his assistant N. S. Khrushchev, was most involved with the development of Moscow, requested a new plan of the city. Just before the new plan was made public in 1935 a sycophantic letter was sent from the Organizing Committee of the Union of Soviet Architects to Kaganovich praising his wonderful 'iron' leadership in the plan for the rebuilding of Moscow. It was signed by Shchusev, Ginzburg, Vesnin and many others. There was no longer any question that the planners and architects might work unfettered by the demands of the Party and state. Moscow received the most attention because it was the seat of all the central apparatus and because most of the Soviet leaders lived there.

In July 1935 the plan was announced with a great fanfare, proclaiming that the barbarous Russian city built by capitalism was to be come a socialist city, the most beautiful in the world. The plan attempted to avoid two extremes: on the one hand it did not leave the centre of Moscow untouched but on the other it did not propose that all existing buildings should be destroyed as, it was alleged, Le Corbusier had recommended.

The most important aspect of the plan was the widening of the main arteries, the extension and regulation of the lines of the squares – in a passion for the straight line, as Grabar put it – and the retention of the radial, circular historical development of the city. However, if all the widening and straightening envisaged in the plan had been carried out Moscow would have been changed almost beyond recognition. Red Square was to have been doubled in width and GUM, the large department store, was to have disappeared. The Garden Ring Road was to be widened. In every district there was to be a large square for administrative buildings. Many large arteries were to be built particularly these linking the centre with the Palace of Soviets. But of all the projected broad criss-crossing roads only a few were ever started. Prospekt Marksa was widened and all the buildings in the huge space of Revolution Square were removed as part of the grand design to form an avenue leading to the Palace of Soviets. The Garden Ring Road was indeed widened but at the expense of the lovely old lime trees that fronted all the buildings and that gave it its name. Although more parks were to be added in the outskirts, they could not compensate for the removal of these breathing spaces in the centre of a city otherwise devoid of greenery. Red Square remained untouched and it was only in the new districts that the new central squares were built. The plan also predicted that as many flats would be built in the succeeding ten years as had been built in the previous one hundred but this aspect did not receive primacy of place.

The main achievement of the plan in the late thirties was the radical reconstruction of Gorky Street. Here the mania for rectilinear development and

Реконструируемые магистрали   Существующая граница города

Проектируемые магистрали   Проектируемая граница города

81 The 1935 plan of Greater Moscow. Most of the main arteries have not been built.

wide streets took precedence over any other consideration. The Tverskaya, as it was known until 1935, had been the principal road of Moscow since ancient times when it formed the main artery leading to Tver and Novgorod. Attempts had been made in the rebuilding of Moscow after 1812 to make it more regular, but it remained a winding, curving narrow street about three kilometres long, symbolic of the tortuous and Byzantine forms of Moscow compared with the wide, open avenues of the more rational St Petersburg. Now all that was to change. There were already new buildings on Gorky Street, such as the Lenin Institute, the Telegraph and the *Izvestiya* building. In the first years of the Five Year Plan so much effort was put into the expansion of industry that capital, labour and materials were in extremely short supply for building. Two solutions were tried; one was to build temporary prefabricated two-storey houses of wooden panels but this method was discontinued in 1935, in favour of more permanent dwellings; the other method was far cheaper, involving the addition of an upper storey or stories to already existing buildings. This method was used all over Moscow, especially in Gorky Street.

The few churches on Gorky Street, the Passion Monastery, and the Triumphal Gate at the entrance to the street from the north were all pulled down. To straighten the street and more than double its width it was decided to rebuild on the east side from Revolution Square and to leave the west side with the National Hotel and the Telegraph building unaltered. Further up, near Pushkin Square and beyond, reconstruction took place on both sides of the street. The new construction went on behind the existing buildings which were then pulled down when the new ones were completed, although in some cases parts of the old buildings were incorporated into the new. In 1937–38 the first large building, the eight-storey Block A, was erected opposite the National Hotel. Seven or eight stories were considered the right proportion to the widened street. Block B followed on from Block A. Further up, Pushkin Square neatly denuded of its convent, was to be the site of a cinema and a museum about Pushkin (not yet built) and the statue of the writer was transferred from the square to the entrance to Tverskoi Boulevard across the street. Further up again, the Museum of the Revolution (the former English Club) was to remain but its wings were to be removed. At Mayakovsky Square where the street intersects with the Ring Road, a new, large, rectangular square was to be built to the west of the street with a concert hall. A. G. Mordvinov, who worked in Kharkhov before the Revolution, was the architect of Blocks A and B (Nos 4 and 6) and Blocks V and G (Nos 15 and 17) on the west side of the street. Blocks A and B with the Council of Ministers building and the Moskva Hotel formed an entirely different entrance to the street. The blocks are large, heavy cubes with small windows, hints of classical appurtenances like balconies and belvederes, but utterly lacking the sense of purity, of obedience to specific laws, that was the main gift of classicism. Perhaps the best feature of the blocks is the large archways that lead on the western side to Bryusovsky Lane and Stanislavsky Street. To pass through one of the archways is to step from a ponderous, serious world to the charm of the early nineteenth century, still untouched by redevelopment, full of little shops, ateliers, and embassies, and blessedly quiet after the turmoil of Gorky Street.

One of the main problems of the reconstruction of Gorky Street was the protruding form of Mossoviet, housed in the eighteenth-century Kazakov building which had been the residence of the governors-general of Moscow. Without actually pulling down the old palace, the rebuilders completely changed its appearance and mutilated its once fine proportions so that it is no longer easily recognized as an eighteenth-century mansion. Its wings and entrance porch were taken off and in 1939 it was literally moved back into the courtyard. Then two floors were added and the huge, typically Soviet entranceway cut into the centre of the house. There it stood opposite the Liberty obelisk and the Lenin Institute, flanked by new buildings in the dismal Soviet style, the whole making an incongruous group. Other buildings beside Mossoviet were moved back several feet and finally Gorky Street assumed its modern shape, a mathematical straight line.

Rebuilding went on at an increased pace in many parts of Moscow in the form of ribbon development mostly along the main routes leading out of the city. Thus Leningradskoe Shosse leading north and Bolshaya Kaluga Ulitsa (Leninsky Prospekt) leading south received much attention. The blocks which were used as flats or for administration purposes or even shops were inevitably seven to nine stories high and were very like the Mordvinov designs for Gorky Street but usually without the saving grace of the grand archway. In 1939 of all the flats under construction, 52 per cent were on the main thoroughfares.

82 Mossoviet, the Moscow City Council. Rebuilt by D. Chechulin in 1939–45 from the eighteenth-century Governor's Mansion.

National styles

There is one other trend in the thirties that must be mentioned. Stalin's famous dictum about the arts, 'national in form, socialist in content', was interpreted in architecture as an invitation to design in pseudo-national styles taking for inspiration the ancient architectural forms of the republics. Although ancient Russian forms also made tentative appearances, it was the geometrical features of Central Asia that caught the imagination. Motifs of the ancient mosques and palaces of Uzbekistan and Kazakhstan were used in the national pavilions built for the Agricultural Exhibition of 1937 and appeared on the regular cube of the Chaikovsky Concert Hall of 1940 (in the by now enlarged Mayakovsky Square) where the geometrical design of the exterior competed with statues around the roof.

The war years

In 1941 the Soviet Union was invaded by the German Army and by the autumn of that year the Germans had stormed their way as far as Khimki within five kilometres of Moscow. Here they were halted perhaps as much by the extremely severe winter which set in unusually early as by the fierce resistance of the Soviet forces. In Moscow all building activity ceased except for building work on the metro which was considered part of civil defence. The huge site of the Palace of Soviets was stripped of its metal and the almost equally huge site of the Palace of Industries was left vacant. Stalin refused to abandon the city although government offices and foreign representatives were removed to Kuibyshev. The exigencies of the war, during which the Soviet Union found itself in alliance with Britain and the USA against the Axis Powers, meant that relations improved with the western countries. Many articles began to appear in the Russian architectural press on the achievements of modern architecture in America and in June 1942 an exhibition of English architecture was held in Moscow. For a time it must have seemed to the architects that with the ending of the war a relaxation of the pompous, eclectic architecture of the thirties was a definite possibility. Even Melnikov was given recognition during the war and in 1945 Victor Vesnin was allowed to receive the RIBA gold medal. But the rehabilitation of Melnikov was short-lived and the flirtation of Victor Vesnin with Britain cut short.

In 1946 the Cold War started and Soviet policy became distinctly anti-western. This was felt particularly in the arts, especially literature, and pro-western journals like *Zvezda* and *Leningrad* were forced to cease publication. In architecture there was a resigned return to monumental building. *Kultura i Zhizn* in 1949 published an article attacking a number of architects, including Khiger, Ginzburg and Arkin, for 'grovelling servility before the capitalist architecture of America'. Architects were instead invoked to 'create outstanding works of socialist architecture which reflect the glory and the greatness of the Stalinist epoch'. They set out to do just that. Although there was unremitting criticism of the skyscrapers of decadent America,

Moscow itself gradually began to acquire its own tower blocks. They exceeded by several times the height of the tallest bell-towers of medieval Moscow and changed its landscape beyond anything that had been previously built in Soviet times. Seven of the mammoth buildings were planned and built between 1949 and 1957 ranging from twenty to thirty stories high with central towers, spires, Soviet stars. Some were flanked by lesser buildings, and only one was erected in the unbuilt, relatively empty area on the outskirts of Moscow. Some, like the thirty-floor apartment block on Kotelicheskaya Naberezhnaya (1949–53) by D. N. Chechulin and A. K. Rostovsky, were decorated profusely with sculpture and gothic-style towers giving a 'wedding-cake' appearance. On Ploshchad Vostanyy M. V. Posokhin (now the city architect) and A. A. Mndoyants built a twenty-four-storey tower block. At Komsomolskaya Square near the three most colourful of Moscow's railway stations, the Leningrad Hotel of twenty floors was erected in 1954 by L. M. Polyakov and Boretsky. The corner of Sadovaya-Spasskaya and Kalanchevskaya Street was given a twenty-five-floor tower by A. N. Dushkin and B. S. Mezentsev for the Ministry of Communication. The Foreign Trade Ministry similarly towered over Smolensk Square. The Ukraine Hotel, not finished until 1957, dominated the south-west bank of the city and the huge edifice of the new University on Lenin Hills gazed sternly over the city spread in panorama before it. It would seem strange that so much attention and effort could be spent on buildings such as these when the chronic housing shortage facing Moscow had become even more critical during the war. Although the officially accepted standard is nine square metres of living space person it has never been achieved in the Soviet Union. In 1923 in Moscow there was 6·45 square metres of housing per person but this declined to 4·94 in 1932 and to 4·09 in 1940. By 1950 there was a slight improvement to 4·67 but it still lagged far behind the space available in the early twenties.

5 RESTORATION FROM 1931 TO TODAY

Although many old buildings disappeared in the thirties, especially churches in the anti-religious campaigns, a limited amount of restoration was permitted in the ancient cities of Novgorod, Yaroslav and Vladimir. With the deliberate German destruction of ancient palaces like Peterhof, the eleventh-century buildings of Kiev, the early medieval buildings of Novgorod and the seventeenth-century churches and cells of the New Jerusalem Monastery outside Moscow, the official attitude changed regarding the preservation of old buildings. Immediately the areas were liberated architects and specialists were encouraged to move in and save as much as possible. The work was tackled with great enthusiasm and in time many monasteries and palaces were painstakingly rebuilt. In Moscow only a few buildings had suffered direct attack – the Gagarin House on Novinsky Boulevard was lost this way – but the city itself had been neglected and run down during the war. To mark the celebration

МОСКВА - 14

of eight centuries of Moscow's existence the Kremlin, St Basil's and other important buildings of the centre were repaired and repainted in 1948. For the occasion Stalin ordered that the Liberty Obelisk on Soviet Square, unveiled by Lenin at the first anniversary of the Revolution, be removed and a statue of Yuri Dolgoruky, the founder of Moscow, be put in its place. Stalin, the inheritor of the Revolution, chose to replace its first monument with an insipid impression of the twelfth-century prince.

However, this initial care in the post-war period was distressingly short-lived. By the end of the forties and early fifties Stalin's lavish skyscrapers were going up and more metro lines began to be built. Many churches, palaces and more of the remaining Kitaigorod walls disappeared during this construction. It was not until the middle of the fifties after Stalin died that restoration on a large scale became possible again. The general relaxation, slight as it was after Stalin's death, allowed those with a deep interest in the architecture of the past quietly to get on with the job of studying, surveying and caring for the ancient buildings. It might have been supposed that the years of inactivity would have caused the restorers to drift off into other fields but this was not so. Because of the forcible alignment to the prevailing dogma of Soviet neo-classicism and the crude use of national styles, many architects of principle and feeling sought their careers in other directions, either as art historians, or as painters and lecturers, or as restorers. There was no lack of talent.

In 1955 the Kremlin, which had been a free museum before the Revolution, was opened to the public for the first time since 1918. This marked the watershed of liberation from the tyranny of suspicion and terror that marked Stalin's rule. The ancient Kremlin which no-one had dared to enter uninvited during the entire period of Soviet rule was at last accessible. The government retained its offices, the Senate continued to be used as the Council of Ministers building, and the Great Palace redesigned in the thirties became convenient for government receptions. Sometimes, even today, the Kremlin is arbitrarily closed to the public if important meetings of government and Party are taking place there, but otherwise, it is freely accessible to all.

The restorers began to proliferate all over Moscow, surrounding this or that decaying old building with scaffolding, turning out the tenants who had lived among frescoes and grand rooms since the housing crises of the twenties. Their job was enormous. The Troitsa v Nikitnikakh in Kitaigorod was cleared of numerous tenants and the damaged frescoes and structure of the building were subjected to such careful scrutiny that it was only opened to the public in 1968. One of the most delightful churches in Moscow, the Nikita shto za Yauzy was described in 1948 in Solzhenitsyn's *First Circle* as resembling a bombed-out structure: 'a building of curious shape which had the air of a ruin yet of something that had somehow remained odly intact'. The 'ruin' was most carefully restored in 1958–60 by L. Davyd, a well-known restorer and head of the Central Restoration Workshop.

83 Skyscraper block of flats on Kotelnicheskaya Naberezhnaya, by D. N. Chechulin and A. K. Rostovsky 1949–53.

There were many examples like the Nikita Church but the most impressive is the restoration of the Andronikov Monastery and of its fine centrepiece, the Spassky Sobor (Saviour Cathedral), the oldest building in Moscow. During the most nihilistic period, the end of the twenties and beginning of the thirties, much of the walls and towers and the bell-tower were dismantled but in 1947 the monastery was taken under state care and the people living there were asked to leave. Although some research had taken place in the thirties, when one of the finest architectural restorers and historians, Maksimov, had discovered that the original walls were still extant under the nineteenth-century layer, it was not until the mid-fifties that restoration was tackled properly. The problems were immense. The cathedral had been badly burnt in the 1812 fire and in 1847 had been rebuilt in an altogether different form. Much research had to be carried out before the restorers were sure of the form of the cathedral but finally, in time for the six hundredth anniversary of Rublyev's birth in 1960, the wonderful gabled church was complete. Other buildings in the monastery were likewise restored: the Archangel Church, the Abbot's building, the refectory and monks' cells, and finally the old walls with a lovely fretted wooden gate.

This state of affairs continued until after the Twenty-first Party Congress in 1959 when there was an attempt to expand the industrial sector and to tackle the ever-present housing problem. Again the old parts of Moscow were under threat. From about 1959 to 1964 when Khrushchev was forced to resign, a second period of deliberate dismantling of ancient buildings occurred. There was no-one on the highest councils of Party and state prepared to oppose Khrushchev. His personal attitude was made explicit at the January 1961 plenum when he said scornfully: 'And near Moscow many unnecessary objects of olden times have been put under restoration orders. You will recall, comrades, that people sometimes throw such matters at you, those who want to warm their own hands skilfully coax you. They say something like this: "Here you are, a cultured person, you know and understand the meaning of this ancient monument. You understand and value the fact that this famous person walked here, here he sat and considered his plans, and here he angrily spat." . . . I do not exaggerate, comrades; such outrages happen.' Although not so sweeping as in the thirties the destruction was considerable and many fine buildings were taken off the protected list. Although there were no exact figures, B. V. Talantov, a mathematics teacher in Kiev, estimated that from 1959 to 1964 about 10,000 churches were shut in Russia and that many of these were then demolished.

Khrushchev was removed from power at a meeting of the Central Committee Plenum on 15 October 1964 and after that his 'subjectivism' as it was officially called was no longer a factor. Almost immediately the climate changed with regard to the conservation of old buildings. In 1965 the All-Russian Voluntary Society for the Protection of Ancient Historical and Cultural Monuments was formed and public interest was elicited to help tackle the problem on a national scale. A fund for voluntary contributions was set up and was quickly oversubscribed. Many churches were saved that would otherwise have been demolished. In Moscow a whole street of churches on Ulitsa Razina that were to have been brought down with the construction of the Rossiya Hotel in 1964 were carefully restored: St Barbara, Maxim the Greek, the Znamensky Monastery, Georgi na Pskovksom gore, plus the first English Embassy and the lovely Zachatiya Anny shto v uglu.

Many articles appeared in both the central and specialist press after 1964 extolling the virtues of early Russian architecture. The problems of preservation were also discussed frankly and Krushchev was openly criticised – most unusually considering the otherwise utter silence with which his departure was treated. Writers even felt emboldened enough to suggest that old buildings should be utilized as they were originally intended; thus, churches should be used as places of worship. A growing slavophile movement arose in the mid-sixties under the leadership of writers like Vladimir Soloukhin and artists like Ilya Glazunov and supported oddly enough by the Komsomol, and the movement shared these views.

In recent years there has been an active programme of restoration and repair to Moscow's suburbs as well as the centre, and many lovely buildings, particularly churches, have reappeared from the neglect of previous waves of restoration. In Moscow there are now reckoned to be over 2,000 buildings under state protection and there has even been a start to the proper cataloguing and listing of old buildings according to a broadened category. Although the use to which the newly restored buildings is put is still a subject for controversy and fresh activity in the redevelopment of Moscow has again put whole districts in jeopardy, there is no doubt that recent years have seen advances in the protection of old buildings. Yet the

84 Restoring the sixteenth-century Angliskoe Podvore on Ulitsa Razina in 1970.

essential fickleness of the Soviet system towards issues not considered fundamental to its development means that the protection of ancient buildings will always be vulnerable to abrupt changes of policy.

6 ABOUT FACE: THE RETURN TO MODERN DESIGN

Stalin died on 5 March 1953. His death, at the age of 73, was a great relief; there were indications that even his closest henchmen had had a surfeit of the unremitting capriciousness and intimidation of his rule. Relief at his death led to a tentative 'thaw', the phrase coined by Ehrenburg, but it was not until 1956 that there was a real relaxation. After a certain amount of manoeuvring among the political leaders, Khrushchev emerged as the main figure. His position was not cemented until 1957 when he ousted the anti-Party group (among whom was his former colleague in the Moscow Party Organization, Kaganovich). Hopes for a more liberal attitude led to unrest in eastern Europe of which the most explosive example was the Hungarian Revolution, quickly followed by the reassertion of Soviet control. These liberal aspirations could not fail to be reflected in the arts where literature began to take on a franker air and authors felt able to discuss controversial issues.

The effect of Stalin's death on architecture was dramatic and swift. In December 1954 an All-Union Conference of Builders was held at which Khrushchev and all the members of the presidium and secretariat attended. Khrushchev made an extraordinary speech which announced the death knell of the architecture which had prevailed in the USSR since the June plenum of 1931. His main target was the passion for decoration in Stalinist architecture and the expense and waste that was concomitant with it. In particular he attacked the new skyscrapers in Moscow, some still in the process of being built, and lashed out at Mordvinov, the principal architect and planner of these buildings. He announced that if the trend towards decoration was not stopped it 'will expand excessively' and that 'such architecture has become the stumbling-block on the path to the industrialization of building'. Khrushchev was careful, however, not to criticize the architecture of the thirties in which he himself had played no small part. It was carefully stressed that one of the best periods of Soviet architecture was 1931–35, during which time buildings like the early metro stations and the Dneprostroi were built. In a way this limited criticism, which did not proceed to its logical conclusion, was like the secret speech where the denunciation of Stalin was not intended to be made public or fully discussed. Although in favour of simplicity and more standardization it did not follow that he wanted a reintroduction of modern design – in fact in the same speech he went to some lengths to discredit the constructivists of the twenties. He was obviously most interested in buildings that went up rapidly, were not excessively expensive, and were efficiently organized with prefabricated blocks and partitions. Style did not interest him deeply but ostentation did not suit his temperament and he

---

85 Restoration in the courtyard of the Police Headquarters in 1970.

was impatient to solve the real problems of the USSR, of which housing was one of the most serious. The call for simplicity and functionalism could not but lead in the end to the clean lines of modern architecture.

The old guard architects of the thirties, now entering old age, fell under official disapproval. The work of Fomin, Shchuko, Rudnev and Gelfreikh was criticized as being 'one-sided' but the attack did not result in a change in their positions.

A year later a more forceful attack was launched. On 10 November 1955 *Pravda* published a CPSU resolution signed by Khrushchev and Bulganin. 'On the Removal of Excesses in Planning and Building' only a few days before the second architectural congress was due to open on 26 November. The sentiments were very similar to those expressed in the speech to the Builders' Conference. Architecture should be the epitome of 'simplicity, severity of form and efficiency', an interpretation very similar to the definition of 'formalism' (which then meant constructivism) in the *Large Soviet Encyclopedia* of 1947. The resolution named the culprits and particularly attacked the wedding-cake tower of the Leningrad Hotel which, with its 354 rooms, can make use of only 22 per cent of the total area for the needs of the hotel. Its maintenance costs were said to be exorbitant. The architects, Polyakov and Borevetsky, were deprived of their Stalin prizes. Several others lost their awards or their positions, although Mordvinov, the arch 'excessor' who had given way to Vlasov as President of the Academy of Architecture in May, merely had his 'mistakes' pointed out to him. As chief architect in Moscow, Vlasov was on a visit to study ferro-concrete construction in the United States when the resolution was published. It seemed at first as if he too might be forced to resign but this did not happen and there seems to have been little attempt to get rid of the old guard architects. Certainly, the modern architects of the twenties were not encouraged to make a comeback.

The architectural congress simply endorsed the recommendations of the resolution and concentrated on the themes of economy and simplicity. There were many confessions of 'mistakes'. During the conference it became clear that the size of buildings was to be limited to five stories instead of the seven to eight stories approved in the thirties, or the thirty-storey skyscrapers in the post-war period. The many blocks of flats erected in the greatly increased building programme after 1955 are popularly known as 'Khrushchev boxes'. The magical number of five stories was dictated by the demand for cheaper construction; with more than five stories lifts are required. Built of heavy prefabricated panels to completely standardized designs, such blocks proliferated in the new housing districts in the south-west, Novye Cheremushky and Khorosheve-Mnevniky, and were intended as no more than a short-term expedient, not the final answer to the socialist dream of good housing for all.

During the next twenty years Soviet architecture slowly emerged from the deadening influence of heavily stylized monuments to become an architecture which is almost indistinguishable from contemporary modern design anywhere in the world; in many cases the Soviet examples, like the Comecon building on Prospekt Kalinina or the new Moscow Arts Threatre, are fine additions to the fund of modern architecture. But this transformation did not occur overnight. Exhortations from the Party and government to refrain from the 'excesses' and decorated façades of the past went on unceasingly until the mid-sixties. Khrushchev himself continually demanded that architecture should be simpler and more standardized. He raised the matter in 1958 and again in 1961 at the third Congress of Architects. Articles on foreign architects, such as Niemeyer in Brasilia, Le Corbusier and others, began to appear regularly in Soviet journals. Palaces of culture, the inheritors of the clubs of the twenties, were the worst offenders in the lingering use of neo-classicism; their designers were most reluctant to relinquish the porticos and columns that even today immediately identify them in Soviet cartoons. Eventually the columns were thinned out until finally they disappeared from new buildings altogether, at least in Moscow. The completion of several contemporary buildings in the early sixties like the huge Pioneers' Palace, a grandiose club for children in the Lenin Hills, marks the end of the neo-classical phase. Sparkling with plate glass, wide flat roofs, and straight lines, it sprawls over 56 hectares, boasting a concert hall, rooms for hobbies, a swimming pool, a stadium, winter and summer sports areas, nature trails and even an open-air theatre. It is the realization of the sort of club dreamed of in the twenties but its vast size and the huge area it serves militate against the communal efficaciousness of such facilities.

An interesting development in the early sixties happened with an unusual article in the journal *Moskva* in March 1962 which hinted at a much franker discussion of the problems of Soviet architecture. The *Moskva* article must be seen in the light of developments in the early sixties. The removal of Stalin's body from the Lenin Mausoleum signified an apparent lifting of restraints on many aspects of Soviet culture; among other things Solzhenitsyn's *One Day in the Life of Ivan Denisovich* was published and created a storm of comment, and an exhibition of abstract art was staged in the Manege. Reaction to these liberal trends sparked off by Khrushchev's visit to the Manege exhibition soon set in and in the case of architecture the liberal awakening never really got off the ground. The *Moskva* article was based on a report of a meeting some months earlier of those engaged in working out the general plan of Moscow. The authors of the article reported that at the meeting there was outspoken criticism of Moscow's architectural planners. They were accused of allowing the concentration of too many new buildings in the centre of Moscow, of being responsible for the lamentable rectilinear development of the thirties which cut painfully through the naturally winding streets, of building excessively luxurious façades, of allowing industry to pollute the atmosphere of the city, of not providing enough green spaces in the new residential areas in the south-west, of always insisting on one height for residential buildings at any one time, and of secrecy surrounding planning decisions. The editors of *Moskva* hoped the article would spark off a general discussion on the subject but they were disappointed by a long article in *Pravda* of 11 May signed by twenty-one architects and engineers which refuted the criticisms of the *Moskva* article and accused the authors of trying to preserve Moscow as a museum city. Thus, the first foray into a genuine debate since the twenties was thrust back and the editors of *Moskva* were obliged to apologize humbly for their audacity.

Yet some of these criticisms were taken up in a milder form, especially in connection with the building of the new satellite towns, the micro-rayons recommended by Khrushchev at the Twentieth Party Congress in 1956. Grouped around the outskirts of Moscow, they were a fine idea in the now genuine attempt to solve the housing problem (in 1965 the USSR was building more housing than any other country in the world) but the speed with which new flats were being put up caused problems of construction. The micro-rayons seemed remote and isolated to many Moscow citizens and there were constant complaints about poor transport connections and service facilities. Yet by 1970 housing in Moscow had improved to such an extent that the authorities were able to rehouse those living in basement flats in the centre. The 1935 plan still provided the basis for Moscow's redevelopment and the official attitude to the historical centre was that it should be left as it was unless there was an urgent need to widen roads or to rebuild. Among these priorities were the new Prospekts of Kalinina and Kirova which have cut swathes reaching almost to the Kremlin. With Prospekt Dmitrova, which was later to be widened, they were all part of the original 1935 plan.

The concept that communal housing could assist Soviet man in the 'transformation of the way of life' made a brief reappearance at this time. In a strongly worded article in 1958 Selim Omarovich Khan-Magomedov argued that with the about-turn away from decorative architecture in 1954 it was time to reconsider the achievements of the twenties, in particular communal housing. Some so-called 'experimental housing' was built in the mid-sixties with many facilities not normally provided in residential blocks; these included communal dining-rooms available to these who wished to make use of them, but separate kitchens were also included with every flat and the idea does not seem to have taken hold. In 1973 in an article on future housing in *Arkhitecktura* SSSR the emphasis was on increasing the size of flats to four, five, and six rooms in place of the standard single-room flat. Communal dining facilities would be part of the new scheme but only as a means of relieving women of the chore of cooking, not as an instrument in developing the true socialist society.

The former villains of the thirties, Ginzburg, Melnikov and even Leonidov, were 'rehabilitated' in the course of the sixties with the appearance of serious articles appraising their work. Melnikov was honoured by the staging of an exhibition of his work to mark his seventieth birthday.

In spite of the acceptance of the prevailing international style of architecture

Soviet leaders still yearned for monuments to emphasize the glory of the state. The cult of Lenin had taken on the attributes of a new religion and in every provincial town one or more statues of the great leader presided over the main square. But in Moscow there was an extraordinary dearth of statues of him. Certainly plaster casts could be found in children's play areas and tucked away in odd corners of parks but there was no main statue of Lenin in a central position. To rectify this several competitions were held in the early sixties for a statue to be placed in Lenin Hills in an imposing position in front of the University. It was hoped that the statue could be unveiled in time for the fiftieth anniversary of the Revolution in 1967 or at least in time for the centenary of Lenin's birth in 1970. But it was not to be. The jury criticized the entries as being far too traditional, of not making imaginative use of the site, and the memorial was not commissioned. Finally a small statue was put up in the Kremlin near the Palace of Congresses where it is inconspicuous, the only statue of Lenin in the central part of Moscow.

Looking back over the twentieth century, Moscow, in common with other great capitals of the world, has altered more than at any other time in its history. To take just one indicator, the population, which was under 2 million in 1910, is now approaching 8 million, an expansion that could not but transform the city out of all recognition. Reconstruction continues to tear out and rip apart the gentle old parts of the city and it would be unrealistic to expect the processes of change to halt suddenly. The many fine buildings that are under the precarious protection of the state will probably be preserved but the danger is that they may eventually be isolated, surrounded and overwhelmed by large modern alien buildings like the poor little Zachatiya Anny Church beside the Rossiya Hotel. It is hoped that some odd corners in the centre in addition to the Kremlin and Red Square, like the delightfully quiet streets of the old Ukrainian quarter or the calm nineteenth-century feel of Stanislavskaya Street, will remain untouched and unspoiled by the frenzy of building. Moscow's periphery is quite naturally the most sensible place for its future development and, to be just, it is there that most of the new building has been concentrated. New building is essential if the city is ever to cope adequately with the housing problem. It is a city of all its ages and cannot ignore its immediate needs. It can only be hoped that these needs will be interpreted in such a way that the historical development of the city will not be lost to future generations. From the early simple cubes, gables, and cupolas of the fifteenth and sixteenth centuries to the elaborate Moscow baroque of the late seventeenth, the quiet classical lines of the eighteenth, the lurid eclectic details of the nineteenth, to the frills of Art Nouveau and the strong forms of constructivism, even the monumental architecture of the thirties and the wedding cake skyscrapers of the fifties – all these together add up to a strong blend of history and architecture, a totality that can only mean one city, Moscow.

Bibliography

All sources in Russian can be found at the Lenin Library in Moscow. Most of the periodicals and books in Russian can also be found in London either at the British Museum or at the Library of the Royal Institute of British Architects. The works on restoration of ancient monuments are available only in Moscow. The most important sources are marked with an asterisk. The principal periodical consulted was *Arkhitektura SSSR* which was published from 1933 onwards. Also the main Russian and British architectural journals were used as well as *Pravda, Izvestiya* and some literary publications.

Books in Russian

(a) Works by named authors

Afanasiev, K. N., *Postroenie Arkhitekturnoi Formy*, Moscow 1961.

*Afanasiev, K. N. and V. G. Khazanova (ed.), *Iz Istorii Sovietskoi Arkhitektury, 1917–1932*, 2 volumes, Moscow 1963 and 1970.

Bonch-Bruyevich, V. D., *Vospominaniye o Lenine*, Moscow 1965.

Bondarenko, I. E., *Putevoditel po Moskve*, Moscow 1913.

*Borisova, E. A. and T. P. Kazhdan, *Russkaya Arkhitektura Kontsa XIX Nachaia XX Veka*, Moscow 1971.

Denisev, I. S. *Podmoskovie*, Moscow 1956.

Evangulova, O. S., *Dvortsovo-Parkovye Ansembli Moskvy, Pervoi Poloviny XVIII Veka*, Moscow 1969.

Fedorov-Davydov, A., *Arkhitektura Moskvy Posle 1812*, Moscow 1953.

*Geinike, N. A., *Po Moskve*, Moscow 1917.

Goldenburg, I. E., *Staraya Moskva*, Moscow 1947.

*Golubinsky, E. E., *Istoriya Russkoi Tserkvi*, Moscow 1904.

Gorbunov, N. P., *Kak Rabotal Vladimir Ilich*, Moscow 1933.

Gorky, M., *Sobranie Sochinenii*, Volume 17 (1924–36), Moscow 1952.

Efros, Abram, *Dva Veka Russkovo Iskusstva*, Moscow 1969.

*Grabar, I. E. *Istoriya Russkovo Iskusstva*, Volumes 1–6, Moscow 1910–15.
   Moya Zhizn, Moscow 1937.
   Pamyatniki Iskusstva Razrushennye Fashistkimi Zakhvatchikami SSSR, Moscow – Leningrad 1948.
   Postroiki Bazhenova, Moscow 1951.
   Russkaya Arkitektura Pervaya Polovina XIII Veka, Moscow 1954.
   **Voprosy Restavratsii. Sbornik Tsentralnykh Gosudarstvennykh Restavratsionnykh Masterskikh*, Volume 1, Moscow 1926. Volume 2, Moscow 1928.
   Why, for what reason is it necessary to preserve and collect the treasures of art and the past? (in Russian), Moscow 1919.

Grabar, I. E., V. E. Lazarev and V. V. Kostochkin, *Pamyatniki Kultury, Issledovanie i Restavratssii*, Moscow 1959.

Herzen, A. T., *Byloe i Dumy*, Leningrad 1946.

*Ilin, M. A., *Arkhitektura Moskvy XVIII Veka*, Moscow 1953.

Moskva, Moscow 1963.
Podmoskovie, Moscow 1966.

Ivanov, V. N., *Sokrovishcha Russkoi Arkhitektury*, Moscow 1950.

Karamzin, N. M., *Bednaya Liza*, Moscow 1792.

*Khiger, R. Ya., *Puti Arkhitekturnoi Mysly, 1917–32*, Moscow 1933.

Kim, M. P., *40 Let Sovietskoi Kultury*, Moscow 1957.

*Kuchin, V. N. *Iz Istorii Stroitelstva Sovetskoi Kultury 1917–18, Dokumenty i Vospominaniya*, Moscow 1964.

*Lazarev, V. N., and O. I. Podobedova, *Grabar o Russkoi Arkhitekture*, Moscow 1969.

Lifshits, M., *V.I. Lenin o Kulture i Isskusstve*, Moscow-Leningrad 1938.

Lunacharsky, A. V., *Komy Prinadlezhit Tserkovnoe Imushchestvo?* Moscow 1922.
Stati ob Iskusstve, Moscow 1941.

Malitskii, C. L., *Osnovnye Voprosy Istorii Muzeinovo Dela v Rossii (do 1917)*, Moscow 1950.

Matveyev, A., *Moskva i Zhizn ee nakanune Nashestviya 1812*, Moscow 1912.

Mikhailov, A. I., *Bazhenov*, Moscow 1951.
Arkhitektor D.V. Ukhtomskii, Moscow 1954.

Podobedova, O. I., *Grabar*, Moscow 1965.

Punin, N., *Pamyatnik III Internatsionala. Tatlin*, Petrograd 1920.

Richter, F. F., *Pamyatniki Drevnevo Russkovo Zodchestva*, Moscow 1850.

Ryazanin, M. I., *Arkhitekturnye Ansambli Moskvy XIV–XIX Veka*, Moscow 1950.

Savitsky, Y., *Moskva, Istoriko-Arkhitekturny Ocherk*, Moscow 1947.

Shvarikov, V. A., *Russkaya Arkhitektura*, Moscow 1946.

*Smirnov, I. S., *Lenin i Sovietskaya Kultura*, Moscow (?) n.d.

*Snegirev, V. L., *Moskovie Slobody*, Moscow 1956.
*   *Moskovskoe Zodchestvo*, Moscow 1948.
Zodchii V. I. Bazhenov, Moscow 1950.

Soloukhin, Vladimir, *Pisma iz Russkovo Muzeya*, Moscow 1966.

Stasov, V. V., *Izbrannye Sochineniia*, Moscow 1937.

Sytin, P. B., *Istoriya Planirovki i Zastroiki Moskvy*, Moscow 1954.
Iz Istorii Moskovskikh Ulits, Moscow 1958.
Po Staroi i Novio Moskve, Moscow-Leningrad 1957.

Toropov, S. A. and N. Brynov, *Arkhitekturnye Pamyatniki Moskvy*, Moscow 1947 and 1948.

Voronin, N. N., *Drevnerusskie Goroda*, Moscow-Leningrad 1945.
Lyubite i Sokhranyaite Pamyatniki Drevnerusskovo Iskusstva, Moscow 1960.
Pamyatniki Russkoi Arkhitektury, n.d.

Vselovsky, N. I., *Istoriya Imperatorskovo Russkovo Arkheologicheskovo Obshchestva. 1846–96*, St Petersburg 1900.

Zabelin, I. E., *Istoriya Goroda Moskvy*, Moscow 1905.

(b) Anonymous works

Arkheologicheskie Expeditsii 1919–1956. Index, Moscow 1962.

Arkhitektura Obshchestvennikh Zdanii, Moscow 1948.

* *Arkitekturnoe Nasledstvo*, Moscow 1951–65.

Dokumenty za Sokhranenie i Propogandu Pamyatnikov Kultury, Number 11, Moscow 1966.

* *Istoriya Moskvy*, Volumes 1–6, Moscow 1952–7.

* *Istoriya Russkoi Arkhitektury, Kratkii Kurs*, Moscow 1951.

Istoriya Russkovo Iskusstva, Moscow 1959.

Iz Istorii Sovetskoi Arkhitektury, 1917–25, Moscow 1963.

Iz Istorii Velikoi Oktyabrskoi Sotsialisticheskoi Revolyusii, Moscow 1957.

Izvestiya Arkheologischeskoi Kommissii, Number 63, Petrograd 1917.

Kooperatsiya i Iskusstvo, Moscow 1919.

* *Materialy po Voprosu o Sokhranenii Drevnikh Pamyatnikov*, Imperial Moscow Archaeological Society, Moscow 1911.

Moskva Arkhitekturny Putevoditel, Moscow 1960.

* *Moskva v ee Starina*, Volumes 1–12, Moscow 1913.

Moskva, Sobory, Monastyri, i Tserkvi, Moscow 1880.

Okhranie Istoricheskikh i Arkheologicheskikh Pamyatnikov, Moscow 1949.

O Rossii v Tsarstvovanii Alekseya Mikhailovicha, Moscow 1859.

Polnoe Sobranie Sochinenii V.I. Lenina, 5th edition.

Postanovleniya SNk, SSR, TsK, VKP(B) i shto po Voprosam Stroitelstva, Moscow-Leningrad 1936.

Soobshcheniya Instituta Istorii Iskusstv, Moscow-Leningrad 1951.

Soobshcheniya Nauchno-Metodicheskovo Soveta po Okhrane Pamyatnikov Kultury, Moscow 1969.

Sovietskaya Arkhitektura Ezhegodnik, Moscow, from 1951.

Trudy NIIM, Number 5, Moscow 1961.

Velikaya Oktyabrskaya Sotsialisticheskaya Revolyutsiya, Dokumenty i Materialy Oktyabrskovo Vooruzhennovo Vosstaniya Petrograde, Moscow 1957.

Vestnik Istorii Mirovoi Kultury, Number 3, 158, Moscow.

* *Voprosy Teorii Arkhitektury*, Volumes 1 and 2, Moscow 1955 and 1957.

Vseobshchii Putevoditel po Moskve i Okrestnostyam, Moscow 1911.

Books in English

Baedeker's Russia 1914, London 1971.

*Billington, James, *The Icon and the Axe: an Interpretive History of Russian Culture*, London 1966.

Clarke, E. D., *Travels in Russia, Tartary and Turkey*, London 1810 and 1839.

*Collins, Samuel, *The Present State of Russia*, London 1671.

Custine, Marquis de, *Journey for Our Time: the Journals of the Marquis de Cuistine* (1843), translated by P. Kohler, New York 1953.

Dumas, Alexandre, *Adventures in Czarist Russia*, translated by A. E. Munch, London 1960.

Ehrenburg, Ilya, *Julia Jurenita*, translated by Anna Bostock, London 1958.

*Fitzpatrick, Sheila, *The Commissariat of Enlightenment*, Cambridge 1970.

*Florinsky, M., *Russia: a History and an Interpretation*, New York 1953.

Gabo, Naum, *Constructions Sculpture Paintings Drawings Engravings*, Harvard 1957.

*Gray, Camilla, *The Great Experiment: Russian Art 1863–1922*, London 1962.

*Hamilton, G. H. *The Art and Architecture of Russia*, Harmondsworth 1954.

*Kliuchevsky, V. O., *A History of Russia*, 5 volumes, London–New York 1911–31.

*Kochan, Lionel, *The Making of Modern Russia*, Harmondsworth 1963.

Kochan, Miriam, *Life in Russia under Catherine the Great*, London 1961.

*Kopp, Anatole, *Town and Revolution: Soviet Architecture and City Planning, 1917–35*, London 1970.

Lawrence, J. W., *Russia*, London 1965.
  Russia in the Making, London 1957.
  Russians Observed, London 1969.

*Lissitsky, El, *Russia: an Architecture for World Revolution*, London 1970.

*Milyukov, P. N., *Outlines of Russian Culture*, Philadelphia 1942.

Oldenburg, Zoe, *Catherine the Great*, London 1965.

Oman, Charles, *The English Silver in the Kremlin, 1557–1663*, London 1961.

Palmer, William, *The Patriarch and the Tsar*, London 1871–6.
  A Picture of Moscow, London 1812.

Radishchev, A. N., *A Journey from Moscow to St Petersburg*, London 1958.

Rice, Tamara Talbot, *Elizabeth, Empress of Russia*, London 1970.
  A Concise History of Russian Art, London, 1963.

*Shvidkovsky, O. A., *Building in the USSR 1917–32*, London 1971.

Souvarine, Boris, *Stalin*, London 1939.

Sukhanov, Nikolai, *The Russian Revolution, 1917*, London 1955.

Troyat, Henri, *Daily Life in Russia under the Last Tsar*, London 1961.

Voyce, A., *Moscow and the Roots of Russian Culture*, Newton Abbot, 1972.
* *Russian Architecture: Trends in Nationalism and Modernism*, New York 1948.

Wells, H. G., *Russia in the Shadows*, London 1920.

Williams, Albert Rhys, *Through the Russian Revolution*, New York 1921.

Wilson, Francesca, *Muscovy: Russia Through Foreign Eyes*, London 1970.

Wright, Frank Lloyd, *An Autobiography*, New York 1945.

Books in French

Beyle, M. H., *Vie de Napoléon*, Paris 1930.

Le Corbusier, *Oeuvres complètes 1929–34*, Paris 1947.
  Oeuvres complètes 1934–38, Paris 1947.

Martynov, A., *Environs de Moscou. Anciens monuments*, Moscow 1889.

*Reau, Louis, *L'Art russe des origines à Pierre Legrand*, Paris 1921–2.

*Violet-le-Duc, *L'Art russe*, Paris 1877.

Index

Page numbers in italics refer to illustrations

Credits

The following have kindly supplied illustrations for use in this book:
The British Library 75; The British Museum 81; Hal Doyne-Ditmas 20; Michael Duncan 47; The Mansell
Collection 7, 39, 40, 55; Konstantin Melnikov 72; R. Morphet 66; The Moscow History Museum 51, 53; The
Novosti Press Agency 45, 51, 53; Valery Plotnikov 4, 4(a), 9, 13, 14, 15, 18, 19, 21, 23, 24, 25, 26, 27, 30, 31, 33,
34, 60, 61, 64, 84; The Radio Times Hulton Picture Library 10, 28, 38, 52, 54, 65, 68, 71; K. Smith 36, 42;
Stan Tough 3, 12, 57, 59